HEAVEN
OBSERVED

HEAVEN OBSERVED

GLIMPSES

OF

TRANSCENDENCE

IN

EVERYDAY

LIFE

BARRY L. MORROW

NAVPRESS

Bringing Truth to Life
P.O. Box 35001, Colorado Springs, Colorado 80935

The Navigators is an international Christian organization. Our mission is to reach, disciple, and equip people to know Christ and to make Him known through successive generations. We envision multitudes of diverse people in the United States and every other nation who have a passionate love for Christ, live a lifestyle of sharing Christ's love, and multiply spiritual laborers among those without Christ.

NavPress is the publishing ministry of The Navigators. NavPress publications help believers learn biblical truth and apply what they learn to their lives and ministries. Our mission is to stimulate spiritual formation among our readers.

© 2001 by Barry L. Morrow
All rights reserved. No part of this publication may be reproduced in any form without written permission from NavPress, P.O. Box 35001, Colorado Springs, CO 80935.
www.navpress.com
Library of Congress Catalog Card Number: 2001026700
ISBN 1-57683-232-5

Cover design by Dan Jamison
Cover photo by © 2000 M. Vavrik/Alaska Stock.com
Creative Team: Don Simpson, Greg Clouse, Amy Spencer, Laura Spray

Some of the anecdotal illustrations in this book are true to life and are included with the permission of the persons involved. All other illustrations are composites of real situations, and any resemblance to people living or dead is coincidental.

Unless otherwise identified, all Scripture quotations in this publication are taken from the *New American Standard Bible* (NASB), © The Lockman Foundation 1960, 1962, 1963, 1968, 1971, 1972, 1973, 1975, 1977. Other versions used include The *HOLY BIBLE: NEW INTERNATIONAL VERSION*® (NIV®). Copyright © 1973, 1978, 1984 by International Bible Society. Used by permission of Zondervan Publishing House. All rights reserved; and the *Good News Bible Today's English Version* (TEV), copyright © American Bible Society 1966, 1971, 1976.

Excerpts from LETTERS TO MALCOLM: CHIEFLY ON PRAYER, copyright © 1964, 1963 by C. S. Lewis Pte. Ltd. And renewed 1991, 1992 by Arthur Owen Barfield, reprinted by permission of Harcourt, Inc. GOD IN THE DOCK by C. S. Lewis copyright © C. S. Lewis Pte. Ltd. 1970. Extract reprinted by permission. MIRACLES by C. S. Lewis copyright © C. S. Lewis Pte. Ltd. 1960. Extract reprinted by permission. THE PROBLEM OF PAIN by C. S. Lewis copyright © C. S. Lewis Pte. Ltd. 1940. Extract reprinted by permission. THE GREAT DIVORCE by C. S. Lewis copyright © C. S. Lewis Pte. Ltd. 1946. Extract reprinted by permission. MERE CHRISTIANITY by C. S. Lewis copyright © C. S. Lewis Pte. Ltd. 1942. Extract reprinted by permission.

Printed in the United States of America

1 2 3 4 5 6 7 8 9 10 / 05 04 03 02 01

To Caroleeta, Anna, and Jonathan, whose lives continually show me that this life is a joyful journey, brimming with pleasures and delights, "hints" of a loving Father who desires our company in that undiscovered country, Heaven.

CONTENTS

FOREWORD

"As the deer pants for the water brooks, so my soul pants for Thee, O God. My soul thirsts for God, for the living God; when shall I come and appear before God?" (Psalm 42:1-2).

LONGING TO SEE GOD AND TO ENTER HIS CONSUMMATE PRESENCE IS AN oft-repeated theme in the writings of the great saints throughout church history, but it is rarely seen in the Christian literature of our time. This is why I welcome the publication of *Heaven Observed*. As you will discover, my colleague Barry Morrow has a penchant for leveraging culture to illuminate timeless spiritual issues.

Six hundred years ago, Julian of Norwich, in her *Revelations of Divine Love*, wrote: "The reason why we have no ease of heart or soul [is because] we are seeking our rest in trivial things which cannot satisfy, and not seeking to know God, almighty, all-wise, all-good....We shall never cease wanting and longing until we possess Him in fullness and joy. Then we shall have no further wants. Meanwhile His will is that we go on knowing and loving until we are perfected in heaven. ... The more clearly the soul sees the blessed face by grace and love, the more it longs to see it in its fullness."

C. S. Lewis, in *The Weight of Glory*, spoke of the stab and pang of acute longing as homesickness for a place and a time we have not yet visited that is beyond the edge of the imagination. "The door on which we have been knocking all our lives will open at last....Apparently, then, our lifelong nostalgia, our longing to be reunited with something in the universe from which we now feel cut off, to be on the inside of some door which we have always seen from the outside, is no mere neurotic fancy, but the truest index of our real situation. And to be at last summoned inside would be both glory and honour beyond all our merits and also the healing of that old ache."

There have been times when a walk in the woods, a painting, a photograph, or a piece of music created a sudden and profound sense of longing within me. When I thought about it, I realized that in each case, the vehicle that caused the longing pointed not to itself, but to that which is beyond the created order, to God Himself. These are fleeting moments, but they are enough to remind me of the reality of my pilgrim status and to awaken desire for something more than this world can offer.

Along similar lines, Henri Nouwen in his perceptive book, *The Return of the Prodigal Son,* describes his encounter with Rembrandt's painting of this parable and its remarkable effect on his self-understanding. "It had brought me into touch with something within me that lies far beyond the ups and downs of a busy life, something that represents the ongoing yearning of the human spirit, the yearning for a final return, an unambiguous sense of safety, a lasting home."

Laying hold of our true desire is the theme of *The Sacred Romance* by Brent Curtis and John Eldredge and of *The Journey of Desire* written by John Eldredge after the loss of this beloved co-laborer and friend. These books portray heaven as the great restoration of the beauty we long to see on a cosmic scale; the grand affair of complete intimacy among the people of God; and the great adventure of fruitful, creative, activity without frustration and disappointments.

"Jesus took it for granted that all human beings are 'seekers.' It is not natural for people to drift aimlessly through life like plankton. We need something to live for, something to give meaning to our existence, something to 'seek,' something on which to set our hearts and our minds" (John Stott, *Christian Counter-Culture*).

God waits to be wanted, but He must be wanted for Himself, not for some lesser good He may provide. May we ask for the grace to long for the beatific vision, for the vision of God Himself.

Kenneth Boa, Ph.D., D.Phil.,
President, Reflections Ministries

ACKNOWLEDGMENTS

I AM CONVINCED THAT, IN THE WORDS OF FREDERICK BUECHNER, ALL OF life is a "sacred journey." While many people have influenced my life and thinking, I'm especially thankful for the education I received at Dallas Theological Seminary. I deeply treasure that they not only gave me a good grasp of the Scriptures, but also taught me how to think well. In a day when serious reflection and thinking are no longer in vogue, we need to be reminded of the importance of the Christian mind if we are to live faithfully in our post-Christian culture. As Thomas Traherne once said, "To think well is to serve God in the interior court." Yet I claim no originality for anything I have written in the book, for I have traveled in the company of giants like C. S. Lewis, George MacDonald, and G. K. Chesterton. Like the medievals, we should remember that we are, as Bernard of Chartres once declared, "dwarfs standing on the shoulders of giants. If we see farther than the ancients, it is only because we have their shoulders to stand on."

I'm also grateful to the people of Dunwoody Community Church in Atlanta. During my time in ministry there, they helped me process many of these ruminations on Heaven. I'm sure that God will amply reward them for patiently enduring my frequent quoting of C. S. Lewis!

Special thanks are also due to the team at NavPress in bringing this book to publication. Don Simpson was of particular help in the early stages of the project, and Greg Clouse and Amy Spencer made helpful suggestions in the editing process.

Thanks are especially due to my colleague Ken Boa, and the Reflections Ministries staff. Ken, along with Len Sykes and George Grove, has been an encouragement through these past few years of ministry in the marketplace. Through his friendship, counsel, and encouragement, Ken has been a tremendous help during the writing of this manuscript.

INTRODUCTION

Everywhere the apostle Paul went, there was either riot or revival. Everywhere I go, they want to serve tea.

—former Archbishop of Canterbury

IN ONE OF HIS MOST POPULAR SHORT STORIES, "PIGEON FEATHERS," NOV-elist John Updike tells the story of a fourteen-year-old boy named David who has recently moved to his mother's birthplace in the small farm community of Firetown. David is a voracious reader curious about his Christian heritage. After reading H. G. Wells' account of Jesus as an obscure political agitator who was crucified and presumably died a few weeks later—only to have a religion founded after him—David begins to wonder whether or not Christianity is true. After he is visited by a horrid vision of his own death—a revelation amounting to extinc-tion—he looks to his parents to provide answers, but they are no help.

David then turns to his pastor, Reverend Dobson, a sophisti-cated and enlightened preacher and a bit misplaced in Firetown, who teaches the catechism class to the young people on Sunday after-noons. When the time comes for questions, David asks about the resurrection of the body and about whether we are conscious between the time we die and the Day of Judgment. "What will heaven be like?" David asks Reverend Dobson.

When Dobson suggests to David that Heaven might be best understood as "the goodness Abraham Lincoln did living on after him," David feels betrayed. The only thing David wants is to hear Reverend Dobson repeat the words about the Christian hope of immortality that he said every Sunday morning. But David leaves that afternoon with a sense of indignation, not only at being betrayed, but of seeing Christianity betrayed. When he returns home and sits down with his grandfather's Bible, attempting to read it, his mother joins him on the green sofa to see what is troubling him.

> "I asked Reverend Dobson about Heaven and he said it was like Abraham Lincoln's goodness living after him."
>
> "And why didn't you like it?"
>
> "Well, don't you see? It amounts to saying there isn't any Heaven at all."

"I don't see that it amounts to that. What do you want Heaven to be?"

"Well, I don't know. I want it to be something. I thought he'd tell me what it was."

"David," she asked gently, "don't you ever want to rest?"

"No. Not forever."

"David . . . when you get older, you'll feel differently."

"Grandpa didn't. Look how tattered this book is."

"I think Reverend Dobson made a mistake. You must try to forgive him."

"It's not a question of his making a mistake! It's a question of dying and never moving or seeing or hearing anything ever again."

"But"—in exasperation—"darling, it's so greedy of you to want more. When God has given us this wonderful April day, and given us this farm, and you have your whole life ahead of you—"

"Mother . . . don't you see . . . if when we die there's nothing, all your sun and fields and what not are, ah, horror? It's just an ocean of horror."[1]

Few stories better capture the modern-day sentiment of our culture's belief—or disbelief—in Heaven than Updike's "Pigeon Feathers." While many, like David's mother, have some wistful, ethereal idea about the afterlife, it is not saying too much to suggest that our culture at large has lost its sense of transcendence in the biblical hope of Heaven. And while modernity has largely jettisoned the Christian view of Heaven, believing the message to be irrelevant, there has never been a time when the message of Christianity—and the hope of Heaven—is more relevant.

We, like David, want more than wonderful April days, beautiful vistas, and all that this life can offer. Our souls cry out that life has meaning and purpose and that ultimate meaning and purpose must transcend this temporal life. I am reminded of Walker Percy's likening of his prophetic role as a writer to the canary that coal miners used to take down into the shaft to test the air:

> The novelist feels more and more like the canary being taken down the mine shaft with a bunch of hearty joking sense-making miners while he, the canary, is already getting a whiff of something noxious and is staggering around his cage trying to warn the miners, but they can't understand him nor he them.[2]

Despite the unprecedented affluence and enlightened thinking that characterize our modern world, there is a tremendous amount of pain, purposelessness, and futility. Perhaps it is time for the miners to "surface and think things over." I hope this book will help the reader to do just that.

While culture has largely abdicated any serious belief in the reality of Heaven, it is the premise of this book that God has provided "signals of transcendence" in our everyday lives that hint of another world to come. Many books today deal with Heaven and the afterlife, written from both Christian and nonChristian perspectives. The distinctive of *Heaven Observed* is that it deals with the topic through these intimations from our daily lives, these "inconsolable longings" we feel. This idea of inconsolable longings — desires that cannot be fully satisfied in this life — is rooted in the German word *sensucht* and is powerfully portrayed in the writings of C. S. Lewis. Despite the abundant delights and pleasures of this world, these feelings of incompleteness keep us asking the question, Is there nothing more?

If you are like me, sometime in your life you set your hopes and affections on some person or thing or on an experience that you believed would make you happy. Yet what happened? Even when we get it, we are not satisfied. So what does this have to do with Heaven? Simply this: If I find in myself a desire that no experience in this world can satisfy, the most probable explanation is that these longings intimate that I was made for *another* world, as C. S. Lewis observes in his classic *Mere Christianity*.

To that end, the book is divided into three sections: The Imitation of Heaven, The Intimations of Heaven, and The Implications of Heaven. In the first chapter of part 1 we deal with how culture, having rejected a transcendent worldview of life with God as the Author, has trivialized the very idea of Heaven. When we don't want to deal with the important issues of life (like God and death), we trivialize them. In the second chapter, through Solomon's words in the book of Ecclesiastes we discover that a person can have *everything* under the sun and yet have *nothing*. Oscar Wilde once put it so well: "There are two tragedies in life. One is not getting what you want. The other is getting it!" Mankind may seek to imitate Heaven by creating its own Utopia, but it does not provide lasting satisfaction. Why? Solomon gives us a hint when he declares that God has put eternity in our hearts (see Ecclesiastes 3:11). Our feeble attempts to find significance and satisfaction apart from the living God do not lead to fulfillment but to disillusionment.

In part 2, The Intimations of Heaven, we consider a number of these "hints" of transcendence that suggest another world awaits us. Using Blaise Pascal's famous dictum, "The heart has its reasons, of which reason knows nothing," we suggest that the heart is a reliable guide to teach and instruct us about Heaven. These intimations of Heaven include our universal unhappiness, our sense of alienation, our encounters with literature and film, our pain and suffering, our pleasures and joys, the daily humdrum of life, our work, and our play.

In part 3 we consider The Implications of Heaven. In this section, we first discuss why the Christian can have an abiding confidence that Christianity is true and is therefore a reliable guide in matters pertaining to Heaven. Based on the testimony and reliability of the Scriptures, in addition to the person and work of Jesus Christ culminating in His resurrection, we will see that belief in Christianity is not a *blind* faith. Faith is not, as H. L. Mencken once defined it, "an illogical belief in the occurrence of the improbable," but rather a *reasonable* response to the evidence at hand. Chapter 13 deals with the "choice" of Heaven and covers the complex and difficult doctrine of Hell. As problematic as the doctrine of Hell is (arguably the most difficult of Christianity), if there is a Heaven, then it is only logical that there is a "non-Heaven." In chapter 14 we consider what may be called the "character" of Heaven, and we do some theological musing on a number of questions that are often asked about Heaven: Where is Heaven? Is there time in Heaven? Will we have bodies in Heaven? What will we do in Heaven? Will we recognize others in Heaven? Will we all be equal in Heaven?

While the world may reject such longings for Heaven, some with listening hearts and a burning desire to find ultimate security and happiness will be reminded and encouraged to know that their hopes and aspirations for Heaven are indeed true.

One day God will fulfill our deepest expectations and desires, and those who know God will be united with Him and other saints throughout eternity. It is in the Eternal City not made with hands, whose architect and builder is the living God (see Hebrews 11:10), where our greatest hopes and dreams shall come to pass. There, as the apostle Paul declares, we will experience "things which eye has not seen and ear has not heard, . . . all that God has prepared for those who love Him" (1 Corinthians 2:9).

> *We want something else which can hardly be put into words —*
> *to be united with the beauty we see, to pass into it, to receive it*
> *into ourselves, to bathe in it, to become part of it. . . . At present*
> *we are on the outside of the world, the wrong side of the door.*

We discern the freshness and purity of morning, but they do not make us fresh and pure. We cannot mingle with the splendors we see. But all the leaves of the New Testament are rustling with the rumor that it will not always be so. Some day, God willing, we shall get in.

—C. S. Lewis, *The Weight of Glory*

PART I

THE IMITATION OF HEAVEN

This Life's dim window of the soul
Distorts the Heavens from Pole to Pole
And leads you to believe a lie
When you see with, not through, the eye.

—William Blake

I can't understand why people are frightened by new ideas—
I'm frightened of the old ones!

—John Cage

CHAPTER I

The Trivialization of Heaven

I had far rather walk, as I do, in daily terror of eternity, than feel that this was only a children's game in which all the contestants would get equally worthless prizes in the end.

—T. S. Eliot

WITH THE PREVIOUS PENETRATING WORDS, POET AND LITERARY CRITIC T. S. Eliot confronts us with the greatest wager any mortal will ever face. Is there a true Heaven, a place where God and righteousness dwell? Or could life be no more than a child's game with everyone getting "equally worthless prizes in the end"? Does Heaven actually exist, or is it a figment of our imagination, drummed up by religious people to help us cope with a harsh and cruel world?

Whatever our personal belief, it is clear that we are experiencing an unprecedented interest in Heaven and the afterlife. National surveys by Gallup and other organizations show that the vast majority of people believe in Heaven. People from various religious backgrounds make confident assertions about the afterlife.

A few years ago *USA Today* reported on a seventeen-day international conference in Scottsdale, Arizona, where some one thousand "immortals" convened to discuss the hot topic: If you believe strongly enough that you won't die, your body creates a "cellular awakening," a constant renewal of healthy cells so that you won't experience physical death.[1] In the movie industry, films such as *Ghost, Flatliners, Defending Your Life,* and more recently *What Dreams May Come* have raised provocative questions about what lies on the other side of this mortal existence.

The story is told of a church choir director who was attempting to be innovative in the worship service. Instead of the men singing one verse and the women another, he thought he would have the women sing the first line and the men respond. As it turned out, he had made a terrible mistake and swore never to do it again. In a hymn celebrating the Christian's hope of Heaven, the women sang, "I will go home someday," and the men thundered back, "Glad day, glad day!"

Such a story humorously illustrates that the American landscape has divergent hopes and aspirations about the afterlife. Yet one thing is certain: the traditional Christian worldview of Heaven and Hell has been seriously undermined in recent years. While the Bible abounds with references to the reality of the Christian hope of the afterlife,[2] we live in a culture that no longer embraces a Christian worldview.

In his book *Lost in the Cosmos: The Last Self-Help Book,* Catholic novelist Walker Percy pokes fun at fundamentalist Christians when he playfully promises to inform his readership, "How you can survive in the Cosmos about which you know more and more while knowing less and less about yourself, this despite 10,000 self-help books, 100,000 psychotherapists, and 100 million fundamentalist Christians."[3] While Percy was never comfortable in the conservative fundamentalist camp of Christendom, he once lamented that the Christian novelist nowadays is like a person who has found a "treasure hidden in the attic of an old house." Yet he concluded that he is writing for people who have "moved out to the suburbs" and who are "bloody sick of the old house of orthodoxy" and everything in it.

A World Come of Age

What has caused this disdain for orthodox, evangelical Christianity? What has happened that has made people "bloody sick of the old house of orthodoxy"? Why has the biblical concept of Heaven become so trivialized? While many factors have led to the present state of affairs, there is little question that Western society has undergone a tremendous philosophical shift in its thinking as it relates to God, humanity, and the afterlife. More importantly, such questions as What can I know? (*truth*), What should I do? (*goodness*), and In what may I place my hope? (*joy*) are no longer addressed by modernity. Perhaps the greatest tragedy of life is that—far worse than death—we have no reason to live but only to exist.[4]

What then has led to humanity's "agnosticism" about transcendent matters? In his excellent book *The Universe Next Door,* author James Sire makes this important observation:

> In the Western world, up to the end of the seventeenth century, the theistic worldview was clearly dominant. Intellectual

squabbles—and there were as many then as now—were mostly family squabbles.... During the period from the early Middle Ages to the end of the seventeenth century, very few challenged the existence of God or held that ultimate reality was impersonal or that death meant individual extinction.... Christianity had so penetrated the Western world that, whether people believed in Christ or acted as Christians should, they all lived in a context of ideas influenced and informed by the Christian faith.[5]

Sire contends that Christian theism was the dominant worldview for approximately the first eighteen centuries after Christ. But as human reason was exalted over biblical revelation as the source of man's authority, Enlightenment sentiment led to the eventual shift in worldviews away from theism. This shift was increasingly characterized by the absence of God and a deemphasis in propositional revelation (that is, that God could reveal Himself through the Bible, the written Word). Sire observes that when Christian theism was rejected in favor of human reason, humanity lost its God-given meaning and purpose for life, which led to despair and utter hopelessness. This worldview, known as nihilism, is best described as

more a feeling than a philosophy.... It is a denial of philosophy, a denial of the possibility of knowledge, a denial that anything is valuable.... In other words, nihilism is the negation of everything—knowledge, ethics, beauty, reality. In nihilism no statement has validity; nothing has meaning. Everything is gratuitous, *de trop*, that is, just there.[6]

This shift in philosophical worldview was especially evident in the world of literature. American poet and author T. S. Eliot divided modern literature into three periods in regard to its attitude toward

Christianity. The first period, he said, "took the Faith ... for granted, and omitted it from its picture of life." This era may be said to have lasted until the middle of the nineteenth century, or more precisely, until the publication of Darwin's *The Origin of Species* in 1859. The second period, Eliot contended, "doubted, worried about, or contested the Faith." Here he was perhaps thinking of such writers as Herman Melville, Thomas Hardy, Fyodor Dostoyevsky, and Emily Dickinson. It was Eliot's contention that we are living in the third period: "It is the phase of those who have never heard the Christian faith spoken of as anything but an anachronism." Eliot noted that as a result "the whole of modern literature is corrupted by what I call Secularism." To him, secularism is "simply unaware of, simply cannot understand the meaning of the primacy of the supernatural over the natural life." [7]

The Abdication of Belief

In the early 1880s, a plain-faced, middle-aged woman sat in her father's house in Amherst, Massachusetts, musing on the dying. She'd had the opportunity to observe many people on their deathbeds. She knew well the difference between those who died in confidence of spending eternity with God and those who looked fearfully upon the vast unknown of death. In light of these experiences, Emily Dickinson wrote a poem:

> Those dying then,
> Knew where they went—
> They went to God's Right Hand—
> That Hand is amputated now,
> And God cannot be found—
>
> The abdication of Belief
> Makes the Behavior small—
> Better an *ignis fatuus*
> Than no illume at all[8]

In Dickinson's poem "those dying then" represent the age of complacent faith. The amputation of "God's Right Hand" fittingly describes the subsequent assaults upon belief in God in an age of skepticism and doubt. We then come to "the abdication of Belief," which represents the age of secularism, characterized by a rejection of transcendent knowledge.[9]

While attempts to achieve meaning and purpose in recent years have been sought in the West through the Eastern religions and the new age movement (something of a halfway house between the East and the West), humanity has indeed become "lost in the Cosmos." The modern person is a forlorn cosmic orphan who has thrown off the shackles of orthodoxy to pursue freedom and self-enlightenment—for what reason, he or she is not sure. Blaise Pascal, writing over three centuries ago, accurately diagnosed the malady of modernity when he observed that, because of hubris, man has severed himself from God and the knowledge of transcendent affairs:

> It is in vain, oh men, that you seek within yourselves the cure for your miseries. All your insight only leads you to the knowledge that it is not in yourselves that you will discover the true and the good. . . . Your principal maladies are pride, which cuts you off from God, and sensuality, which binds you to the earth.[10]

Malcolm Muggeridge, following the thought of Pascal, delivered the inaugural addresses of The Pascal Lectures on Christianity at the University of Waterloo in 1978. In his own unique style, Muggeridge described Christendom in somber terms: "A dying civilization, Christendom, on a swiftly moving, ebbing tide, clutches at any novelty in art and literature, ready to accept and then almost at once reject whatever is new no matter how perverse or abnormal." We have a "weariness with striving to be men," as the

American critic Leslie Fiedler put it,

> the more desolating because there's no God to turn to. . . . We
> continue to insist that change is progress, self-indulgence is
> freedom, and novelty is originality. . . . Western man has
> decided to abolish himself, creating his own boredom out of
> his own affluence, his own vulnerability out of his own
> strength, his own impotence out of his own erotomania,
> himself blowing the trumpet that brings the walls of his own
> city tumbling down. . . .[11]

Even contemporary writers who are entrenched nihilists exude
a great despair in finding purpose to life. Musing upon the existential despair that pervades much of contemporary life, writer
Kurt Vonnegut once poignantly observed that the mind is a marvelous instrument, but unfortunately, "it did not come with direc-
tions. We could say the same for life. And the more we miss the key
to living a full life, the more people invent guide books that tell us
how to 'find life.' " Boston College philosophy professor Peter Kreeft
accurately captures the malaise of contemporary culture when he
declares,

> Millions all around us are living the tragedy of a meaningless
> life, the "life" of spiritual death. That is what makes our soci-
> ety most radically different from every society in history . . . it
> does not know why it exists. . . . How is it that the society that
> "knows it all" about everything knows nothing about Every-
> thing? How has the knowledge explosion exploded away the
> supreme knowledge? Why have we thrown away the road
> map just as we've souped up the engine? We must retrace the
> steps by which we have come to this dead end; to recapture
> hope we must diagnose the causes of our hopelessness before
> we begin to prescribe a remedy.[12]

The Banality of Our Age

When contemporary culture rejects the traditional Christian perspective dealing with life, faith, and God, it often resorts to humor, banality, and trivialization. Better to ridicule and trivialize God and religion, society reasons, than to think deeply about them. Author Tom Willett has gleaned some humorous quotes on how a few well-known Americans in our post-Christian culture view God, religion, and the afterlife:[13]

> If there is a God, give me a sign! . . . See, I told you that the knlpt smflrt glpptnrr . . .
> —Steve Martin

> Not only is there no God, but try getting a plumber on weekends.
> —Woody Allen

> I do not believe in God. I believe in cashmere.
> —Fran Lebowitz

> Most people past college age are not atheists. It's too hard to be one in society, for one thing, because you don't get any days off. And if you're an agnostic, you don't know whether you get them off or not.
> —Mort Sahl

> Millions long for immortality who do not know what to do with themselves on a rainy Sunday afternoon.
> —Susan Ertz

Because the concept of Heaven no longer carries ultimate meaning and significance in our culture, the afterlife often elicits humor rather than serious reflection. Sports enthusiasts perhaps caught actor Burt Reynolds playing the role of God several years ago on the ESPN commercial for the PGA; he requests "fewer blimp shots because they are so boring!" Gary Larsen, famous for *The Far Side*, portrays in one of his cartoons a group of people in Hell walking around drinking coffee under the supervision of several devils. One man remarks to another, "Oh man! The coffee's *cold!* They thought of *everything!*"[14] One of the most memorable advertisements dealing with Heaven is the slick print ad for Godiva chocolates. The advertisement reads,

> NOW EVERYONE CAN GET TO HEAVEN
> Perhaps you've sinned once or twice. But when you indulge in the luscious richness of our delectable milk chocolate truffles, you too will experience your own little moment in heaven.

Heaven: Escapism or Realism?

While such advertising may make us laugh, Heaven raises fundamental questions for the thoughtful person. Do we believe in Heaven because we think it is *true*, that is, because we believe it is part of ultimate reality? Or do we believe in Heaven because we think it is a *nice* doctrine, a comforting solace in this cruel world? In other words, is our belief in Heaven based on realism or escapism? C. S. Lewis criticized a simplistic, "feel-good" Christianity when he responded to the question, "Which of the religions of the world gives to its followers the greatest happiness?"

> While it lasts, the religion of worshipping oneself is the best. . . . As you perhaps know, I haven't always been a Christian. I didn't go to religion to make me happy. I always knew a bottle of Port would do that. If you want a religion to make you feel really comfortable, I certainly don't recommend Christianity.[15]

Lewis went so far as to make the astounding statements that

"it is more important that Heaven should exist than that any of us should reach it"[16] and that "If Christianity is untrue, then no honest man will want to believe it, however helpful it might be: if it is true, every honest man will want to believe it, even if it gives him no help at all."[17] What Lewis is addressing is the fact that, in our heart of hearts, what all people truly desire is the Real, the True.

Christians may be quite shy in our modern world of even mentioning Heaven because we fear the jeers of people who make light of it as "pie in the sky" and who tell us we are trying to escape from the duty of making the world a happy place. But the real issue is whether Heaven exists. In reality, either there is pie in the sky or not, and if there is not, then Christianity is false, for Heaven is woven into the very fabric of the Christian faith.[18]

So then, is Heaven relevant to the human situation? What difference does a genuine belief in Heaven make? In many ways, it makes all the difference in the world, for it is the difference between hope and despair. Why? Because in the end, there are only two possible visions about life, and those two visions involve seeing life as either "chance or the dance."[19] At death we find out which vision is true. Does life all go down the drain in the end, or are all the loose threads finally tied together into a gloriously perfect tapestry? Do the tangled paths through the forest of life head to the golden castle or over the cliff and into the abyss? In other words, is death a door or a hole?[20]

While modernity is reluctant to see life in such either-or terms, those who reflect seriously on such weighty issues must come to either one or the other conclusion about life. Either this physical, material life is all that exists, or there is another world that transcends this temporal, material existence. If this temporal life is all that exists, then the Christian faith is an elusive dream at best. The apostle Paul put it in the starkest terms: if Christ was not bodily raised, then we of all people should be pitied because we have only hoped in Christ in this life (see 1 Corinthians 15:19). But if the Christian faith is true, then another world beyond the grave awaits us all. Jesus Himself told His followers, "He who hears My word, and believes Him who sent Me, has eternal life, and does not come into judgment, but has passed out of death into life" (John 5:24).

Flannery O'Connor was a master of the short story and one of the most original and provocative writers to emerge from the South. Her apocalyptic vision of life was expressed through grotesque, often comic situations. Yet her novels and short stories of a Christ-haunted South were frequently too bizarre for readers to comprehend. In one of her most chilling short stories, "A Good Man Is Hard to Find," she vividly portrays the relevance to the saint of Christ's "raising the dead." Listen to the latent theology expressed through words of the Misfit, who has just had his accomplices murder a woman's family and who is about to kill the grandmother:

> "Jesus was the only One that ever raised the dead," The Misfit continued, "and He shouldn't have done it. He thrown every-thing off balance. If He did what He said, then it's nothing for you to do but throw away everything and follow Him, and if He didn't, then it's nothing for you to do but enjoy the few minutes you got left the best way you can — by killing some-body or burning down his house or doing some other mean-ness to him. No pleasure but meanness," he said and his voice had become almost a snarl.[21]

O'Connor believed that when people begin taking the Christian faith for granted, it is necessary to take extreme measures to awaken their spiritual sensibilities. She believed that it was some-times necessary to "shout" to get the attention of her readership. O'Connor says that "the grandmother's head cleared for an instant" before she reached for the Misfit. But it was the terror of death, not the recognition of her own mortality, that brings her to this point. Death is a powerful instructor![22]

Heaven and Belief in God

As we reflect on the reality of Heaven, it is important to realize that our belief or disbelief about Heaven is closely related to our fundamental belief in the existence of God. We cannot have Heaven without God. British historian Paul Johnson has noted that God's existence carries tremendous implications for our eternal destinies:

> The existence or non-existence of God is the most important question we humans are ever called to answer. If God does exist, and if in consequence we are called to another life when this one ends, a momentous set of consequences follows, which should affect every day, every moment almost, of our earthly existence. Our life then becomes a mere preparation for eternity and must be conducted throughout with our future in view. If, on the other hand, God does not exist . . . this life then becomes the only one we have, we have no duties or obligations except to ourselves, and we need weigh no other considerations except our own interests and pleasures. . . . In a Godless world, there is no obvious basis for altruism of any kind, moral anarchy takes over and the rule of the self prevails.[23]

Yet many people who might trivialize the biblical hope of Heaven would be reluctant to dismiss the existence of God. In the world of film, renowned director Ingmar Bergman confronts his audience with the dilemma we must face if there is no God. Listen to the dialogue between Death and the questing knight in his cinematic classic *The Seventh Seal:*

> Knight: Why can't I kill God within me? Why does he live on in this painful and humiliating way even though I curse him and want to tear him out of my heart? Why, in spite of everything, is he a baffling reality that I can't shake off? Do you hear me?

Death: Yes, I hear you.

Knight: I want knowledge, not faith. . . . I want God to stretch out his hand toward me, reveal himself and speak to me.

Death: But he remains silent.

Knight: I call out to him in the dark but no one seems to be there.

Death: Perhaps no one is there.

Knight: Then life is an outrageous horror. No one can live in the face of death, knowing that all is nothingness.[24]

Can we believe, deep within ourselves, that this mortal existence is all that exists? Can life truly be "an outrageous horror"? Does it all lead to nothingness? Deep down, we sense that the answer is no. We yearn for something more, something that this world cannot fulfill. Despite the supposed wisdom of the sophisticates of modernity, in our heart of hearts we believe that there is more to life than just *this* life. Frederick Buechner recounts a poignant story that characterizes the dilemma of the modern world:

It is a peculiarly twentieth-century story, and it is almost too awful to tell: about a boy of twelve or thirteen who, in a fit of crazy anger and depression, got hold of a gun somewhere and fired it at his father, who died not right away but soon afterward. When the authorities asked the boy why he had done it, he said that it was because he could not stand his father, because his father demanded too much of him, because he was always after him, because he hated his father. And then later on, after he had been placed in a house of detention somewhere, a guard was walking down the corridor late one night when he heard sounds from the boy's room, and he stopped to listen. The words that he heard the boy sobbing out in the dark were, "I want my father, I want my father."[25]

Buechner suggests that this story is a "kind of parable of the lives of all of us." Modern society is like that boy in the house of detention. We have killed off our Father, but deep down inside we cry out for our Father. We desperately want Him to exist, and we want to believe that this life is more than simply a brief temporal existence leading to nothingness.

Before we embark on our journey to consider the clues in our lives that serve as signals of transcendence for another world (these are discussed in part 2), we'll first consider how our attempts to find lasting meaning, significance, and happiness in this present world cannot truly be satisfied. Despite the modern world's attempts to create a virtual secular Utopia—a Heaven on earth—genuine happiness and fulfillment cannot be achieved. Rather, we were made for another world. On this deep, insatiable longing for another world, Lewis writes,

> In speaking of this desire for our own far-off country, which we find in ourselves even now, I feel a certain shyness. . . . These things—the beauty, the memory of our own past— are good images of what we really desire; but if they are mistaken for the thing itself they turn into dumb idols, breaking the hearts of their worshippers. For they are not the thing itself; they are only the scent of a flower we have not found, the echo of a tune we have not heard, news from a country we have never yet visited.[26]

CHAPTER 2

THE SECULARIZATION OF HEAVEN

There are two tragedies in life. One is not getting what you want. The other is getting it.

— Oscar Wilde

Man finds it hard to get what he wants, because he does not want the best; God finds it hard to give, because He would give the best, and man will not take it.

— George MacDonald

Of all that I have ever seen or learned, [the biblical book of Ecclesiastes] seems to me the noblest, the wisest, and the most powerful expression of man's life upon this earth, and also the highest flower of poetry, eloquence and truth. I am not given to dogmatic judgments in the matter of literary creation, but if I had to make one, I could only say that Ecclesiastes is the greatest single piece of writing I have ever known, and the wisdom expressed in it the most lasting and profound.

— Thomas Wolfe

IN THE FIRST CHAPTER WE OBSERVED THAT MODERN CULTURE, HAVING rejected a perspective of life with God as its focus, has resorted to triviality when it comes to issues of transcendence. Having turned from the orthodox, biblical perspective of finding meaning, purpose, and significance through the Creator, people attempt to fulfill these needs through secular pursuits. If people will not bow to the Creator, then they will bow to the work of their hands. As G. K. Chesterton once observed, "When man stops believing in God, it's not that he believes in nothing, but that he will believe in anything." Because by nature people are worshipers, it only remains to be determined what will be the object of that worship. And because contemporary culture has jettisoned the transcendent God of the Bible and His values, it aspires to create a secularized "Heaven on earth." Our culture asks, Can all that this world has to offer make us happy? Can we find meaning and purpose without a transcendent dimension in our lives?

Perhaps no other book of the Bible so vividly portrays this attempt to create a secular Utopia than the Old Testament book of Ecclesiastes. Likewise, no other book of the Bible speaks so powerfully and prophetically to our twenty-first-century culture. Great literary minds have long admired this seemingly pessimistic but timeless tome on life. In addition to Thomas Wolfe's praise, the God-haunted agnostic Herman Melville declared in *Moby Dick,* "The truest of all books is Ecclesiastes." Commenting on the uniqueness of the book in the Scriptures, British theologian Derek Kidner observes,

> Anyone who spends time with Ecclesiastes (that least ecclesiastical of men) finds himself in the company of a highly independent and fascinating mind. . . . The voice of the Old Testament has many accents. . . . But there is no-one quite like Qoheleth (to give him his untranslatable title);[1] no book in this whole great volume speaks in quite his tone of voice. His natural habitat, so to speak, is among the wise men who teach

us to use our eyes as well as our ears to learn the ways of God and man. . . . Wisdom—quite practical and orthodox—is his base-camp; but he is an explorer. His concern is with the boundaries of life, and especially with the questions that most of us would hesitate to push too far.[2]

Despite the prophetic wisdom contained in Ecclesiastes, because its writer, Qoheleth (the Preacher), pushes the boundaries of life, the book is often regarded as a classic work of despair, cynicism, and ambiguity.

The Ambiguity of Ecclesiastes

Because the Preacher in Ecclesiastes confronts us with some very uncomfortable questions, the church has largely neglected his sage advice. This neglect is born of a general cynicism and pessimism about life that the modern reader, especially the more "ecclesiastical" person, encounters in Ecclesiastes. Yet, as we saw in the first chapter, when our culture loses the transcendent dimensions of life, the result is trivialization and cynicism, not only about God and religion but about many other things as well.

In virtually every arena of life, cynicism is the prevalent mood of the day. Alexander Pope declared, "Blessed is he who expects nothing, for he shall never be disappointed." Lily Tomlin mused, "Things are going to get a lot worse before they get worse." Woody Allen observed, "Life is divided into the horrible and the miserable." James Hagerty declared, "One day I sat thinking almost in despair; a hand fell on my shoulder and a voice said reassuringly: 'Cheer up, things could get worse.' So I cheered up and, sure enough, things got worse." George Burns made the witty observation, "Happiness is having a large, loving, caring, close-knit family . . . in another city."

A primary reason for the cynicism in Ecclesiastes is that life presents us with many ambiguities. It is sometimes assumed, especially among religious people, that "The Good Life" will always be the reward for faithfulness to God. This prosperity theology promises blessings, riches, and a life of comfort if we will only "give our lives to Jesus" and become His devoted followers. Such thinking goes along the lines of "God has a wonderful plan for your life." But Ecclesiastes does not fit easily into the prosperity theology that pervades segments of the contemporary church. Rather, the Preacher shows us that this present life is greatly characterized by ambiguity and does not necessarily reward the righteous nor punish the guilty. He declares in Ecclesiastes 8:14:

> There is futility which is done on the earth, that is, there are righteous men to whom it happens according to the deeds of the wicked. On the other hand, there are evil men to whom it happens according to the deeds of the righteous. I say that this too is futility. (Compare Ecclesiastes 7:15.)

Eugene Peterson concludes his book *Run with the Horses* with this insightful comment on the prophet Jeremiah, which is reminiscent of the cynical and ambiguous nature of Ecclesiastes:

> Flannery O'Connor once remarked that she had an aunt who thought that nothing happened in a story unless somebody got married or shot at the end of it. But life seldom provides such definitive endings. Life is ambiguous. There are loose ends. It takes maturity to live with the ambiguity and the chaos, the absurdity and the untidiness. If we refuse to live with it, we exclude something, and what we exclude may very well be the essential and dear—the hazards of faith, the mysteries of God. . . . Jeremiah ends inconclusively. We want to know the end, but there is no end. . . . We want to know that he was finally successful so that, if we live well and courageously, we also will be successful. Or we want to know that he was finally unsuccessful so that, since a life of faith and

integrity doesn't pay off, we can go on with finding another means by which to live. We get neither in Jeremiah. He doesn't get married and he doesn't get shot.[3]

The Modernity of Ecclesiastes

Because modern culture has "come of age" (to use Dietrich Bonhoeffer's phrase) and no longer considers God as necessary to account for mankind and the world, we must look to a book that addresses the thinking and mood of modern people. In many ways, Ecclesiastes' modernity makes it a powerful apologetic for today. Peter Kreeft rightly observes,

> Ecclesiastes is the one book in the Bible that modern man needs most to read, for it is Lesson One, and the rest of the Bible is Lesson Two, and modernity does not heed Lesson Two because it does not heed Lesson One. Whenever I teach the Bible as a whole, I always begin with Ecclesiastes. In another age, we could begin with God's beginning, Genesis. But in this age, the Age of Man, we must begin where our patient is: we must begin with Ecclesiastes.[4]

Qoheleth sets forth an appraisal of life that is brutally honesty. Robert Short authored *A Time to Live and a Time to Die,* a book of contemporary photographs, one for each verse of Ecclesiastes. Similarly, Ecclesiastes is a series of *word photographs,* or "light writings," pictures taken with light "under the sun" (a key phrase that occurs some twenty-nine times in Ecclesiastes). Unlike the other biblical writers, Qoheleth informs us about life by using only the available light "under the sun": observation and human reason. He has no flashbulb of faith to reveal life's ambiguities.

Because the Preacher is only using natural revelation "under the sun," without the aid of faith, the book is inviting us not so much to think as to *feel*. Ecclesiastes is an existential book. Does my existence have any meaning? While earlier ages debated what the meaning of human existence was, our day asks the more fundamental question, *Is* there meaning in our existence? If there is one fate for all, namely death, can anything have significance? If every card in our hand will be trumped, does it really matter how we play?[5] Listen to Qoheleth's similar lament:

> For there is no lasting remembrance of the wise man as with the fool, inasmuch as in the coming days all will be forgotten. And how the wise man and the fool alike die! So I hated life, for the work which had been done under the sun was grievous to me; because everything is futility and striving after wind. Thus I hated all the fruit of my labor for which I had labored under the sun, for I must leave it to the man who will come after me. (Ecclesiastes 2:16-18)

Hence, Ecclesiastes assaults modernity's greatest fear, which is not so much the fear of death (ancient man's deepest fear) or the fear of sin, guilt, or Hell (medieval man's deepest fear), but the fear of meaninglessness.[6] Throughout the book, Qoheleth uses the word "vanity" (Hebrew *haval*) thirty-five times to stress the fact that all of life is vanity, ephemeral, transient, purposeless. But in Ecclesiastes, the word no longer means simply what is slight and passing, but more ominously, what is pointless. It is a *desperate* word. A dialogue from the movie *Holiday* wonderfully captures the unsettledness of contemporary culture in its quest for meaning and purpose. These lines spoken by Cary Grant to Katherine Hepburn sound like a modern-day Qoheleth:

> Linda: How does your garden grow, Case? Is life wonderful where you are?
>
> Johnny: It can be.

Linda: But it hasn't been?

Johnny: Well, I don't call what I've been doing living.

Linda: And what do you recommend for yourself, Doctor?

Johnny: A holiday.

Linda: For how long?

Johnny: As long as I need.

Linda: Just to play?

Johnny: No, no. I've been working since I was ten. I want to find out why I'm working. The answer can't be just to pay bills and to pile up more money. Even if you do, the government's going to take most of it.

Linda: Yes, but what is the answer?

Johnny: Well, I don't know. That's what I intend to find out.[7]

The Strategy of Ecclesiastes

The strategy Qoheleth uses in getting us to consider the purpose and meaning of life is in keeping with the general air of cynicism that pervades the book. In many ways, he is seeking to knock the props out from under our lives—such props as money, fame, and fortune—to get us to look at life from a new perspective. Kidner accurately describes his strategy:

> He is demolishing to build. The searching questions he has asked are those that life itself puts to us, if we will only listen. He can afford to ask them, because in the final chapters he has good news for us, once we can stop pretending that what is mortal is enough for us, who have been given a capacity for the eternal.[8]

We also see the Preacher's strategy within the disconcerting structure of Ecclesiastes. The book clearly defies any logical outline. It seems to ramble, going nowhere in particular, containing bits of wisdom here and there sprinkled over a desert landscape of futility and meaninglessness. It is kind of like a collage of photos taken through the porthole of a sinking ship,[9] yet this rambling is deliberate, for this form ideally suits the book's content. Just as life rambles, going nowhere (from a naturalistic, horizontal perspective), so Ecclesiastes practices what it preaches.

Yet a subtle structure is given at the outset of the book, a cameo of Ecclesiastes in the first three verses: "The words of the Preacher, the son of David, king in Jerusalem. 'Vanity of vanities,' says the Preacher. 'Vanity of vanities! All is vanity.' What advantage does man have in all his work which he does under the sun?" Because "all toil" (*any* work, everything we do, all human pursuits) is "under the sun," and because everything under the sun is vanity, it follows naturally that all our toil is vanity. In these few terse verses, we are confronted with a worldview that seems to put the lie to everything of seeming importance.

In addition to the key words "vanity" and "under the sun," which stress desperation, the phrase "what does man gain?" strongly supports Qoheleth's contention that life, for all its success, is *undone* in the end. A free translation of this verse might read, "You spend your life working, laboring, and what do you have to show for it?"[10] When one samples all that this life has to offer and still lacks happiness and fulfillment, where is one to turn? In a covert manner, the Preacher is exposing the bankruptcy of the world in its ability to provide ultimate meaning and purpose to life.[11]

Five Candidates for the Greatest Good

Qoheleth is no ordinary teacher. He invites us on a journey that he himself has taken to see if any candidate under the sun can provide lasting happiness and fulfillment. At least five candidates, five efforts, five "toils," are introduced throughout the book. These are perhaps the five most universal lifestyles that humanity follows to find meaning and significance in life: *wisdom, pleasure, power and riches, altruism,* and *naturalistic religion.*[12]

The first of these candidates is philosophical intellectualism, or the pursuit of *wisdom.* Qoheleth desperately wants to know what is the ultimate end, the *summum bonum* of life. Where are true happiness and fulfillment found? He is a philosopher at heart, a lover of wisdom, so naturally he hopes that wisdom will provide this fulfillment.

> I, the Preacher, have been king over Israel in Jerusalem. And I set my mind to seek and explore by wisdom concerning all that has been done under heaven. It is a grievous task which God has given to the sons of men to be afflicted with. I have seen all the works which have been done under the sun, and behold, all is vanity and striving after wind. . . . I said to myself, "Behold, I have magnified and increased wisdom more than all who were over Jerusalem before me; and my mind has observed a wealth of wisdom and knowledge." And I set my mind to know wisdom and to know madness and folly; I realized that this also is striving after wind. Because in much wisdom there is much grief, and increasing knowledge results in increasing pain. (Ecclesiastes 1:12-14,16-18)

Despite his quest for happiness through filling his mind with knowledge and wisdom, even considering madness and folly, the only wisdom he attained was that "in much wisdom there is much grief, and increasing knowledge results in increasing pain." Qoheleth's discovery bears a remarkable similarity to those in our own day, when we are unparalleled in our ability to discover, learn, and access information about virtually anything under the sun. Yet we too, if we are wise, will come to realize the futility of looking to wisdom and information to bring us lasting meaning and purpose. T. S. Eliot, the celebrated poet and literary critic, expresses this sentiment well in his "Choruses from 'The Rock,'" when he declares that our knowledge leads us only to our "ignorance" and our ignorance "nearer to death," not God. Eliot then asks us to consider, "Where is the wisdom we have lost in knowledge."[13]

The second candidate for true meaning and fulfillment is *pleasure*. If happiness cannot be found through stimulating the mind (wisdom), then perhaps bodily pleasures will work (hedonism). Qoheleth's experiment with pleasure involved a virtual sensory overload, including wine, women, and song. He experienced an almost Disneyesque lifestyle. Listen to how he describes it:

> I said to myself, "Come now, I will test you with pleasure. So enjoy yourself." And behold, it too was futility. I said of laughter, "It is madness," and of pleasure, "What does it accomplish?" I explored with my mind how to stimulate my body with wine. . . . I enlarged my works: I built houses for myself, I planted vineyards for myself; I made gardens and parks for myself, and I planted in them all kinds of fruit trees; I made ponds of water for myself from which to irrigate a forest of growing trees. I bought male and female slaves. . . . Also I possessed flocks and herds larger than all who preceded me in Jerusalem. Also, I collected for myself silver and gold, and the treasure of kings and provinces. I provided for myself male and female singers and the pleasures of men—many concubines. . . . Thus I considered all my activities which my hands had done and the labor which I had exerted, and behold all was vanity and striving after wind and there was no profit under the sun. (Ecclesiastes 2:1-8,11)

Just as modernity is enraptured with a quest for wisdom and information, the quest for pleasure as the purpose in life also holds a prominent place in our culture. In a world devoid of an eternal, transcendent dimension, the "pleasure principle" rules supreme. Mirroring the eighteenth-century French philosopher Rousseau, who declared that "happiness is a good bank account, a good cook, and good digestion," the late comedian George Burns once put his own inimitable twist on the quote: "Happiness is a good meal, a good cigar, and a good woman. Or a bad woman, depending on how much happiness you can stand!"

Because modernity has become anesthetized to the spiritual world, this present temporal world has become its haven of rest. Consequently, the *summum bonum* is to be found largely through the pleasures of this life. In Carnegie Hall's concert program an advertisement selling luxury apartments captured the spirit of our age: "Nobody gets out of life alive. So it makes superb common sense to live as beautifully, as comfortably, and as creatively as possible while one has the time. Life is too short to settle for second best."[14]

To many of us who do not "have it all," pleasures promise to fill the empty void, to bring happiness. Yet the truth of the matter is that we, like Qoheleth, become disillusioned with hedonistic aspirations. Why? Because in the end we sense that even pleasures are "vanity and striving after wind," because pleasure seeking inevitably produces boredom and apathy. And to overcome the inertia of boredom and apathy, we must experience even stronger doses of pleasure. There is a paradox to hedonism: the more we hunt for pleasure, the less we are able to find and sustain it.[15]

The third candidate in Qoheleth's experiment for ultimate meaning and purpose is *power and riches*. If he cannot find happiness from filling his mind with wisdom (intellectualism), or his body with pleasure (hedonism), then perhaps filling his wallet with money (materialism) is the answer. In his world as ours, if we have wealth and power, we can buy the pleasures we desire. As we saw earlier, his goal in life was amassing great wealth, the most obvious form of power, and relatively speaking, he had no equal: "Also, I collected . . .

silver and gold, and the treasure of kings and provinces. . . . Then I became great and increased more than all who preceded me in Jerusalem" (Ecclesiastes 2:8-9).

It seems to be a part of the human condition to believe that wealth and money can bring genuine and lasting happiness. Over a hundred years ago, novelist Jane Austen mused, "A large income is the best recipe for happiness I ever heard of." In reality, wealth often confuses us with what is really important in life. In Deadwood, South Dakota, there is a Wild West museum that displays artifacts from a past era. On display is a note left by an unsuccessfully successful prospector, which reads,

I lost my gun.

I lost my horse.

I am out of food.

The Indians are after me.

But I've got all the gold I can carry.

We laugh at such folly, but deep down we know that it may describe our approach to living. We don't comprehend what a powerful influence the desire for wealth exerts on all of us. So Qoheleth would have us realize, as many wealthy and powerful people have discovered, that fame and fortune do not bring ultimate happiness. Contentment and satisfaction do not lie in amassing what this world has to offer. Rather, what we need is the perspective of contentment. Listen to the conversation years ago between Jed Clampett and Cousin Pearl in the television program *The Beverly Hillbillies:*

Jed: Pearl, what d'ya think? Think I oughta move?

Cousin Pearl: Jed, how can ya even ask? Look around ya.

You're eight miles from yore nearest neighbor. Yore overrun with skunks, possums, coyotes, bobcats. You use kerosene lamps fer light and you cook on a wood stove summer and winter. Yore drinkin' homemade moonshine and washin' with homemade lye soap. And yore bathroom is fifty feet from the house and you ask "Should I move?"

Jed: I reckon yore right. A man'd be a dang fool to leave all this![16]

Somehow we need to capture the secret of contentment that characterized Jed Clampett. We need to come to the realization, as Helen Keller once observed, that "contentment is not the fulfillment of what you want, but the realization of how much you already have." Leo Tolstoy once told a story about a peasant who was offered all the land he could walk around in one day. The man hurried to encircle as much land as possible, but his exertion was so great he fell dead just as he got back to where he had begun. He ended with nothing.[17] Similarly, John D. Rockefeller declared, "I have made many millions, but they have brought me no happiness." John Jacob Astor left five million dollars to his heirs, but at the end of his life lamented, "I am the most miserable man on earth." Andrew Carnegie once commented, no doubt from personal experience, "Millionaires seldom smile."

Like the paradox of hedonism, there is a paradox of materialism. The more we look for happiness through wealth and power, the more disillusioned we become. Only the hunger remains. No, we need something more substantial than toys and trinkets to make this life meaningful. Perhaps novelist John Steinbeck was on to something when he declared, "Money is easy to make if it's money you want. But with few exceptions people don't want money. They want luxury and they want love and they want admiration."[18]

Qoheleth reasons that if the key to life is not to be found in the selfish pursuit of filling his mind, body, or pocketbook, then perhaps it lies in service to others. This is Qoheleth's fourth *summum bonum* candidate, *altruism*. Perhaps through philanthropy and living for others — especially for posterity — life can have lasting significance. Having experimented with vain pursuits to bring happiness, he hints at the importance of relationships and friendships:

> Two are better than one because they have a good return for their labor. For if either of them falls, the one will lift up his companion. But woe to the one who falls when there is not another to lift him up. . . . A cord of three strands is not quickly torn apart. (Ecclesiastes 4:9-10,12)

But as noble as this may seem, it is not enough to overcome a life of vanity:

> Thus I hated all the fruit of my labor for which I had labored under the sun, for I must leave it to the man who will come after me. And who knows whether he will be a wise man or a fool? Yet he will have control over all the fruit of my labor for which I have labored by acting wisely under the sun. This too is vanity. (Ecclesiastes 2:18-19)

Qoheleth has come to the stark realization that it is meaningless to work for posterity because posterity may very well be a fool! As he has already discovered that wisdom, pleasure, wealth, and power are vanity for him, they will be equally vain for his posterity. It is all well and fine to work for the good of others, to put altruism over narcissism, but one must ask the fundamental question, What *is* the good of others?

The desire to place altruistic aspirations as the greatest good in one's life finds many contemporary expressions. A number of years ago, David Frost interviewed media mogul Ted Turner in what turned out to be a very enlightening and honest intimation of

Turner's purpose in life. Having been raised in a Christian home with the hopes of becoming a missionary, Turner jettisoned the God of Christianity during his adolescence. This was due in part to his sister's death from cancer and, he says, because he could not find adequate answers for his searching questions.

Turner admitted to Frost that he had instead chosen to focus his attention and financial resources toward world peace and ecological concerns. To this statement Frost asked him the penetrating question, "But haven't you simply exchanged one gospel for another? A spiritual gospel for a social gospel?" Turner, mental wheels turning, had no answer for Frost. Interestingly, in recent years Turner has established the Turner Foundation, which has become the world's largest financial supporter of environmental causes. Most curious is the fact that Turner, mirroring the Judeo-Christian Ten Commandments, has laid out his foundation's core values in "Ten Voluntary Initiatives." [19]

If intellectualism, hedonism, materialism, and altruism prove unsatisfactory in providing ultimate purpose and meaning to life, then perhaps religion will work, reasons Qoheleth. Conventional, *naturalistic religion* is his fifth candidate for the *summum bonum*. While biblical faith or religion—an understanding of the true knowledge of God—would provide an adequate explanation of Qoheleth's penetrating search for significance and happiness, his God is merely the God of reason and human experience. As mentioned earlier, his beliefs stem from sensory observation and human reason, "photographs" of life taken with the only available light "under the sun." Consider his sobering words:

> Consider the work of God, for who is able to straighten what He has bent? In the day of prosperity be happy, but in the day of adversity consider—God has made the one as well as the other so that man may not discover anything that will be after him. I have seen everything during my lifetime of futility; there is a righteous man who perishes in his righteousness,

and there is a wicked man who prolongs his life in his wickedness. Do not be excessively righteous, and do not be overly wise. Why should you ruin yourself? Do not be excessively wicked, and do not be a fool. Why should you die before your time? (Ecclesiastes 7:13-17)

One thing is certain about Qoheleth's musings on religion: he is an honest observer. While the rest of the Scriptures will extol the benevolence and goodness of God, Ecclesiastes is content to describe God, like the universe, as impersonal and uncaring. Qoheleth's God is the God of nature and reason, who can only be known by observation and experience. While such a God may elicit fear and belief, such a God could not be genuinely loved or trusted. Kreeft rightly declares,

> Such a God is merely "the Force" of *Star Wars*. . . . Such a God is . . . a thing to acknowledge, not a person to love and listen to and long for. The Great Unknown, however great, cannot fill the hole in our heart or the hole in our head. He must become known. But that story is in the rest of the Bible.[20]

Having considered the major candidates that would give ultimate meaning and happiness, Qoheleth comes to the end of his experiment, a disillusioned but wiser man. He may fill his mind with wisdom, his body with pleasure, his pockets with wealth, his conscience with good works, or his spirit with religion, but in the end all his striving and accomplishments are futile. Man must look for something greater to bring lasting meaning and satisfaction. The French mathematician and Christian philosopher Blaise Pascal rightly mused, "Anyone who does not see the vanity of life is vain indeed."

The End of the Journey
As Qoheleth discovers, all of life has a built-in fizzle to it. The world's promise to deliver ultimate happiness, significance, and satisfaction

is at best inadequate and fleeting. Tennis great John McEnroe candidly remarked in an interview several years ago, "I haven't quite figured out how to enjoy losing. As you get older, the pain of losing is greater, and the joy of winning is diminished." [21]

After the assassination of John F. Kennedy, Daniel Patrick Moynihan was heard to say, "To be Irish is to know that in the end the world will break your heart." [22] And in the end, we know that he is right. The world will break our hearts. In the end, death will trump even the most glorious earthly existence. Where is God in all of this futility? Does He care? Not only is Qoheleth's God known only from nature and reason, but more significantly, He is a God of silence.

Yet even that silence has a purpose. Ecclesiastes is the only book in the Bible in which God is totally silent. Qoheleth's appeal is, as we have seen, only to human reason and sense observation. He claims to know nothing of divine revelation; thus Ecclesiastes is all monologue, not dialogue. Nonetheless, the book is divine revelation. "How is it divine revelation?" Kreeft asks.

> It is inspired monologue. God in his providence has arranged for this one book of mere rational philosophy to be included in the canon of Scripture because this too is divine revelation. It is divine revelation precisely in being the absence of divine revelation. It is like the silhouette of the rest of the Bible. . . . In this book God reveals to us exactly what life is when God does not reveal to us what life is. Ecclesiastes frames the Bible as death frames life. [23]

It has been suggested that while Qoheleth penned the Song of Solomon in his youth and his writings in Proverbs in middle age, it was not until he looked back upon a long life of futility—a life lived without God—that he authored Ecclesiastes. Having surveyed everything under the sun that promised to give lasting happiness and meaning, he waits until the end of the book to suggest the only thing that can transcend a world of futility and meaninglessness: our Creator. At last we are ready, if we ever intend to be, to look beyond earthly vanities to God, who made us for Himself.

> Remember also your Creator in the days of your youth,
> before the evil days come and the years draw near when you
> will say, "I have no delight in them"; before the sun, the light,
> the moon, and the stars are darkened, and clouds return after
> the rain; in the day that the watchmen of the house tremble,
> and mighty men stoop, the grinding ones stand idle because
> they are few, and those who look through windows grow dim;
> and the doors on the street are shut as the sound of the grind-
> ing mill is low, and one will arise at the sound of the bird, and
> all the daughters of song will sing softly. Furthermore, men
> are afraid of a high place and of terrors on the road; the
> almond tree blossoms, the grasshopper drags himself along,
> and the caperberry is ineffective. For man goes to his eternal
> home while mourners go about in the street. Remember Him
> before the silver cord is broken and the golden bowl is
> crushed, the pitcher by the well is shattered and the wheel at
> the cistern is crushed; then the dust will return to the earth as
> it was, and the spirit will return to God who gave it. "Vanity of
> vanities," says the Preacher, "all is vanity!" (Ecclesiastes 12:1-8)

This passage, one of the most beautiful of all sequences of word pictures in the Old Testament, serves as a poignant reflection of a wise old man who has achieved wisdom through living. It is an eloquent allegory, the picture of a great house in decline that speaks of our mental as well as physical aging. Qoheleth then concludes his book with these powerful words: "The conclusion, when all has been heard, is: fear God and keep His commandments, because this applies to every person. For God will bring every act to judgment, everything which is hidden, whether it is good or evil" (Ecclesiastes 12:13-14).

Up to this point in the book, we have seen that all of our paths and strivings come to nothing. And yet in this last chapter the Preacher sets us on a path that will not disappoint, the path to God. Here is the goal for which we were made, the Eternal toward whom the eternity of man's heart was intended to gravitate and find its home (see Ecclesiastes 3:11).

This is the driving force behind the words of Qoheleth in Ecclesiastes. The world offers abundant pleasures and temporal happiness, but in the end life adds up to futility and despair, because everything comes to nothing. Qoheleth suggests that God purposefully has us taste of this emptiness and futility that we might seek Him, our true resting place. C. S. Lewis contended in many of his writings that, however grand the pleasures of this life are, they are in fact "drippings of grace," intended by God to whet our appetites, to awaken our thirst for eternal pleasures. To Lewis, however great this world's pleasures may be, there still remain these inconsolable longings (*sensucht*), intimations of a redeemed world to come.

As we turn from our futile attempts to find lasting meaning, purpose, and significance, Ecclesiastes reminds us that we can have no sustained purpose and significance apart from God. The modern world may seek desperately to create a secular Heaven on earth, but in the end such a Utopia is reduced to nothing. This is Qoheleth's cry: "Vanity of vanities! All is vanity." The confession of Augustine, used as a prelude to his own story, could easily serve as a coda to the book of Ecclesiastes:

> Thou hast made us for Thyself,
> And our heart is restless till it rests in Thee.[24]

A fitting postscript to the book of Ecclesiastes is a poem by George Herbert entitled "The Pulley."[25] Herbert poignantly extols the truth that our feeble attempts to find significance and satisfaction apart from the living God lead not to rest, but to weariness.

Hopefully, in God's providence, that weariness will lead to our true resting place, God Himself.

> When God at first made man,
> Having a glass of blessing standing by;
> Let us (said He) pour on him all we can:
> Let the world's riches, which dispersed lie,
> Contract into a span.
>
> So strength first made a way;
> Then beauty flowed, then wisdom, honor, pleasure,
> When almost all was out, God made a stay,
> Perceiving that alone of all His treasure,
> Rest, in the bottom lay.
>
> For if I should (said He)
> Bestow this jewel also on My creature,
> He would adore My gifts instead of Me,
> And rest in nature, not the God of nature:
> So both should losers be.
>
> Yet let him keep the rest,
> But keep them with repining restlessness:
> Let him be rich and weary, that at least,
> If goodness lead him not, yet weariness
> May toss him to My breast.

Part II

The Intimations of Heaven

The difference between the old Narnia and the new Narnia was like that. The new one was a deeper country: every rock and flower and blade of grass looked as if it meant more. I can't describe it any better than that: if you ever get there you will know what I mean. It was the Unicorn who summed up what everyone was feeling. He stamped his right fore-hoof on the ground and neighed and then cried: "I have come home at last! This is my real country! I belong here. This is the land I have been looking for all my life."

—C. S. Lewis

In part 1, we observed that our modern world has lost a sense of transcendence and consequently has abdicated any true sense of belief in Heaven. To our contemporary world, the idea of Heaven has become either too trivial or secularized to teach us anything of real substance about what lies beyond this present life. Yet, as we saw from the book of Ecclesiastes, our attempts to find meaning and purpose solely in this world—apart from God—are doomed to futility and failure.

Let us now turn to consider some of the clues along the way, the "signals" that may help us recapture a sense of awe and wonder with our world and point us onward—"further up and further in"—to discover that undiscovered country for which we have been looking all of our lives.

CHAPTER 3

THE HEART HAS ITS REASONS

Never lose a holy curiosity.

—Albert Einstein

Earth's crammed with heaven,
And every common bush aflame with God;
But only he who sees takes off his shoes,
The rest sit 'round and pluck blackberries.

—Elizabeth Barrett Browning

There is a road from the eye to the heart that does not go through the intellect.

—G. K. Chesterton

DO YOU REMEMBER THE OWL IN *ALICE'S ADVENTURES IN WONDERLAND?* Alice sought out the Owl because she had heard that he had the Answer. When she found him, she said, "It is said that you alone have the Answer." The Owl replied, "My friend, as much as is said of me is true." So she asked the Owl her question. And he answered carefully, "You must find out for yourself." Alice said angrily, "Did I need the Owl to tell me I must think for myself?" "But, my friend," the Owl replied. "*That* is the Answer."

Perhaps in no other generation is the need so great for clear thinking about the significant issues of life. Is there hope for life beyond the grave? Is there a Heaven? What is the Answer? Can there even *be* answers to life's most important questions? What are we to make of this life? Some time ago a friend sent me a fax that expresses a common sentiment:

> LIFE IS A TEST. It is only a Test. If this were your actual life, you would have been given better instructions.

Many of us wander through life searching for clues to make ourselves happy and our lives meaningful. Yet skepticism and cynicism concerning answers to life's big questions characterize our age. The modern world is deeply suspicious of anyone claiming to have knowledge about transcendent affairs. Actor Steve Martin captured the mood of our day when he declared, "It's so hard to believe anything anymore. . . . I guess I wouldn't believe in anything if it weren't for my lucky Astrology Mood Watch."

In an interview with the magazine *College People*, filmmaker Woody Allen mused, "More than any other time in history, mankind faces a crossroads. One path leads to despair and utter hopelessness. The other, to total extinction. Let us pray we have the wisdom to choose correctly." [1] In one of the essays in his book *Without Feathers,* Allen questions the possibility of divine revelation as he spoofs the biblical story of Abraham and Isaac. As Allen tells the story,

Abraham reports to his wife, Sarah, (and son, Isaac) that God has commanded him to sacrifice their only son. Listen to this brooding dialogue as both Isaac and Sarah challenge Abraham to demonstrate how he knows for sure that he has heard from God:

> And Abraham awoke in the middle of the night and said to his only son, Isaac, "I have had a dream where the voice of the Lord sayeth that I must sacrifice my only son, so put your pants on." And Isaac trembled and said, "So what did you say? I mean when He brought this whole thing up?" "What am I going to say?" Abraham said. "I'm standing there at two A.M. in my underwear with the Creator of the Universe. Should I argue?" "Well, did he say why he wants me sacrificed?" Isaac asked his father. But Abraham said, "The faithful do not question. Now let's go because I have a heavy day tomorrow." And Sarah . . . said, "How doth thou know it was the Lord?" . . . And Abraham answered, "Because I know it was the Lord. It was a deep, resonant voice, well modulated, and nobody in the desert can get a rumble in it like that." [2]

A Doglike State of Mind

How did the modern world come to have such suspicion and disregard for those who embrace a confident faith in the world to come? While this subject was largely dealt with in chapter 1, it needs to be reiterated that the modern scientific method, with the reign of empiricism, has given us a false sense of reality and truth. In essence, the scientific method has been employed by the modern world as the controlling paradigm for all objectively true knowledge, with the result that anything that is not empirically verifiable is automatically suspect. If it is not scientifically provable, then it must be a dogma of faith. In other words, the scientific community has often suggested that what we can verify through the physical senses is considered material, real, and objective while that which lies beyond the scope of the physical senses is considered spiritual, matters of faith or opinion, and subjective.

C. S. Lewis addressed the blinding effect of such a reductionistic worldview in his essay "Transposition." He observes that a dog cannot understand what you are doing when you point to its food. Invariably, it will sniff your finger rather than look down at the food. Lewis contends that our world, like the dog's world, is all fact and no meaning. Empiricism has led to this doglike state of mind.[3] This world of all fact and no meaning that Lewis describes, a world of great knowledge but meager insight, is well portrayed in a poem by Robert Short:

> Lots of know-how, but little know-why;
> Lots of sight, but little insight.

This dilemma of modernity was evidenced by one of the high priests of philosophy and science of the twentieth century, George Bernard Shaw. Toward the end of his life he made this candid admission concerning the failure of his beloved science to find answers to life's ultimate questions:

> The science to which I have pinned my faith is bankrupt. Its counsels, which should have established the millennium, led instead directly to the suicide of Europe. I believed them once. In their name I helped to destroy the faith of millions of worshippers in the temples of a thousand creeds. And now they look at me and witness the great tragedy of an atheist who has lost his faith.

Looking Through the Eye

For all of our sophistication and knowledge, we as a culture are still left wanting for answers to ultimate questions. Recall the William Blake poem quoted at the beginning of part 1:

This Life's dim windows of the soul
Distorts the Heavens from Pole to Pole
And leads you to believe a lie
When you see with, not through, the eye.[4]

This poem suggests that when we look only on the surface of things, reality may very well be distorted. If not distorted, then at least minimized or trivialized. We need to look beneath the surface of the material world for answers to life's challenging questions. Why? Because it is only beneath the surface of this material, visible world that transcendent answers can be found. We, like Alice, need to ask the deep questions.

In his essay "Meditation in a Toolshed," Lewis recounts his standing in a dark toolshed with the sun brilliantly shining outside but only a sunbeam coming through the crack at the top of the door. While everything else in the toolshed was pitch black, the beam of light, by which he could see flecks of dust floating about, was the most striking thing in that toolshed.

> I was seeing the beam, not seeing things by it. Then I moved, so that the beam fell on my eyes. Instantly the whole previous picture vanished. I saw no toolshed, and (above all) no beam. Instead I saw, framed in the irregular cranny at the top of the door, green leaves moving in the branches of a tree outside and beyond that, 90 odd million miles away, the sun. Looking along the beam, and looking at the beam are very different experiences.[5]

In our modern world, which provides largely surface answers to life's questions, where can we turn? If looking at the world only *with* our eyes (to use Blake's image) leads us to believe a lie, then perhaps we should look *through* the eye, to see life as it really is. Or, to use Lewis's image, perhaps we should step *inside* to the transcendent nature of life. Both Blake and Lewis challenge us to look for clues to life's meaning through the "eye of faith."

Listening to Our Hearts

What Blake and Lewis are encouraging us to do is to let our interior lives inform us about life. They are fundamentally challenging us to let our heart be our teacher and guide. When we hear the word "heart," we often make the mistaken assumption that the business of the heart is to feel but not to see or think. Blaise Pascal's most famous and probably most misunderstood dictum reads, "The heart has its reasons, of which reason knows nothing. . . . It is the heart which perceives God and not the reason. That is what faith is: God perceived by the heart, not by the reason."[6]

More often than not, Pascal's statement is understood as an argument favoring sentimentalism and subjectivism over reason. Yet if one properly understands Pascal, who was a brilliant mathematician and Christian apologist, it is clear that he is not saying we should jettison thinking in favor of sentimentality. Rather, he is suggesting that learning and reason by themselves are cul-de-sacs and have their limits: "Reason's last step is the recognition that there are an infinite number of things which are beyond it. It is merely feeble if it does not go as far as to realize that."[7]

Pascal is arguing that our heart, that deepest core of our individual lives, does in fact *see,* and we must look at life with it if we are to avoid the muddled thinking that Blake and Lewis address. A scene from Harriet Beecher Stowe's classic *Uncle Tom's Cabin* beautifully captures this idea. In it Tom, the slave, is talking to his skeptical owner, Augustine St. Clare, about his religious convictions following the death of St. Clare's devout daughter, Eva:

> St. Clare: Who knows anything about anything? Was all that beautiful love and faith only one of the ever-shifting phases of human feeling, having nothing real to rest on, passing

away with the little breath? And is there no more Eva,—no heaven,—no Christ,—nothing?

Tom: O, dear Mas'r, there is! I know it; I'm sure of it. Do, do, dear Mas'r, believe it!

St. Clare: How do you know there's any Christ, Tom? You never saw the Lord.

Tom: Felt Him in my soul, Mas'r,—feel Him now!

St. Clare: Tom, this is all real to you!

Tom: I can jest fairly see it, Mas'r.

St. Clare: I wish I had your eyes, Tom. But Tom, you know that I have a great deal more knowledge than you; what if I should tell you that I don't believe this Bible? Wouldn't it shake your faith some, Tom?

Tom: Not a grain.[8]

Tom was not advocating an anti-intellectual approach to life. He was merely pointing out to St. Clare that there is a knowledge that transcends the intellect. That knowledge comes from the fundamental conviction of the heart.

The Role of the Heart in the Bible
It is interesting that the biblical usage of "heart" more closely resembles Pascal's idea than the commonly associated meaning. From an Old Testament perspective, the heart serves as a vital component enabling us to comprehend life. Hans Walter Wolff, professor of Old Testament at the University of Heidelberg, comments on the various usages of "heart" in the Old Testament:

In by far the greatest number of cases it is intellectual, rational functions that are ascribed to the heart—i.e., precisely what we ascribe to the head and, more exactly, to the brain. . . . We must guard against the false impression that biblical man is determined more by feeling than reason. This mistaken anthropological direction is all too easily derived from an undifferentiated rendering of *leb*. The Bible sets before men clear alternatives, which have to be recognized.[9]

These observations suggest that the heart is life's primary instrument of discernment and insight. Far from the stereotypical Western mindset, the biblical notion suggests that the heart knows and sees life—and possesses intuitive insight. We are therefore invited to listen with our heart, for it will intimate to us the transcendent nature of life.

The Scriptures are replete with examples of how our world powerfully points to the transcendent nature of this world and to the God who governs it. David extols the beauty of the created order as a signpost pointing to God when he declares,

The heavens are telling of the glory of God;
And their expanse is declaring the work of His hands.
Day to day pours forth speech,
And night to night reveals knowledge. (Psalm 19:1-2)

In his famous sermon at the Areopagus on Mars Hill, the apostle Paul spoke passionately to a pagan Greek culture with a pantheon of gods but without a knowledge of the one true God. Commending their religious fervor, he proclaimed to them that what they worshiped in ignorance, he would now declare to them. In these verses he appeals not only to God as the transcendent Creator, but also to the living God as the immanent One who is close to each one of them. In Paul's estimation, the Athenians could seek and find the true God if they sought Him with their hearts:

"The God who made the world and all things in it, since He is Lord of heaven and earth, does not dwell in temples made with hands; neither is He served by human hands, as though He needed anything, since He Himself gives to all life and breath and all things; and He made from one, every nation of mankind to live on all the face of the earth, having determined their appointed times, and the boundaries of their habitation, that they should seek God, if perhaps they might grope for Him and find Him, though He is not far from each one of us; for in Him we live and move and exist, as even some of your own poets have said, 'For we also are His offspring.'" (Acts 17:24-28)

In perhaps the most highly theological book of the New Testament, the epistle to the Romans, Paul declares that our world bears eloquent testimony to the presence of God. He argues that our world provides for us a profound *heart* knowledge about God, even though many people may suppress this knowledge of God born out of nature:

Because that which is known about God is evident within them; for God made it evident to them. For since the creation of the world His invisible attributes, His eternal power and divine nature, have been clearly seen, being understood through what has been made, so that they are without excuse. (Romans 1:19-20)

The Scriptures suggest that, in addition to the witness of the creation, there is an inner witness to God. The Preacher of Ecclesiastes makes the bold declaration that we intuitively know that we were made for more than *this* world. In our heart of hearts, we know that we will live forever, that we are creatures made for eternity. Why? Because God "has also set eternity in their heart" (Ecclesiastes 3:11).

Paul refers to the "eyes of the heart" as the intuitive organ of spiritual enlightenment that allows Christians to understand God's gracious provisions for them in this life and the life to come: "I pray that the eyes of your heart may be enlightened, so that you may know what is the hope of His calling, what are the riches of the glory of His inheritance in the saints, and what is the surpassing greatness of His power toward us who believe" (Ephesians 1:18-19).

In these passages the heart, that intuitive sixth sense that we possess, plays a prominent role in our ability to grasp the transcendent nature of life. Concerning the primacy of the heart in our desire for another world, Peter Kreeft makes this important observation:

> Many books have explored the heaven-shaped hole in the modern head, the meaninglessness of atheist and secularist philosophies. But there is not a single book in print whose main purpose is to explore the heart's longing for heaven. For the heart is harder to explore than the head and has had fewer explorers. The field of the heart has largely been left to the sentimentalists. But sentiments are only the heart's borders, not its inner country. We must discover this "undiscovered country." [10]

The Vertical Search

If the heart serves as an adequate guide in matters pertaining to God and transcendence, the question must be asked, Why are so few people listening to their hearts concerning these signals? While the dominance of the scientific, empirical worldview is much to blame, many people do not listen to their hearts simply because they are "sunk in the everydayness" of life.

Novelist Walker Percy describes this dilemma through Binx Bolling, the central character in his National Book Award-winning novel, *The Moviegoer*. Binx is a small-time stockbroker who lives quietly in suburban New Orleans, pursuing an interest in the movies, affairs with his secretaries, and living out his days. But he soon finds himself on a search for something more important, something that will change his life forever. Listen to his words early on in the novel:

> What is the nature of the search? . . . Really it is very simple. . . . The search is what anyone would undertake if he were not sunk in the everydayness of his life. . . . To become aware of the possibility of the search is to be onto something. Not to be onto something is to be in despair. . . . What do you seek— God? you ask with a smile. I hesitate to answer, since all other Americans have settled the matter for themselves. . . . Have 98% of Americans already found what I seek or are they so sunk in everydayness that not even the possibility of a search has occurred to them? On my honor, I do not know the answer.[11]

As Percy suggests, most Americans are caught up in the every-dayness of life, a refusal to stop and reflect on significant issues, such as whether God exists and what role He might play. Rather, they are trapped by the tyranny of the urgent and consequently are too busy to reflect on the transcendent. A little later in the novel, Percy describes Uncle Jules, who finds his niche in this present world— the City of Man—to be so pleasant that he has little time for the City of God.[12]

Percy's words serve as an important prompting for us to resist spiritual inertia and to attentively listen to our hearts, which point not only to God, but also to another world that awaits us. As we begin to consider these clues of transcendence, I am reminded that this desire to know about God is deeply embedded in our human psy-che and that it matters greatly not only that there is a God, but also that He is involved in our daily affairs. Novelist Frederick Buechner beautifully expresses that our desires run deeper than to simply know that God exists. If we will but listen to our hearts, we will realize that He has provided signposts of the world to come.

> What we need to know, of course, is not just that God exists, not just that beyond the steely brightness of the stars there is a cosmic intelligence of some kind that keeps the whole show going, but that there is a God right here in the thick of our day-to-day lives who may not be writing messages about himself in the stars but who in one way or another is trying to get messages through our blindness as we move around down here kneedeep in the fragrant muck and misery and marvel of the world.[13]

CHAPTER 4

Our Universal Unhappiness

And I still haven't found what I'm looking for.

—U2

You need chaos in your soul to give birth to a dancing star.

—Friedrich Nietzsche

You don't know quite what it is you want, but it just fairly makes your heart ache you want it so.

—Mark Twain

HUMANS ARE CURIOUS AND RESTLESS CREATURES, ALWAYS LOOKING TO THE world to make us happy. And while it may seem odd to consider unhappiness a hint of Heaven, in reality it is our disappointments — not unlike Qoheleth's experiences reflected in Ecclesiastes — that prepare us for something more, something greater than this life can possibly provide.

Relationships that have gone sour between men and women provide fertile ground to illustrate this unhappiness. And there is probably no greater testimony to the unhappiness that stems from failed relationships than the lyrics of country songs. Some of the all-time classic lines from country music that lament these broken relationships have been compiled by Paula Schwed in her little book, *I've Got Tears in My Ears from Lyin' on My Back in My Bed While I Cry Over You.*[1]

> I don't want no more of the cheese, I just want to get out of the trap.
> > —Glenn Barber, 1968

> Ever since we said "I do," there's so many things you don't.
> > —Johnny Slate and Red Lane, 1970

> She got the goldmine, I got the shaft.
> > —Tim Dubois, 1983

> If the phone doesn't ring, it's me.
> > —Jimmy Buffett, Wyland Arnold Jennings, and Michael E. Utley, 1985

> You're so cold, I'm turning blue.
> > —Harlan Howard and Don David, 1967

I only miss you on days that end in "Y."
—Jim Malloy, Even Stevens,
1975

While we may get a good laugh out of these lines, many of us know firsthand that failed relationships can be a source of great heartache. They show us that while we may look for happiness in relationships, exhilarating mountaintop experiences, career advancements, or the amassing of "stuff," in reality we are often disappointed. Life simply doesn't satisfy.

The story is told of a young author who was writing a book about the people of Appalachia. As he traveled through a mountain valley, he noticed a large old house with an elderly cigar-smoking man rocking on the front porch. He thought to himself, *I ought to interview this old man to see what keeps him going!* He sat down by the old man and inquired, "Tell me, you men of Appalachia live to be so old, what's the secret?" The man responded, "It's no secret to me! I drink a quart of homemade whiskey every day, I smoke at least a half-dozen cigars like these every day, and I chase women at night." With a look of astonishment, the young writer replied, "That's incredible! Just how old are you?" With a calmness in his voice, Gramps said, "I'll be thirty-two this October."

While most of us don't live life like this man from Appalachia, many of us lament the frantic pace of contemporary life. In pursuit of happiness, we find ourselves performing the ultimate juggling act with work, family, and leisure time. A new term has even been coined for multi-tasking: time stacking. Time stackers are busy people who juggle two or more tasks at once, a behavior that has become rampant, especially among professionals.

Two college professors studied the time diaries of 8,500 people in 1965, 1975, and 1985 and noticed that time stacking is a relatively recent phenomenon. Geoffrey Godbey and John P. Robinson, coauthors of *Time for Life: The Surprising Way Americans Use Their Time*, discovered that the primary reason for time stacking is the increased expectation of what's necessary to accomplish. With the onslaught of technology (personal computers, faxes, e-mail, and cell phones), not only has the ease of communication been enhanced, but there is also a heightened *expectation* of how productive we should be. The authors observe that since time is perceived as the new currency, time stacking is becoming a way of life; consumers want to get the maximum return from their investment.

Our Restless Culture

Ours is a restless culture in a quest for happiness, a culture in pursuit of The Good Life. And how do we seek happiness? Deeply embedded in the Western mindset is the fundamental belief that acquiring more things, bigger and better things, will ultimately make us happy. Musing on the fickleness in the American consciousness, Daniel Boorstin suggests that Americans suffer from extravagant expectations. In his much-quoted book, *The Image: A Guide to Pseudo-Events in America,* Boorstin makes this observation of Americans:

> We expect anything and everything. We expect the contradictory and the impossible. We expect compact cars which are spacious; luxurious cars which are economical. We expect to be rich and charitable, powerful and merciful, active and reflective, kind and competitive. . . . We expect to eat and stay thin, to be constantly on the move and ever more neighborly, to go to a "church of our choice" and yet feel its guiding power over us, to revere God and to be God. Never have people been more the masters of their environment. Yet never has a people felt more deceived and disappointed. For never has a people expected so much more than the world could offer.[2]

Boorstin describes how American journalism, entertainment, and advertising create and sustain our illusions because "ever enlarging our extravagant expectations we create the demand for the illusions with which we deceive ourselves. And which we pay others to make to deceive us."[3]

Great sophistry lies behind contemporary advertising that promises fulfillment and happiness. Advertisers have spent untold fortunes to probe our psyches so they can pitch their products to our deepest longings. Today "spirituality is in," says Sam Keen, author of *Hymns to an Unknown God*. Today it has become financially profitable to exploit the spiritual hunger of America. "A car that can help save your soul." Would that commercial entice you to buy a Volvo? Ironically, this deep spiritual longing that is implicit in much of modern advertising has its origin with Christians in the early twentieth century. Writing in *Christianity Today*, Charles Colson observes,

> According to James Twitchell in *Adcult USA*, the people who developed the art of modern advertising in the early part of this century were largely Christians, often sons of clergymen, who imported the methodology of religious revivalism into the commercial arena. The spiritual sequence of sin-guilt-redemption was transposed into the psychological sequence of problem-anxiety-resolution.[4]

According to Twitchell, the typical television commercial is "a morality play for our time . . . the powerful allure of religion and advertising is the same." Both reassure us, Twitchell concludes, because "we will be rescued." Novelist John Updike has compared the effort put into commercials with the fanatical care medieval monks put into decorating sacred books. The goal of all this labor, Updike writes, is "to persuade us that a certain beer or candy bar, or insurance company or oil-based conglomerate, is, like the crucified Christ . . . the gateway to the good life."[5]

But the more we try to find fulfillment and happiness in the accumulation of goods and living life to the hilt, the more often we are greeted with a certain disillusionment and emptiness. A few years ago the *Wall Street Journal* published one of its quarterly American Opinion surveys covering politics, economics, and values. In an article entitled "Americans Have It All (But All Isn't Enough)," the writer observes,

> With so many people owning so many things, their talk often turns to the question: What now? The answer seems to be something less tangible than a Rolex watch or a mink coat: a good college education for their children, more involvement in community activities, the time to watch the tide come in. . . . "On the one hand, people say they have larger houses, amazing cars, and they can go places," says Peter Bahouth, executive director of the nonprofit Turner Foundation, which funds environmental projects. "But people also think about what their town was like when their grandfather lived there, when they could ride their bikes downtown and leave their doors unlocked."[6]

In many ways, we are getting everything we want, but enjoying it less. In his book *Margin: Restoring Emotional, Physical, Financial, and Time Reserves to Overloaded Lives,* Richard A. Swenson, M.D., observes that all of the advantages granted to Americans have not delivered the longed-for happiness. Whatever formula we concoct for ourselves to be happy, it often shows itself to be more elusive than we could have imagined, and it frequently leaves us with stress, frustration, and even despair. Prosperity does not equal Utopia.[7]

In Swenson's opinion, modern-day living devours the necessary "margin" that we need to lead truly healthy, balanced lives. All the trumped-up promises of happiness and fulfillment from our achievements and accomplishments often leave us frazzled and disillusioned. Some years ago country singer Peggy Lee recorded the hit song "Is That All There Is?" Many of us have found ourselves asking that question. All of this leads to the fundamental question that sooner or later we have to confront: Can this world really make us happy?

Can This World Really Make Us Happy?

Christians boldly pronounce that life can have no meaning, purpose, or happiness apart from a transcendent perspective that includes a relationship with God. Yet, from a purely secularist perspective, this world does deliver a modicum of temporal meaning and happiness. For periods of pleasure-induced narcosis, all may be well. As Malcolm Muggeridge observes, "Contrary to what is often suggested, a hedonistic way of life, if you have the temperament for it and can earn a living at it, is perfectly feasible. The earth's sounds and smells and colors are very sweet; human love brings golden hours; the mind at work gives great delight."[8]

French existentialist Albert Camus often addresses the issue of mankind and conscience in our troubled world. The author of *The Fall* and the recipient of the Nobel Prize for Literature, he frequently deals with the theme of humanity being condemned by its nature and circumstances to a spiritual exile, ever seeking an inner kingdom in which it might find new life.

In one of his short stories, Camus tells of a French couple, Marcel and Janine, who are together on one of Marcel's business trips. They are childless, and over the twenty years of their marriage, their relationship has come to be characterized more by necessity than love. In fact, Marcel's love for Janine has waned, as "the only joy he gave her was the knowledge that she was necessary." But Janine is not content with her marriage or her life, and she seeks to be liberated and fulfilled. One late evening she leaves Marcel's side and goes into town to taste the illicit pleasures of the night. She returns to her room, only to awaken Marcel as she gets back into bed:

> He spoke and she didn't understand what he was saying. He got up, turned on the light, which blinded her. He staggered

toward the washbasin and drank a long draught from the bottle of mineral water. He was about to slip between the sheets when, one knee on the bed, he looked at her without understanding. She was weeping copiously, unable to restrain herself. "It's nothing, dear," she said, "it's nothing."[9]

The loneliest time in life occurs when we experience that which we believe will deliver the ultimate satisfaction and we are still let down. That was Janine's experience and it is ours. This bitter irony meets us not so much in our disappointments, but amidst our joys and happiness. As Kreeft observes,

> It is precisely when life treats us best that the deepest dissatisfaction arises. As long as we lack worldly happiness, we can deceive ourselves with the "if only" syndrome: If only I had this or that, I would be happy. But once we have all our thises and thats and are still unhappy, the deception is exposed. . . . Our greatest bitterness comes not only in the sham sweetness of riches and power but also in the middle of our truest earthly sweetness: hearing a symphony, seeing a sunset, complete sexual love. It is highest life that sets us longing for something more than this life.[10]

At the core of our greatest pleasures lies a sadness that transcends this world, a sadness that cannot be quenched. I previously mentioned the vertical search of Binx Bolling, the stockbroker in Walker Percy's novel *The Moviegoer*. From that same novel, listen to Binx's description of the malaise resulting from The Good Life in the fictional Louisiana town of Gentilly:

> The closer you get to the lake, the more expensive the houses are. . . . The swimming pools steam like sleeping geysers. These houses look handsome in the sunlight; they please me with

their pretty colors, their perfect lawns and their clean airy garages. But I have noticed that at this hour of dawn they are forlorn. A sadness settles over them like a fog from the lake.[11]

Percy's words contain a certain pathos. And they accurately diagnose the malaise that characterizes modernity. Try as we may to find happiness and fulfillment by accumulating possessions and experiencing the best life has to offer, we still are a restless and unhappy people.

But there is a classical wisdom, certainly not in vogue today, that says we are not *supposed* to be happy in this present life. The idea that no one is really happy in this life—nor should be—sounds quite strange to our modern ears. This is the case especially when, according to the U.S. Declaration of Independence, we deserve the "pursuit of happiness" as an "inalienable right." In his thoughtful work *Jesus Rediscovered*, Muggeridge goes so far as to suggest that the pursuit of happiness as one of our inalienable rights is one of the surest ways to unhappiness:

> The pursuit of happiness, included along with life and liberty in the American Declaration of Independence as an inalienable right, is without any question the most fatuous that could possibly be undertaken. This lamentable phrase—the pursuit of happiness—is responsible for a good part of the ills and miseries of the modern world.[12]

One would think that in a country such as ours, we would be a happier people. Peggy Noonan, a former newswriter and political speechwriter, comments on this issue in her book *What I Saw at the Revolution*. Noonan believes that much of our unhappiness is born out of a huge cultural revolution within the baby boomer generation. The salient feature of this revolution, Noonan contends, is the *expectation* of happiness:

It is 1956 in the suburbs, in the summer. A man comes home from work, parks the car, slouches up the driveway. His white shirt clings softly to his back. He bends for the paper, surveys the lawn, waves to a neighbor. From the house comes his son, freckled, ten. He jumps on his father; they twirl on the lawn. Another day done. Now water the lawn, eat fish cakes, watch some TV, go to bed, do it all again tomorrow.

Is he happy? No. Why should he be? We weren't put here to be happy. But the knowledge of his unhappiness does not gnaw. Everyone is unhappy, or rather everyone has a boring job, a marriage that's turned to disinterest, a life that's turned to sameness. And because he does not expect to be happy the knowledge of his unhappiness does not weigh on him. He looks perhaps to other, more eternal forms of comfort.[13]

Noonan suggests that when we believe we are entitled to be happy in this world, we will be sorely let down. Consequently, we lose hope. We despair. We run around, harried, hassled, and complaining that we never have enough time—though we really don't want to simplify our lives. In reality, we want the very thing we complain about. We gripe about not having enough leisure time to kick back, reflect, and unwind. Yet for many of us, more time for leisure and reflection would be unbearable. Why? We seek to be diverted from thinking about transcendent things. They are too threatening to us. We crave diversions to keep us from genuine solitude. Kreeft believes that our fear of solitude belies a deeper fear of our mortality. In his book *Christianity for Modern Pagans,* he writes,

If you are typically modern, your life is like a rich mansion with a terrifying hole right in the middle of the living-room floor. So you paper over the hole with a very busy wallpaper pattern to distract yourself. You find a rhinoceros in the middle of your house. The rhinoceros is wretchedness and death. How in the world can you hide a rhinoceros? Easy: cover it with a million mice. Multiply diversions.[14]

Kreeft's book is devoted to explaining Blaise Pascal's *Pensées,* and it was Pascal's contention that we seek diversions in life to assuage our unhappiness. According to Pascal,

> If our condition were truly happy we should not need to divert ourselves from thinking about it. . . .

> I have often said that the sole cause of man's unhappiness is that he does not know how to stay quietly in his room. . . . What people want is not the easy peaceful life . . . but the agitation that takes our mind off it and diverts us. That is why we prefer the hunt to the capture. That is why men are so fond of hustle and bustle.[15]

These *pensées* are arguably the most powerful and relevant for our modern culture, which ironically has more leisure than our ancestors ever experienced. Despite all of our labor-saving devices, we are still a society that is largely discontent. Pascal's words even suggest that the society that has the most diversions and amusements is in fact the unhappiest!

A few years ago, we were greeted with the revealing slogan, emblazoned on car bumpers and T-shirts, "He who dies with the most toys wins." In a society that has lost its sense of purpose and meaning — its divine center — banality is the prevailing sentiment of the day. And our culture of amusement and entertainment bears eloquent testimony that we are an unhappy people who seek to anesthetize our unhappiness by busyness and diversions. If life felt like a holiday, we would not want holidays from it.[16]

Many years ago, our frenetic pace was captured by the American poet W. H. Auden in his poem "September 1939." He describes the average man in 1939 as barely aware of his emptiness and, despite the diversions in life, still finding himself to be lost in a haunted wood:

> Children afraid of the dark
> Who have never been happy or good.[17]

What Lies Behind Our Unhappiness?

Beneath the surface of our strivings for fulfillment and happiness is a void or hollowness in our hearts as wide as the ocean. In this troubled, unhappy world of ours, it is typically the artist who, living on the cutting edge of culture, reflects the true sentiment of the age. Percy often writes about the prophetic role of the novelist in our culture. He makes the following observation in his essay "Novel-Writing in an Apocalyptic Time":

> If the novelist's business is, like that of all artists, to tell the truth . . . he had better tell the truth no matter how odd it is, even if the truth is a kind of upside-downness. . . . Whenever you have a hundred thousand psychotherapists talking about being life-affirming and a million books about life-enrichment, you can be sure there is a lot of death around. . . . Could it be that this paradoxical diminishment of life in the midst of plenty, its impoverishment in the face of riches, is the peculiar vocation of the novelist. . . . There is something worse than being deprived of life: it is being deprived of life and not knowing it. The poet and the novelist cannot bestow life but they can point to instances of its loss.[18]

Percy's words are directed to us, an absorbed and distracted people who, despite our exhaustive efforts to find fulfillment, remain unhappy. But the truth of the matter is that this world cannot provide us with a lasting happiness. The Preacher of Ecclesiastes, you will recall, discovered this after years of vain pursuit. His abiding legacy of unhappiness serves as a divine reminder to us some three millennia removed that our home is not of this world. Truly, our deepest desire is for Heaven, the dwelling of God.

In the retelling of the ancient myth of Cupid and Psyche, C. S. Lewis's *Till We Have Faces* (his favorite though perhaps most obscure book) beautifully illustrates this longing (*sensucht*) for another world beyond our own. Listen to the words of Psyche to her sister, Orual:

> "I have always—at least, ever since I can remember—had a kind of longing for death."
>
> "Ah, Psyche," I said, "have I made you so little happy as that?"
>
> "No, no, no," she said. "You don't understand. Not that kind of longing. It was when I was happiest that I longed most. It was on happy days when we were up there on the hills, the three of us, with the wind and the sunshine. . . . And because it was so beautiful, it set me longing, always longing. Somewhere else there must be more of it. Everything seemed to be saying, Psyche come! But I couldn't (not yet) come and I didn't know where I was to come to. It almost hurt me. I felt like a bird in a cage when the other birds of its kind are flying home."[19]

Many people today have reached the pinnacle of personal, financial, and career success, but they have what some have called "destination sickness." They have arrived, but they are sick and disillusioned. They may have all the outward appearances of success, but deep inside they are hollow and empty. They are hungry for things spiritual, because this world alone cannot sustain a lasting happiness.

A contemporary example of this spiritual hunger and restlessness is seen in the journey of Jon Katz, a former executive producer with CBS. In his book *Running to the Mountain: A Journey of Faith and Change,* Katz describes his spiritual pilgrimage through the writings of Thomas Merton.

> Ten years earlier, as executive producer of the two-hour program *The CBS Morning News,* I had stood in a control room one day before dawn, staring at a wall of high-tech color monitors. The co-anchor of the spectacularly unsuccessful show I produced, a former beauty queen and sports commentator named Phyllis George, was smiling back at me surreally from all of them. An assistant dabbed at her makeup and fluffed her hair. I was powerful, well-compensated, lost. A few minutes later, I was locked in my office, weeping. I had reached a rung in my life a lot of people would have coveted, and I would rather have thrown myself off a bridge than stay there for another month. So, tentatively, with equal parts of determination and terror, I set off on what Thomas Merton liked to call a journey of the soul.[20]

Katz came to the important realization that one can have all that this world has to offer and still be miserable. He, like many an "up-and-outer," had reached the upper tier of success by worldly standards, yet was in despair. He came to the conclusion that the true journey of life is a spiritual journey, a journey of the soul.

As we conclude this chapter we would do well to reflect on a passage from the pen of Lewis that, interestingly enough, is taken from his little classic *The Problem of Pain.* Lewis suggests that, behind our lack of long-lasting happiness in this world, there is a divine intent. Despite the abundant pleasures God brings our way, He does not want us to mistake this world for home.

The settled happiness and security which we all desire, God withholds from us by the very nature of the world: but joy, pleasure, and merriment He has scattered broadcast. We are never safe, but we have plenty of fun, and some ecstasy. It is not hard to see why. The security we crave would teach us to rest our hearts in this world and oppose an obstacle to our return to God. . . . Our Father refreshes us on the journey with some pleasant inns, but will not encourage us to mistake them for home.[21]

CHAPTER 5

OUR SENSE OF ALIENATION

It's not that I'm afraid to die. I just don't want to be there when it happens.

— Woody Allen

If time were the wicked sheriff in a horse opera, I'd pay for riding lessons and take his gun away.

— W. H. Auden

When once you have got hold of a vulgar joke, you may be certain that you have got hold of a subtle and spiritual idea.

— G. K. Chesterton

IN ADDITION TO OUR UNIVERSAL UNHAPPINESS, ANOTHER SIGNAL OF TRAN-
scendence that another life awaits us is our sense of discord or alienation in this life. The New Testament resonates with the perspective
that this world is not our home, and that we are "aliens and strangers"
(1 Peter 2:11). Try as we may, we are not really at home in this world.

Malcolm Muggeridge once declared that "to accept this world as
a destination rather than a staging post would seem to me to reduce
life to something too banal and trivial to be taken seriously or held
in esteem."[1] Coming to the Christian faith late in life, he considered
his deep abiding sense of alienation in this world to be an important
safeguard for his eternal hope.

> I had a sense, sometimes enormously vivid, that I was a
> stranger in a strange land; a visitor, not a native . . . a displaced
> person. . . . The feeling, I was surprised to find, gave me a
> great sense of satisfaction, almost of ecstasy. . . . The only ulti-
> mate disaster that can befall us, I have come to realize, is to
> feel ourselves to be at home here on earth. As long as we are
> aliens, we cannot forget our true homeland.[2]

Muggeridge's words bear eloquent testimony to the idea that
our ultimate destiny lies beyond this world. While our sense of alienation, of being a stranger in this world, manifests itself in numerous
ways, we will consider three primary ones: our fear of death; our
uneasiness with time; and our sense of humor.

Our Fear of Death

The late Joseph Bayly was flying from Chicago to Los Angeles some
years ago and found himself engaged in conversation with an articulate, middle-aged woman. "Where are you from?" he asked.

"Palm Springs," she answered.

Knowing Palm Springs to be a city of the rich and famous, he
asked, "What's Palm Springs like?"

"Palm Springs is a beautiful place filled with unhappy people."

Curious about her unusual response, he posed the question, "Are you unhappy?"

"Yes, I certainly am."

"Why?"

"I can answer it in one word: mortality. Until I was forty, I had perfect eyesight. Shortly after, I went to the doctor because I couldn't see as well as I could before. Ever since that time, these corrective glasses have been a sign to me that not only are my eyes wearing out, but I'm wearing out. Some day I'm going to die. I really haven't been happy since."

These words capture the feelings and angst of millions of Americans today. We don't want to be reminded that death will one day greet us, as it will everyone else in the human race. We don't want to lose this precious thing called life. And it's little consolation to imagine living on in the memory of our friends and loved ones. Woody Allen, in an interview with *Rolling Stone* magazine some years ago, was being realistic when he declared,

> Someone once asked me if my dream was to live on in the hearts of my people, and I said I would like to live on in my apartment. And that's really what I would prefer. . . . You drop dead one day, and it means less than nothing if billions of people are singing your praises every day, all day long.[3]

I'm reminded of the story of the English vicar who was asked by a colleague what he expected after death, and he replied, "Well, if it comes to that, I suppose I shall enter into eternal bliss, but I really wish you wouldn't bring up such depressing subjects."

The Denial of Death

The words of the vicar express the prevalent response of our culture toward death. In a word, it is *denial*. Contemporary culture, having largely lost its sense of the sacred and belief in the afterlife, hates and fears death and strives to wish it away. Modernity plays death down, euphemizes it, and attempts to conceal it. This denial of death takes on various guises in our culture. One way is through aspirations to achieve immortality. *Forbes* magazine reported that afterlife insurance is the newest thing in financial services. As more people request to be preserved by the ingenuity of cryonics, insurance companies such as New York Life are covering the costs. The concept of reviving a human embedded in ice was first developed as a story line for W. Clark Russell's 1887 yarn, "The Frozen Pirate." In 1974 the American Cryonics Society began freezing bodies, and now a half-dozen cryonics providers, such as the Scottsdale, Arizona-based Alcor Life Extension Foundation, promise to pickle their clients in liquid nitrogen in the hopes of bringing them back if and when technology allows. The tab? Fifty thousand dollars for the head, $120,000 for the whole body.[4]

And if we cannot cheat death through achieving immortality, let's simply ignore the obvious. Society reasons, let's look at death in purely naturalistic terms. Life and death. We are born, and then we die. Thomas Lynch, an author and poet who serves as the funeral director in the small town of Milford, Michigan, writes in *Esquire* magazine about the death of old George Horton, his friend for years, who served as the cemetery sexton. He recalls George's comments on our mortality:

> "Do the math" I heard him give out once, from the cab of his backhoe, for no apparent reason. He was backfilling a grave in Willow Creek. "You gonna make babies, you've gotta make some room — it's biblical." Or once, leaning on a shovel, waiting for the priest to finish: "Copulation, population, inspiration, expiration. It's all arithmetic — addition, multiplication, subtraction, and long division. That's all we're doing here, just the math. Bottom line, we're buried a thousand per acre or

burned into two quarts of ashes, give or take." There was no telling when such wisdoms would come to him.[5]

Such secular thinking pervades our modern consciousness. Death is the most inconvenient thing in life, yet also the most obvious—like an elephant in the kitchen. Better to live like an ostrich with our head in the sand than to face the hard facts of mortality. In his critically acclaimed book *The Undertaking: Life Studies from the Dismal Trade*, Lynch laments the modern embarrassment of death with a curious analogy:

> The thing about the new toilet is that it removes the evidence in such a hurry. The flush toilet, more than any single invention, has "civilized" us in a way that religion and law could never accomplish. No more the morning office of the chamber pot or outhouse, where sights and sounds and odors reminded us of the corruptibility of flesh . . . having lost the regular necessity of dealing with unpleasantries, we have lost the ability to do so when the need arises. . . . It is the same with our dead. We are embarrassed by them in the way that we are embarrassed by a toilet that overflows the night that company comes. It is an emergency. We call the plumber.[6]

Lynch is not the only writer who has observed modernity's embarrassment with death. Muggeridge, who spent many of his remaining days writing on the shortcomings of contemporary, atheistic culture, commented on our denial of death:

> It is, of course, inevitable that in a materialist society like ours death should seem terrible, and even inadmissible. If Man is the very apex of creation, with nothing greater than himself in the universe; if his earthly life exhausts the whole content

of his existence, then, clearly, his definitive end, his death, is too outrageous to be contemplated, and so is better ignored.[7]

While today's culture denies the reality of death, the one sure thing about our mortal existence is that it will come to an end; the moment we are born, we begin to die. Samuel Beckett declared, "We give birth astride a grave." Alexander the Great is said to have directed that he be buried with his naked arm hanging out of his coffin, with his hand empty, to show one and all that the man who conquered the world left it as he entered it. Job declares, "Naked I came from my mother's womb, and naked I shall return there" (Job 1:21).

The Trivialization of Death

Because death has become such a taboo subject in modern culture, we seek diversions not only to make us happy, but also to keep us from reflecting on our mortality. (As Blaise Pascal said, "If we were truly happy, we should not need to divert ourselves from thinking about it.") When society cannot offer satisfying answers or explanations dealing with transcendent issues (in this case, death), the tendency is to trivialize the matter.

There's a scene in the movie *Moonstruck* where Cher asks a middle-aged man why middle-aged men chase after young women. He responds with the offhanded remark, "Maybe it's the fear of death." Cher stops dead in her tracks, reflects on the comment, and declares, "That's it!" Better (or safer) to trivialize an issue that is too discomforting to talk about than to really come to grips with it.

In this manner, humor helps to allay our uneasiness with painful reminders of our mortality. *Prairie Home Companion* radio host Garrison Keillor once created a character who specifies that "his ashes be divided up and put in manila envelopes and mailed to people he admired, such as writers, actors, teachers, healers, religious people and rock stars—hundreds of them—as gifts."

Humorous musings on mortality have also become strange

bedfellows in recent years in the advertising arena. A few years ago the Comedy Central cable channel employed the Grim Reaper as a pitchman. The commercial began conventionally enough:

"To keep my thighs silky smooth I use a pollen extract from Romanian Royal bees," purred actress Sean Young. "To keep my navel taut and resilient I use African antelope musk oil." Then, the shocker: "For up here" (pointing to her head), "I use a combination of sublimation and denial. To keep from remembering that all this is absolutely meaningless." Cut to the new ad campaign's slogan: "We're all going to die. Watch Comedy Central." [8]

About the same time, Nike tried a similar experiment. Their ad showed a near-perfect nude with the headline, "Yes, this is a goddess." Then came the cold shower: "But you are not a goddess and you aren't ever going to be a goddess so maybe you should just get used to it. . . . Someday, since you are human, you will notice your body has changed and your face has changed and your kneecaps look more like Winston Churchill than ever before." The ad went on to suggest that it might just be worth strapping on a pair of running shoes anyway and forget about looking like Kim Basinger. [9]

Hope Beyond the Grave

However society may attempt to deny death by wishing it away or ignoring it, the fact remains that from earliest times humanity has tenaciously believed in an afterlife. We might go so far as to say that part of our humanness is to desire Heaven, even as we face death. I recall visiting The British Museum in London, where an entire floor is dedicated to the Egyptians' practice of mummification to preserve their royalty for the journey to the world beyond. However various the forms, belief in an afterlife is coterminous with humanity. [10] On this hope in the afterlife, British historian Paul Johnson observes in his book *The Quest for God*:

The first fact of life primitive man accepted, and pondered, was death. Mankind has been thinking about it ever since, for tens of thousands of years, during which billions of our species have met their deaths and disappeared; and after all that anxious cogitation, we are not much the wiser. . . . The Ancient Egyptians crowded their tombs with exact replicas of all the good things of this life to persuade themselves that continuity of living and enjoyment was a fact. . . . The famous Egyptian papyrus, "The Book of the Dead,". . . is not a celebration of death at all, but a denial of death, a manifesto against death, a celebration rather of immortality, of the continuity of life, but in a different place.[11]

While many tell us to accept death as "natural," the truth of the matter is that deep down we resist such a notion. Why? Because we feel a sense of dissonance with death. In fact, we are immortals trapped in mortal surroundings, our bodies. While the pop psychologists of our day try to convince us that death is just another stage of growth, deep down we resist such a calm assessment. Such advice from our therapeutic professionals is "like telling a quadriplegic that paralysis is a stage of exercise, or a divorcée that divorce is a stage of marriage. It's the kind of joke only a moron or a sadist would tell."[12]

While modernity seeks to deny death, in earlier Victorian times—with a decidedly Christian worldview—death was perceived differently. Death was magnified, talked about, and even relished. Johnson observes,

> The Victorians with their death-masks, their elaborate funeral processions and carriages . . . looked death squarely and ceremoniously in the face. Deathbed scenes were elaborately recorded or committed to memory, and became part of family folklore, reverently told to children and grandchildren. . . . Death was a domestic, household, family affair,

with the dying person upstairs in a well-attended bedroom
with a fire in the grate, people downstairs walking softly and
talking in whispers, straw in the street outside to muffle the
noise of carriage-wheels, the neighbors alerted to the
impending event and sending regular and anxious
enquiries.[13]

Needless to say, death is observed much differently in today's
world. Most people die in the hospital, sparsely attended—if at all—
by their loved ones and often alone except for medical professionals. In a world where physical life and well-being are the *summum
bonum*, death has become an insult and absurdity that we would
rather forget.

Even those of us in the West, with our traditional belief in the
afterlife, seem obsessed with ritually denying what obviously happens. We embalm our corpses, dress them up in new suits, pronounce last rites over them, and bury them in airtight caskets and
concrete vaults in order to postpone the inevitable decay. Through
our rituals we act out our stubborn reluctance to yield to this most
powerful of human experiences. While nature treats death as normal and everyday, the human species treats it with shock and dismay. Perhaps these feelings we have toward death should be seen not
as unnatural but as natural, if we accept a biblical view of mankind.
That view is essentially that mankind is an immortal spirit trapped
for a time in matter, a body. C. S. Lewis went so far as to suggest that
all the commotion surrounding death was a strong indicator of the
truthfulness of Christian theology:

Almost the whole of Christian theology could perhaps be
deduced from the . . . fact that (men) feel the dead to be
uncanny. . . . It is idle to say that we dislike corpses because we
are afraid of ghosts. You might say with equal truth that we
fear ghosts because we dislike corpses—In reality we hate the

division which makes possible the conception of either corpse or ghost. Because the thing ought not to be divided, each of the halves into which it falls by division is detestable.[14]

Lewis suggests that this division between the material and immaterial parts of a person evidences that man was originally created as a unity. This alienation with death, therefore, provides a transcendent clue that this life is not all there is. Indeed, the pages of the New Testament are rustling with that very rumor. Our feelings about death suggest that this is not our ultimate home.

John Updike often muses in his writings about our mortality and what may lie beyond this temporal existence. In his Pulitzer Prize-winning *Rabbit at Rest*, he penned one of the funniest novels ever written about death. In his fourth and final appearance, Harry "Rabbit" Angstrom, Updike's jockish alter ego, munches various junk foods that thicken his body while thinning his arteries as he makes his way toward his Maker. Updike himself seems to be having a wonderful time contemplating eternity with his wistful observations about the afterlife that come out of Rabbit's mouth. At one point, while Rabbit looks for his car at a Florida airport, the narrator deep within Rabbit's consciousness thinks to himself, "He doesn't remember which of these rows he parked the car in. He parked it in the patch of dead blank brain cells like all of our brains will be when we're dead unless the universe has cooked up some truly elaborate surprise."[15]

Our Uneasiness with Time

One of Grimm's fairy tales, "The Duration of Life," tells the story of God originally determining thirty years as the ideal life span for all animals, including mankind. The donkey, dog, and monkey all consider it much too long, however, and beg God to reduce their years by eighteen, twelve, and ten. The man, being healthy, vigorous, and somewhat greedy, asks to be given those extra years. God agrees, so man's years total seventy. The first thirty are his own and pass quickly. The next eighteen are the donkey years, during which he has to carry countless burdens on his back. Then come the dog years, twelve years where he can do little but growl and drag himself along. And finally, the monkey years, his closing ten, when he grows strange and does things that make children laugh at him.

While the tale suggests that the latter years of a person's life are painful, we still yearn to see no end to our days. We have an uneasiness with time and are startled at the concept of time — or rather at its passing. In the film *The Doctor*, Elizabeth Perkins plays a terminally ill cancer patient who cries out to a doctor who has befriended her, "Time is rushing past me, and I want to savor it!"

In his book *When I Relax I Feel Guilty*, Tim Hansel recalls reading the thought-provoking article entitled "If You Are 35, You Have 500 Days to Live." Its thesis was that when you subtract the time spent sleeping, working, tending to personal matters, hygiene, odd chores, medical care, eating, traveling, and miscellaneous time-stealers, in the next thirty-six years you will have roughly the equivalent of only five hundred days left to spend as you wish.[16]

In a wonderfully odd and beguiling inquiry, physicist Alan Lightman, who teaches physics and writing at Massachusetts Institute of Technology, has written the highly acclaimed work *Einstein's Dreams*. Set in Bern, Switzerland, in 1905, the book tells of a young patent clerk named Albert Einstein who has been dreaming marvelous dreams about the nature of time and has almost finished his special theory of relativity. What were his dreams during those last pivotal few months? In this enchanting work, thirty fables conjure up as many theoretical realms of time dreamt in as many nights.

In one of these vignettes, Lightman portrays how the people of Bern attempt to slow the passing of time by curious means. In this particular world, it is apparent that something is a bit odd. No houses are visible in the valleys or plains. Everyone lives in the mountains.

At some time in the past, Lightman suggests, scientists discovered that time actually flows more slowly the farther one is from the center of the earth. And while the effect is miniscule, it can be measured with extremely sensitive instruments. Once the phenomenon was determined, some people, anxious to stay young, moved to the mountains. Now all houses are built on Dom, the Matterhorn, Monte Rosa, and other high ground, so that it is virtually impossible to sell living quarters anywhere else. And because many people are no longer content simply to locate their homes on a mountain, to get the maximum effect they have constructed their houses on stilts! Consequently, mountaintops throughout the world are nested with such houses, which from a distance look like a flock of fat birds squatting on long skinny legs. Furthermore, the people most passionate about living the longest have built their houses on the highest stilts. Indeed, some houses rise half a mile high on their spindly wooden legs. Height has become status.

> When a person from his kitchen window must look up to see a neighbor, he believes that neighbor will not become stiff in the joints as soon as he, will not lose his hair until later, will not wrinkle until later, will not lose the urge for romance as early. . . . Now and then some urgent business forces people to come down from their houses, and they do so with haste . . . completing their transactions, and then returning as quickly as possible to their houses, or to other high places.[17]

Lightman's playful novel beautifully portrays how we try to slow down time, to savor this life. And we are reminded of the sobering truth that as time marches on, our joys and cherished dreams are ruined or come to naught. Yet when we experience tragic losses in our brief lives, we are subtly reminded of a certain nostalgia that is reminiscent not just of more time, but also of another *kind* of time.

As Peter Kreeft observes,

> What is home? What are we longing for? Not just our lost youth, but humanity's. . . . We long not for 1955 or 1255 but for Eden, where we lost not just our youth but our identity. . . . Our nostalgia for Eden is not just for another time but for another *kind* of time. Time in Eden was the pool in which we swam. . . . The experience of longing for the past that is unattainably gone is our deep nostalgia brought about by the knowledge of death. . . . Time and death make life precious, but they do not make it eternal. But that is what we long for ("thou hast put eternity into Man's heart").[18]

But not only does the passing of time bring a tragic dimension to life and remind us of our Edenic past. We are also so little reconciled to time that we are amazed at its passing. Time, then, is yet another signal of transcendence intimating that we were not made for this world alone. In a letter to Sheldon Vanauken, a struggling student of his at Oxford University, Lewis penned the following thoughtful words:

> You say the materialist universe is "ugly." I wonder how you discovered that! If you are really a product of a materialistic universe, how is it you don't feel at home there? Do fish complain of the sea for being wet? Or if they did, would that fact itself not strongly suggest that they had not always been, or [would] not always be, purely aquatic creatures? Notice how we are perpetually *surprised* at Time. ("How time flies! Fancy John being grown-up & married! I can hardly believe it!") In heaven's name, why? Unless, indeed, there is something in us which is *not* temporal.[19]

We see, then, that both our fear of death and our uneasiness with time witness to our exile in this world. We encounter frequent hints of the world to come, but they are transitory and ephemeral. Nobody ever gets into the "secret garden." The closest we ever get to it is in some hint of an echo that we hear in a concerto or see in a beautiful face or painting, which fills us with a deep sadness. It is lost for now, and we must turn back to our traffic jams and enemas and red tape.[20]

Our Sense of Humor

Humor also witnesses to our alienation and discord with this life. A natural theology can even be argued from the human phenomena of coarse jokes, especially those jokes that dwell almost entirely on the processes of excretion and reproduction, two of the most "natural" acts that we perform. While we share these processes with all other creatures, we joke and guffaw about such activities because they seem utterly unnatural, even comical! And although we attempt to veil or guard such functions, no one has ever observed embarrassment or shame among the animals as they perform these commonplace functions. Can you imagine a horse, dog, or cat *shy* about the need to excrete in public or reluctant to perform reproductive functions in broad daylight? Similar to his comments concerning a Christian theology that can be deduced from our feelings about the dead, Lewis suggests,

> Almost the whole of Christian theology could perhaps be deduced from the fact . . . that men make coarse jokes. . . . The coarse joke proclaims that we have here an animal which finds its own animality either objectionable or funny. . . . I do not perceive that dogs see anything funny about being dogs: I suspect that angels see nothing funny about being angels.[21]

Despite all the attempts by secularists to make the human race nothing more than a glorified animal at the apex of the evolutionary continuum, deep down our souls resonate with discord, which hints that we are in fact made for more than this world.

In a similar line of thinking, W. H. Auden observed that the human species is distinctive in at least three ways: it features the only animals who work, laugh, and pray. I recall an article a few years ago written by Philip Yancey for *Christianity Today* that dealt with Auden's triad of work, laughter, and prayer as a framework for self-reflection. Yancey observed that while we Americans excel at *work* (didn't our forefathers invent the Protestant work ethic?) and attempt to turn *prayer* into another form of work, it is with *laughter* that we Christians in the West really struggle. To correct this imbalance, Auden proposed resurrecting the medieval practice of Carnival, that raucous holiday preceding Lent. He believed that while Carnival celebrates the unity of our human race as mortal creatures (who eat, drink, defecate, belch, and break wind), we are still uncomfortable about our situation. We in fact oscillate between wishing we were unreflective animals and wishing we were disembodied spirits. In Auden's opinion, the Carnival provides a solution to this ambiguity, for to laugh at ourselves is simultaneously a protest and an acceptance of our mortality.

In fact, the only good reason to find humor in such seemingly crude phenomena as sex, death, burping, and breaking wind is that they parody our mortal existence, just as Auden suggests that the Carnival parodies a being who fell. As G. K. Chesterton once observed, "If it is not true that a divine being fell, then one can only say that one of the animals went completely off its head!" In other words, the Christian has a great advantage over other people, not by being less fallen than they nor less doomed to live in a fallen world, but by *knowing* that he or she is a fallen person in a fallen world. In a way, then, laughter has much in common with prayer, for in both acts we are acknowledging ourselves as fallen creatures.

Along these same lines, it is interesting to observe that the classic materialists who look to this world alone to bring fulfillment and happiness are frequently those who rarely display joy and laughter. Life is too serious to be joked about, they reason. In fact, people who take themselves too seriously (those of the ilk of Charles Darwin,

Bertrand Russell, Karl Marx, or Bill Gates) fail to grasp the irony that informs our human affairs. This biting irony is written into our mortal existence and is beautifully described by Muggeridge in his book *The End of Christendom:*

> This irony ... [is] conveyed beautifully in the medieval cathedrals, where you have the steeple climbing up into the sky symbolizing all the wonderful spiritual aspirations of human beings, but at the same time, set in the same roof, you have these little grinning gargoyles staring down at the earth. The juxtaposition of these two things might seem strange at first. But I contend that they are aspects of the same essential attitude of mind, an awareness that at the heart of our human existence there is this mystery. Interwoven with our affairs is this wonderful spirit of irony which prevents us from ever being utterly and irretrievably serious.[22]

This quote comes from the Blaise Pascal Lectures on Christianity and the University that Muggeridge delivered at the University of Waterloo in the late 1970s. During a question-and-answer sequel to his lectures, he was asked to elaborate on his statement that all believers are truly skeptical.

> The nearer you get to comprehending the true nature of our existence, the more possibility there is of being skeptical about our capacity to express that understanding. ... To believe greatly, it's necessary to doubt greatly. You know, humour is an expression of skepticism, of this disparity between what we aspire after and what we achieve. The greatest humorists, like Cervantes and Rabelais and Gogol and Shakespeare too, have all been believers ... whereas materialists are very serious people indeed because if you believe only in man, then you must hold man in great veneration.[23]

In many ways, then, humor has much to say about humility because it manifests itself in the incongruities of life. Few things are as absurd as people attempting to be God. Is it not rather humorous that God is reported as having to *come down* to see the great building enterprise of the Shemites at the tower of Babel?[24] And while the medieval world had court jesters and grinning gargoyles on cathedral roofs and carved into the ends of the pews to remind worshipers of human pride, the modern world has largely lost these transcendent reminders. As Muggeridge once observed, it is significant that our urban high-rise buildings have no gargoyles—truly, modernity takes itself quite seriously! Perhaps this is why Garrison Keillor once observed, "Some people think it's difficult to be a Christian and to laugh, but I think it's the other way around. God writes a lot of comedy—it's just that he has so many bad actors."

CHAPTER 6

Transcendence in Literature and Film

All of life's riddles are solved in the movies.

> —Steve Martin,
> from the film *Grand Canyon*

Why should a man be scorned, if, finding himself in prison, he tries to get out and go home? Or if, when he cannot do so, he thinks and talks about other topics than jailers and prison-walls? The world outside has not become less real because the prisoner cannot see it.

> —J. R. R. Tolkien,
> "On Fairy Stories"

We never are too old for this, my dear, because it is a play. We are playing all the time in one way or another. Our burdens are here, our road is before us, and the longing for goodness and happiness is the guide that leads us through many troubles and mistakes to the peace which is a true Celestial City.

> —Louisa May Alcott,
> *Little Women*

So far in our journey, we have considered two clues about Heaven. First, despite the pleasures this world affords, our lives are still characterized by a universal unhappiness. Often our greatest dissatisfaction arises amidst our greatest earthly pleasures and joys. Second, we observed that through our discord with death, the passing of time, and our sense of humor, we experience alienation from this world. Truly, we are pilgrims who are not at home here.

We now come to the third intimation of Heaven, which involves the sense of transcendence, or of the numinous, that we observe in all of the arts. What do we mean by the sense of the numinous? It might best be understood as seeing this present life as haunted by something that, although invisible, is nevertheless a real Presence. Implicit in the idea of the numinous is the idea of the Wholly Other, which theologian Rudolph Otto popularized in his book *The Idea of the Holy.* In Otto's thinking, this sense of the numinous pervades all of our experience and inspires fear and awe in us though we are unable to define or articulate precisely what we mean by it. We only know that we meet this sense of the numinous in the strangest of ways: in films, plays, literature, art, and music.

Art moves us and touches something deep within our souls. Who can remain unmoved when observing some of the world's great works of art? How can anyone visit the Louvre in Paris with its collection of over thirty thousand works of art (including the works of Raphael and da Vinci) or the Musee d'Orsay in that same city (boasting Monet, and Renoir, Van Gogh and Cezanne), and not come away with a sense of awe and transcendence?

Or reflect for a moment on how music moves us. I vividly recall a few years ago attending an Evensong service with my good friend Ken Boa at Christ Church in Oxford, England. As the boys' choir sang David's prayer of forgiveness from Psalm 51, we were deeply stirred. It was a transcendent moment that I will never forget. Perhaps this helps explain why the ancients ascribed music to the gods (the Muses), not to human beings. No, music is more than aesthetic pleasure. It is prophetic, a divine haunting that signifies God's presence in the world. If there is a Bach, there is a God.[1]

A physical world stripped of its grandeur, awe, and wonder would be the mere product of an exclusively materialistic universe: without mystery or strangeness. Such a worldview does not feed the soul. What is more, this sense of the numinous that we encounter in art is the basis of our tales and myths that often are populated by elves, fairies, wizards, dragons, even gods and goddesses. Some would suggest that it is this deep-rooted sense of numinous, the *sacramental*, that inspires wonder, awe, and worship.

While we could consider various forms of art, we will confine our discussion to a brief consideration of literature and film. As we shall see, the great writers and filmmakers who have influenced and continue to influence our culture are preoccupied with notions about God and transcendence. Whatever the medium, art reflects the soul of a culture. Marcel Proust observed, "through art we can know another's view of the universe."

But before we consider the transcendence of literature and film, let's first think about why we need this sense of "romance" (to use G. K. Chesterton's idea) to fully account for the idea that life is more than chance — that it is in fact a sacred drama, a dance.

Is Life All Chance or a Dance?

As we have suggested in earlier chapters, much of contemporary culture — impacted by a materialistic, secular worldview — has been robbed of its ability to sense this numinous, sacramental perspective of life. In his book *Chance or the Dance?* Thomas Howard argues that when the scientific method of the eighteenth century was given the authority of dogma, leading to the Enlightenment, a new way of looking at life supplanted the older, traditional way. Fairy tales, magic, wonder, and myth were replaced by empiricism — the new dogma. Listen to Howard's description of what we lost when the Old Myth was replaced by the New:

There were some ages in Western history that have occasionally been called Dark. . . . Men believed in things like the
Last Judgment and fiery torment. . . . They believed that they
had souls, and that what they did in this life had some
bearing in the way in which they would finally experience
reality. . . . And they believed that God was in heaven and
Beelzebub in hell. . . . Altogether, life was very weighty, and
there was no telling what might lie behind things. The ages
were, as I say, dark. Then the light came. It was the light that
has lighted us men into a new age. Charms, angels, devils,
plagues, and parthenogenesis have fled from the glare into
the crannies of memory. In their place have come coal
mining and plastic and group dynamics and napalm and
urban renewal and rapid transit. Men were freed from the
fear of the Last Judgment; it was felt to be more bracing to
face Nothing than to face the Tribunal. They were freed
from worry about getting their souls into God's heaven by
the discovery that they had no souls and that God had no
heaven. . . . The age was called enlightened. The myth
sovereign in the old age was that everything means everything. The myth sovereign in the new is that nothing *means*
anything.[2]

Howard's eloquent observations are an accurate assessment of
the present state of affairs. Under the watchful eye of the Old Myth,
there was a correspondence and significance to life's choices. Things
mattered. Now nothing matters because ultimately there is no transcendent meaning or purpose behind the affairs of life.

Yet we as humans yearn for mystery, awe, wonder, and enchantment. Deep down, we want to believe that life has meaning and purpose, that our choices matter, and that one day goodness and
righteousness will prevail. We are attracted to this God-haunted
aspect of life that informs and yet transcends our world.

Chesterton, who converted to Christianity, was deeply impacted by the strangeness and oddity of our world. He believed deeply that we need "romance" to make sense of this life. Listen to his thoughtful comments in his small but powerful classic, *Orthodoxy:*

> How can we contrive to be at once astonished at the world and yet at home in it? . . . How can this world give us at once the fascination of a strange town and the comfort and honour of being our own town? . . . We need so to view the world as to combine an idea of wonder and an idea of welcome.[3]

Chesterton, who was a pagan at the age of twelve and a total agnostic by the age of sixteen, gradually came to realize that the thin veneer of materialism was not adequate to explain this fascinating world in which we live. He believed that the Christian who embraced mysticism about life was healthy, while the cold and calculating materialist was on the road to insanity:

> The sane man knows that he has a touch of the beast, a touch of the devil, a touch of the saint, a touch of the citizen. . . . But the materialist's world is quite simple and solid, just as the madman is quite sure he is sane. . . . Materialists and madmen never have doubts. . . . Mysticism keeps men sane.[4]

Chesterton in these few words put the lie to the cold, sterile materialism that often informs our contemporary notion about life. Furthermore, he powerfully set forth our need for Christian mysticism, the understanding of life through a sacramental perspective. We earlier observed that the modern world has conditioned us to what C. S. Lewis called a doglike state of mind. When you point to the dog's food, he sniffs your finger because he does not understand the significance of the sign. While "finger sniffing" is the mode of understanding within worldly materialism (which is stripped of mystery and wonder), a sacramental understanding sees the entire world as a sign, a "pointer" toward Something — or rather Someone.

In fact, it is not too much to say that earth is a "mirror," an image of Heaven.[5] In many ways, the whole world becomes God's "mask," His performance; and like all great art, it both instructs and entertains us, providing moral lessons. The whole world is a sacrament, an effective sign that clearly points to what it signifies.[6]

We need desperately to have our imaginations awakened, to daily be reminded that this world is a stage upon which God is acting out His drama in the affairs of daily life. Lewis said his imagination was "baptized" by reading the fantasy works of George MacDonald, particularly *Lilith and Phantastes,* which gave him a greater sense of understanding reality. And when we consider the world of the arts, we are met by the presence of a transcendence that points to another world. Let's now consider literature and film, which see our world as brimming with wonder and awe, signaling that another life awaits.

The American Writer: Quarreling with God?

The present reign of the New Myth is perhaps best seen in the world of literature in the twentieth century, particularly among American writers. While we can only briefly consider the hint of transcendence within literature, we need to first realize that many writers have a gripe with God. What one observes in the American literary landscape is a preoccupation — almost obsession — with God and religion. Alfred Kazin writes of this quest for something akin to faith on the part of these writers in his much-heralded book *God and the American Writer.* He devotes a chapter to some of the most celebrated of America's twentieth-century writers: Hawthorne, Emerson, Stowe, Melville, Whitman, Lincoln, Dickinson, James, Twain, Eliot, Frost, and Faulkner. He presents not so much their personal profession of belief, but rather their "quarreling with God," because they were frequently at odds with their orthodox Christian heritage. Their mindset is aptly displayed in a quote from Emily Dickinson found in the prelude to his book, "We thank thee, Father, for these strange minds that enamor us against thee."[7]

One of the most intriguing authors that Kazin writes about is Herman Melville. While Melville's *Moby Dick* contains over a thousand references to the Bible, he was actually in rebellion against Calvinism, particularly the Dutch Reformed Church of his parents. Like many a lapsed Calvinist, Melville was morbidly apprehensive that the grace and election he had forfeited might prove real after all. Despite his attempts to free himself from Christian orthodoxy, Melville lived life as a spiritual Cain, a wanderer in no man's land, east of Eden.

Concerning Mark Twain and these other prominent American writers, Kazin writes,

Mark Twain, straddling the nineteenth and twentieth centuries, is our contemporary—he is outside the world he sees as mechanism. But like so many nineteenth-century characters who had been severely raised in an orthodoxy he soon escaped, he kept up a grudge against God. In his last years he wrote and wrote feverishly, satirizing everything about God's justice and church tales of heavenly rewards he had been forced to swallow in childhood. But of course he was afraid to antagonize his doting public by saying any heresies aloud. He lamely excused himself on the ground that "only dead men tell the truth." . . . These writers a century ago saw the new urban world with a devastating iciness and brutality. They had all been hardened by the contrast between the forced orthodoxy of their childhoods and the heartlessness of the cities they learned about too well as reporters.[8]

As Kazin observes, the religious certainty that was a central tenet of American Puritan and Calvinist ancestry had now receded into the past, as evidenced by the writings of many Americans in the twentieth century. As a direct result of religious extremism throughout the West, we have witnessed what Malcolm Muggeridge and others call the *end* of Christendom. Unbelief has replaced belief, and apostasy has overtaken faith. Though belief has waned and given way to conventional skepticism or denial about transcendent affairs, the fact that these writers often seem obsessed with God and sought to dismiss orthodox belief suggests that they were in some respects searching *for* the very God they denied. D. Bruce Lockerbie, in his book *Dismissing God,* attempts to answer some of the questions about why leading American writers have neglected their Christian heritage.

> While some writers . . . have not been timid about writing from a Christian world-and-life view, other writers have forsaken belief altogether and chosen the vacuum of unbelief; still others, more aggressively, seem obsessed by a warring spirit against belief that compels them to challenge God's supremacy. In a manner of speaking, they seem to have wished to battle God on equal terms. So Emily Dickinson describes an anonymous pugilist who, having worked his way through a roster of lesser opponents, "then, unjaded, challenged God, In presence of the Throne." [9]

Although many American writers have jettisoned a belief in Christian orthodoxy and are content to embrace a skepticism that derides faith in God and the Christian hope of Heaven—thus reflecting our culture at large—this is not a satisfying view of life. Deep down we yearn for a return to those supposed "dark" ages that Howard wrote about. We desire a world where life has meaning and purpose, where it is generally agreed that there is a Heaven and a Hell, and where there are consequences that put "bite" into this drama we call life.

The Literary Classics: What Does It Mean to Be Human?

We often encounter a sense of the transcendent when we read the great classics of literature, because they transport us to other worlds, times, and places. While reading in our culture is sometimes considered a lost or dying art due to the proliferation of the visual and technological media, the classics keep us in touch with the past. By knowing the past we are liberated from the bondage to the contemporary and temporal. Lewis wrote,

> We need intimate knowledge of the past. . . . A person who has lived in many places is not likely to be deceived by the local errors of his native village: the [person who knows the past] has lived in many times and is therefore in some degree immune from the great cataract of nonsense that pours from the press and the microphone of his own age.[10]

In great literature not only are we challenged to know the past, but we are also inspired to live in the present and future. The classics have a way of pointing beyond the immediate and the ordinary to another world. There is something almost magical about getting into a good novel that has interesting characters and an intriguing plot. In many ways, stories have a way of drawing us into their world. We come to appreciate through the joys and travails of characters what it is to be a part of the human drama. American playwright Arthur Miller, author of *Death of a Salesman,* when once asked how he knew he had discovered a great script, said it was when he found himself saying of the characters, "My God, that's me!" Perhaps one of the central elements behind great literature is that it transcends the immediate and applies to the universal human condition. In a way, good literature mirrors real life.

It is no accident that the classics often deal not only with universal human themes but also with how humanity views the existence and involvement of God in our world. The issues of life and God are central to the Western classics. Even from a nonChristian or atheistic perspective, such existential works as Jean-Paul Sartre's *Nausea,* Albert Camus' *The Stranger,* or Samuel Beckett's *Waiting for Godot* demonstrate the consequences of what it means to live in a world that from their vantage point is God-forsaken.

From a Christian worldview, such writers as Dante, Shakespeare, Milton, Tolstoy, Dostoyevsky, and more recently, Flannery O'Connor, Walker Percy, and John Updike, have powerfully crafted works that portray life as a sacred drama with a moral order. In his great work *Anna Karenina,* Tolstoy portrays the moral deterioration of Anna due to her unfaithfulness. In his classic *Crime and Punishment,* Dostoyevsky asks the reader to enter into the psychology of a crime and the issue of guilt through his character Raskolnikov. The crowning achievement of Dostoyevsky's life, *The Brothers Karamazov,* confronts the reader with sobering questions pertaining to the very existence of God, especially in the great chapter "The Grand Inquisitor."

Graham Greene, author of *The Power and the Glory* (with the inimitable whiskey priest) and *The Heart of the Matter,* was one of the greatest novelists and playwrights of the twentieth century. He once declared that "every creative writer worth our consideration is a victim: a man given over to an obsession." Greene's obsession was the inescapability of sin. "The basic element I admire in Christianity," he said, "is its sense of moral failure." When asked toward the end of his life, "Are you still hounded by God?" he replied, "I hope so. I'm not very conscious of His presence, but I hope He is dogging my footsteps."[11]

Philosopher Mortimer Adler was given the task of coediting a fifty-five-volume series for *Encyclopedia Britannica* titled *The Great Books of the Western World* and containing selections from the finest thinkers in the history of Western civilization. When Adler was asked why the series index contains more entries on God than any other topic, his answer was interesting: "It is because more consequences for life follow from that one issue than from any other."

Truly, the classics of Western civilization have withstood the test of time because they grapple with these universal issues of humanity: What does it mean to live life? How do I achieve significance and purpose in this present life? How am I to relate to God, my Maker? What happens at death? Is there life after death? The classics have the *scent* of transcendence.

Reynolds Price, author and professor of English at Duke University, has written of his abiding belief in orthodox Christianity as reflected in the Apostles' Creed. Price, who acknowledges that such a creed can be stated but not "defended with a satisfying dossier of empirical evidence," concludes,

> The final help I can offer the proof-hungry is a reminder that virtually identical beliefs powered perhaps a majority of the supreme creative minds of our civilization—Augustine, Dante, Chaucer, Michelangelo, Durer, Milton, Rembrandt, Pascal, Racine, Bach, Handel, Newton, Haydn, Mozart, Wordsworth, Beethoven, Kierkegaard, Dickens, Tolstoy. . . Auden, O'Connor (to begin a long roll that includes only the dead). Pressed by their unanimous testimony to a dazzling but benign light at the heart of space, what sane human will step up to say "Lovely, no doubt, but your eyes deceive you"? Not I, not now or any day soon.[12]

The Enchanted World of Fairy Tales

While the classics of Western civilization continue to have an enduring impact on society and instruct us about what it means to be human, it is in fairy tales that we frequently encounter a sense of awe, wonder, and enchantment with this world. Memorable are the magical worlds of Kenneth Grahame's *The Wind in the Willows,* J. R. R. Tolkien's *The Hobbit,* and Lewis's *The Chronicles of Narnia.* And while some critics may suggest that fairy tales are only for children, Lewis explains their abiding importance for all ages:

> I never met *The Wind in the Willows* . . . till I was in my late twenties, and I do not think I have enjoyed them any less on that account. I am almost inclined to set it up as a canon that a children's story which is enjoyed only by children is a bad children's story. The good ones last. . . . Now the modern critical world uses "adult" as a term of approval. It is hostile to what it calls "nostalgia." . . . Critics who treat *adult* as a term of approval, instead of as a merely descriptive term, cannot be adult themselves.[13]

Lewis is chiding modernity, which attempts to be sophisticated or grown-up and thereby delights to ridicule and mock a world characterized by a sacramental perspective, a world that is embued with the supernatural, magic, enchantment, and awe. He pokes fun at this worldly, adolescent approach to life in one of his most memorable characters of the Narnia series, Eustace Clarence Scrubb (even the name strikes one as odious!). Eustace is the only son of Harold and Alberta Scrubb and a cousin of the four Pevensie children, who are the main characters in the adventures into the magical world of Narnia. Eustace is a precocious and obnoxious nine-year-old whose imagination and sense of adventure have been stunted by his upbringing. His education at Experiment House had not cultivated his sense for the extraordinary:

> Harold and Alberta . . . were very up-to-date and advanced people. They were vegetarians, non-smokers and teetotalers and wore a special kind of underclothes. . . . Eustace Clarence liked animals, especially beetles, if they were dead and pinned

on a card. He liked books if they were books of information and had pictures of grain elevators or of fat foreign children doing exercises in model schools.[14]

While Eustace is reformed from his shallow thinking as the story unfolds, more importantly, Lewis is intimating that a sense of enchantment, such as that found in fairy tales, arouses within us longings that go beyond this present world. It speaks of Heaven.[15]

When we look at the world through the window of the fairy tale, we are met with astonishment and awe, and we discover a heightened sense of the numinous (the haunting of this world), which points us toward worship. Through the fairy tale we come to see this life in a new and sacramental way. It was Tolkien, Lewis's literary companion in the Oxford gathering known as the Inklings, who once declared, "If the story succeeds, you look out of it; if it fails, you look into it."[16]

While the wise and sophisticates wish to strip this world of its supernatural, its splendor and mystery, and to ridicule those who embrace such a universe, only a world of romance brimming with wonder and awe is truly satisfying to the human experience. If such a universe turns out to be a mistake, then it would still have been worth believing! Better to believe that this life is a sacred drama, that things matter—and to live life accordingly—than to live as though this world is devoid of meaning and purpose.

A scene from Lewis's *The Silver Chair* beautifully portrays this idea that an enchanted world is to be preferred to a hollow, materialistic existence. In the fourth adventure of the *Chronicles of Narnia*, two cousins of the Pevensies, Eustace Scrubb (who has already been mentioned) and Jill Pole, are carried away at the beginning of their term at the horrid Experiment House to the heart of Narnia and the castle of Cair Paravel. On instructions from Aslan, the great lion and king of Narnia, they are commissioned along with the Marsh-wiggle Puddleglum to find Prince Rilian.

The prince had gone northward to slay a large green snake that had killed the queen, but he met a beautiful woman with a green dress who had persuaded him to stay with her. After much travail, Eustace, Jill, and Puddleglum discover a fair-haired young man who turns out to be Prince Rilian. He has no recollection of his past, and all his interests center on the beautiful woman he adores and who has promised him a great kingdom in Narnia. He explains to them that for a short period each night he becomes abnormal and turns into a serpent unless he allows himself to be tied to a silver chair. When the fit comes upon him, however, the children discover that this is the only time he is normal, for he then insists that the beautiful woman is actually a wicked witch who has kept him in bondage for years.

When the children honor Prince Rilian's request to cut his cords, they break the spell upon him. But the witch returns immediately and enchants the prince and his three new friends by casting a green powder into a fire that emits a sweet and drowsy smell. As she weaves her magic, she denounces the existence of Narnia, the sun, and Aslan, the great lion. She suggests to them that it is all a dream.

At this point, Puddleglum does a very brave thing. With his bare foot (being a Marsh-wiggle, his feet were bare, "webbed and hard and cold-blooded like a duck's"), he stomps on the fire, "grinding a large part of it into ashes on the flat hearth." The "sweet, heavy smell" wanes and, along with the smell of burnt Marsh-wiggle (which is not very enchanting at all!), makes everyone's thinking much clearer. And Puddleglum boldly declares to the Witch:

> "One word, Ma'am," he said, coming back from the fire; limping, because of the pain. "One word. . . . Suppose we *have* only dreamed, or made-up, all those things—trees and grass and sun and moon and stars and Aslan himself. . . . Suppose this black pit of a kingdom of yours *is* the only world. Well, it

strikes me as a pretty poor one. . . . We're just babies making up a game, if you're right. But four babies playing a game can make a play-world which licks your real world hollow. That's why I'm going to stand by the play-world. I'm on Aslan's side, even if there isn't any Aslan to lead it. I'm going to live as like a Narnian as I can even if there isn't any Narnia. So, thanking you kindly for our supper, if these two gentlemen and the young lady are ready, we're leaving your court at once and setting out in the dark to spend our lives looking for Overland. Not that our lives will be very long, I should think; but that's small loss if the world's as dull a place as you say." [17]

We have seen, then, that literary classics and fairy tales not only instruct us about what it means to be human, but also remind us of another world that lies beyond this temporal, visible world. Even the phenomenal success of the recent *Harry Potter* series by J. K. Rowling can be attributed not just to the fact that the stories tell a good yarn, but also because they tap into that longing most of us feel for that better, magic-filled world. When we trudge up a dusty hill with Frodo and Samwise in Tolkien's Middle Earth or explore the enchanted world of Narnia with the Pevensie children, where the "inside is bigger than the outside," [18] or fly in a purple car with Harry Potter and his friends, our present experience of pain and sorrow is diminished, and our longings for Heaven become more real.

Transcendence in Film

As much as we may encounter an enchanted world signifying Heaven through literature, it is clear that the influence of literature has waned significantly since the days of Tolstoy or Dostoyevsky. With the decline in reading skills starting in the late 1960s, some studies have suggested that only slightly over half of all Americans spend thirty minutes a day reading anything at all. Indeed, in our media-frenzied culture where the Internet, cable and satellite television, and film have become ubiquitous, going to the movies may be the *last* cultural experience shared by a majority of Americans.

Although the impact of television on the traditional values of our culture cannot be minimized,[19] our purpose here is only to underscore the impact of film on culture. That film has largely replaced the novel as the dominant mode of artistic expression is undeniable, especially for Americans under age thirty, who tend to be more image- than word-oriented. Some movie critics and scholars have even gone so far as to suggest that movies are permeating our culture with a new paradigm for comprehending reality. Neal Gabler, in his book *Life the Movie: How Entertainment Conquered Reality,* says contemporary life has become our very own *The Truman Show,* perhaps aptly retitled "The Human Show." As such, we are all "Trumans," with the difference being that we are witting accomplices to the fictionalization of our lives because we prefer our life movies (or "lifies," as Gabler calls them) to reality, which barely exists anyway.

While literary people lament the fact that movies have superseded the novel as the shaper of our national consciousness (which insinuates that Americans have grown dumber and shallower), it may not be the catastrophic event that it is often imagined to be. Some would argue that the novel, like much of literature, has become obsolete as a form of artistic technology.[20] Although those who automatically reject all cultural change will be disappointed in the decline of the novel (and up to a point, they will be right), Leo Tolstoy made the following remarkable prediction not long before his death in 1910:

> This little clinking contraption with the revolving handle will make a revolution in our life — in the life of writers. It is a direct attack on the old methods of literary art.... This swift change of scene, this blending of emotion and experience — it is much better than the heavy, long-drawn-out kind of writing to which we are accustomed. It is closer to life.[21]

Whatever opinion we may have on the superiority of film to literary art, what is germane to our discussion is that filmmaking, like all art, is preoccupied with transcendent questions about life and God. Indeed, some of the most influential directors and film-makers in the history of cinema have been unabashedly preoccupied with the spiritual dimension to life, though as we saw earlier with many twentieth-century writers, their mindset is frequently one of skepticism or agnosticism. Curiously, it is not unusual for these filmmakers to have had a religious upbringing and to spend their lives artistically exploring the spiritual dimension in the contemporary world.

One of the great masters of modern cinema, Ingmar Bergman, was once asked about his intentions in filmmaking. His response is illuminating and poignantly describes how artists attempt to decipher the human condition and the role of the artist in our world. In describing his aim in filmmaking, he told the old story of how the cathedral of Chartres was struck by lightning and burned to the ground. As thousands of people came from all points of the compass like a giant procession of ants, together they began to rebuild the cathedral on its old site. They worked until the building was completed — master builders, artists, laborers, clowns, noblemen, priests, burghers. But they all remained anonymous, and no one knows to this day who built the cathedral of Chartres.

Bergman contends that in an earlier era, the artist remained unknown. He or she lived and died without being more or less "important" than other artisans, whereas today the individual, not the work of art, is exalted. To Bergman, filmmaking is a gift, like other artistic vocations, and should be attended not only by a sense of assurance (it is to the glory of God), but also by a natural humility. Bergman desired simply to be one of the artists in the cathedral of the great plain. He believed that artistic expression and creative genius cannot be divorced from a sense of transcendence and worship.

Martin Scorsese may be the most consistently passionate and inventive director to have worked regularly in the American cinema over the past two decades. His work is often rooted in his own background; he explores his Italian-American Catholic heritage and regularly confronts the themes of sin and redemption in his works, albeit in a contemporary fashion. Scorsese, best known for *Taxi Driver* (1976), *Raging Bull* (1980), *GoodFellas* (1990), and *Cape Fear* (1991) which all include his good friend Robert De Niro, grew up in New York's Little Italy. As a misbehaving class clown at a Catholic high school, he dreamed of becoming a priest. He went so far as to study briefly at Cathedral College, a junior Catholic seminary. Yet rather than devote himself entirely to the church, he enrolled in New York University and soon discovered that film could serve as a tremendous vehicle for transcendent and religious ideas. One of his more recent works, *Kundun* (or "The Presence," as Tibetans call their Dalai Lama), was a study in nonviolence and included no stars, certainly by Western standards.

In his most overtly spiritual and controversial film, *The Last Temptation of Christ* (1986), based on the novel by Nikos Kazantzakis, Scorsese attempts to dramatize the historical figure of Jesus Christ and His struggle between the spiritual and the secular. The film begins by portraying Christ as a social outcast reviled for making crucifixes. Scorsese's Christ wavers between good and evil, but eventually chooses the path of redemption. In truth, his portrayal of Jesus more resembles a messiah on the verge of a nervous breakdown than the perfect God-Man presented in the pages of the New Testament. The film was criticized by many religious groups as being blasphemous; as a result, many theaters and video chains refused to carry it. In response to what many viewed as a sacrilegious work, Scorsese shot back, "My whole life has been movies and religion. That's it. Nothing else." [22] In a book based on a BBC documentary, *A Personal Journey with Martin Scorsese through American Movies*, he declares, "I don't really see a conflict between the church and the movies, the sacred and the profane. . . . Both are places for people to come together and share a common experience. I believe there is a spirituality in films, even if it's not one which can supplant faith." [23]

Another provocative filmmaker who displays a preoccupation with transcendent themes is Lawrence Kasdan, who has admitted that "movies are my religion." Kasdan, a prolific film writer who is known for his provocative dialogues, has written, directed, or produced over a dozen movies in recent years, including *The Empire Strikes Back, Raiders of the Lost Ark, Return of the Jedi, The Big Chill,* and *The Accidental Tourist.* In *Grand Canyon,* Kasdan's much-ballyhooed film of the early 1990s, Steve Martin, who plays a Hollywood producer, muses early on in the film, "All of life's riddles are solved in the movies." Transcendence permeates the entire film. Mack (Kevin Kline), an immigration lawyer, avoids being run over by a stranger while walking the Miracle Mile on his way to an appointment. He and his wife, Claire (Mary McDonnell), decide to adopt an abandoned infant she discovers while jogging. One evening the two of them discuss recent cataclysmic events in their lives:

> "What if these are miracles, Mack? Maybe we don't have any experience with miracles, so we're slow to recognize them." (Mack, wanting to end the conversation) "I'm getting a terrific headache." "No, you're not." "I'm not?" "I'll tell you why I reject your headache." "Please." "Because it is inappropriate." "Inappropriate." "If I am right, and these are truly miracles, then it is an inappropriate response to get a headache in the presence of a miracle."

Toward the end of the film, Kasdan attempts to answer many of the questions he has raised. Simon (Danny Glover), a tow-truck driver who at the film's beginning had delivered Mack from a group of thugs on his way home from a Los Angeles Lakers' game, takes the entire cast of the "City of Angels" on a day trip to "the end of the line," the Grand Canyon. As they gather around marveling at the canyon, embracing the transcendence of nature, one of the characters remarks, "Perhaps it's not so bad after all."

Yet another filmmaker known for his frequent musings on faith and life is Woody Allen. Allen's oeuvre seems to perennially focus on broken relationships (albeit with much humor), the meaning of life (if there is one), God, death, morality, and our sense of alienation and estrangement in this world. Allen often raises the question, Can we know if God exists? Listen to the conversation between Allen's character, Boris, and Diane Keaton's character, Sonia, as Allen waxes philosophical about God's existence in the comedy *Love and Death* (1975):

> Boris: "Sonia, what if there is no God?" Sonia: "Boris Demitrovich, are you joking?" Boris: "What if we're just a bunch of absurd people who are running around with no rhyme or reason?" Sonia: "But if there is no God, then life has no meaning. Why go on living? Why not just commit suicide?" Boris: "Well, let's not get hysterical; I could be wrong. I'd hate to blow my brains out and then read in the papers they'd found something."

One of the recurring themes in *Love and Death* is Boris's quest to receive some kind of sign from God: "If I could see a miracle, just one miracle. If I could see a burning bush, or the seas part, or my Uncle Sasha pick up a check." Or again, "If only God would give me some sign. If he would just speak to me once, anything, one sentence, two words. If he would just cough."

For Allen (as for French philosopher Jean-Paul Sartre), there is no exit from the conundrum of life. He senses that something must exist beyond this world, some other possibility, but believes we cannot get there. We are caught. In *Broadway Danny Rose* (1984), Allen's character attempts to convince the cynical Tina of the importance of guilt. After all, his rabbi told him that we are "all guilty in the eyes of God." Tina asks him, "Do you believe in God?" To which Danny replies, "No, but I feel guilty about it."

To Allen, there is no God, but there remains a vestige of guilt because of God. There is guilt, but no possibility of forgiveness. In Allen's short story "The Condemned," Cloquet is about to be executed for his murder of Gaston Brisseau when he is visited by a priest, Father Bernard. Cloquet has always been an atheist, but when Father Bernard arrives, he asks if there is still time to convert. Father Bernard shakes his head. "This time of year, I think most of your major faiths are filled. Probably the best I could do on such short notice is maybe make a call and get you into something Hindu. I'll need a passport-sized photograph, though." [24]

Throughout Allen's works, death plays a major role in seeing to it that there is no escape from this life. References abound about what may happen after death, but always with wry humor. In *Love and Death*, Allen's character Boris asks, "What happens after we die? Is there a hell? Is there a God? Do we live again? All right, let me ask one key question: Are there girls?" In his essay "Conversations with Helmholtz," Allen muses on the human condition and religion: "If man were immortal, do you realize what his meat bills would be?... I don't believe in an afterlife, although I am bringing a change of underwear." [25]

While Allen often distances himself from a Christian world-view, he nevertheless explores the dimensions of morality and guilt in his film *Crimes and Misdemeanors* (1989). The film features Martin Landau as a successful Jewish ophthalmologist who hires his brother to murder his mistress. The mistress, played by Angelica Huston, has threatened to tell his wife of their affair. The film, which mirrors Dostoyevsky's classic *Crime and Punishment*, explores whether a person can commit a heinous crime and go on living as though there were no legitimacy to the guilt that results. "What Allen gives us, all in all," commented James Nuechterlein after the release of *Crimes and Misdemeanors*, "is the perspective of a man who wants to believe but cannot bring himself to do so—seemingly the prevailing plight among contemporary intellectuals."[26]

Indeed, Allen's worldview, rooted in his Jewish tradition, pokes and prods the powerful Almighty. His protests against an omniscient, omnipotent God are based on his haunting observations of human suffering and death. He wants a God who will agonize and act with love in response to the human plight. While Allen continually raises questions about conventional religious and philosophical wisdom, he refuses easy answers and cheap comfort. He not only argues with God, like the rabbis, but goes one step further, arguing with the *idea* of God.

Perhaps Allen's real position about God is seen in *Love and Death*. Facing the audience, a man who was promised that he would be saved—only to be executed on time because God did not come through—declares, "The important thing, I think, is not to be bitter. If it turns out that there is a God, I don't think that he's evil. The worst you can say about him is that basically he's an underachiever." In the film *Stardust Memories* (1980), through the character Sandy Bates, Allen declares, "To you, I'm an atheist. To God, I'm the loyal opposition." To Allen, part of living life truthfully is to question, to protest long and loud against the sufferings of humanity—and against any religion that offers superficial answers to humanity's deepest questions.

The film that probably most poignantly portrays a yearning for the Edenic world, Heaven, is Allen's *The Purple Rose of Cairo* (1985). In the film, Allen playfully explores life from two different dimensions. We first see the hero of the film (played by Jeff Daniels) through the eyes of a small-town short-order waitress (Mia Farrow) who attempts to escape her drab existence by going to the movies. She watches the same movie over and over again and is mesmerized by the male lead. One afternoon, as she is watching "her" movie, her hero steps out—literally—from the two-dimensional movie screen and lands in the New Jersey theater. Suddenly, he is in the "real" world with the flabbergasted waitress.

The movie star character discovers that the outside world holds many surprises. When he and the waitress kiss, he pauses, waiting for the fadeout. And when someone attempts to explain the concept of God—"He's the one in control of everything. He's what the whole world is about"—he nods, "Oh, you mean Mr. Mayer, the owner of the movie company." When someone hits him with a fist, he falls down, as he was taught to do on-screen, but rubs his jaw with amazement because blows in the movies don't hurt! The movie also explores the dynamics of friendship, fidelity, and commitment to one another. The actor who has stepped out of the world of celluloid can only identify with harmonious and rewarding relationships. Eventually, he climbs back onto the two-dimensional movie screen and attempts to explain the real world to his supporting cast. They stare at him as if he has lost his mind, believing that he is simply talking nonsense. To the movie cast, there is no other world out there. Only the world of celluloid is real for them.

While it would be presumptuous to suggest precisely what Allen is trying to communicate in this film, he seems to be saying that the world of celluloid, in contrast to real life, presents us with a harmonious and happy existence. To Allen, the movies remove us from the painful realities of our human existence. In the happy ending of his film *Hannah and Her Sisters* (1986), the cinema is a form of storytelling that helps us deal with suffering and injustice. According to Allen, "Gooey finales are what movies are for. They permit us to ride challenges and dangers through to the satisfying ends that don't pan out in life." [27]

But fundamentally, Allen's worldview is one of ultimate despair. In the perspective of Allan Bloom, author of the critically acclaimed book *The Closing of the American Mind,* Allen's work is symptomatic of a dark strain in American culture that is influenced by the German philosopher Nietzsche and that knows only relative values. His work displays nihilism with a happy ending. [28] In Allen's perspective, humanity cannot know ultimate answers about the existence of God or an explanation for human suffering. In a speech to college grad-uates years ago, he mused,

> Mankind faces a crossroads. One path leads to despair and utter hopelessness. The other, to total extinction. Let us pray we have the wisdom to choose correctly. I speak, by the way, not with any sense of futility, but with a panicky conviction of the absolute meaninglessness of existence which could easily be misinterpreted as pessimism. It is not. It is merely a healthy concern for the predicament of modern man. (Modern man is here defined as any person born after Nietzsche's edict that "God is dead." But before the hit recording "I Wanna Hold Your Hand.") . . . How comforting life must have been for early man because he believed in a powerful, benevolent Cre-ator who looked after all things. Imagine his disappointment when he saw his wife putting on weight.[29]

While it would be saying too much to say that Allen's works function *evangelistically* to bring the world to faith in God, it is fair to say that his films and writings do show us something of the absur-dity of life if there is no God. In many ways, he is a modern-day Qoheleth, whose musings on life and faith resemble Ecclesiastes. I think it was Bishop Fulton Sheen who spoke of "black grace," of see-ing the great message of redemption and our need for a merciful and omnipotent God amidst the darkness of human misery, with all our sufferings and unanswered questions.

Allen stands in line with other existential writers and artists, such as Sartre and Camus. And we cannot be too thankful for these great atheists, for they often show us the shape of God by His *absence* more clearly and starkly than believers do by His *presence*. To some degree, their works represent a silhouette, for they show us the need for God in a seemingly God-forsaken world.

While the Christian faithful may be disturbed by filmmakers

such as Allen, in our post-Christian culture these artists may very well serve a redemptive purpose. In a way, they show the world the need for a moral universe, where truths are absolute, where the violation of these truths results in legitimate guilt and estrangement, and where a life lived without facing its absurdities would be a life lived in denial. Thomas Merton would have appreciated Allen.

> It is only when the apparent absurdity of life is faced in all truth that faith really becomes possible. Otherwise, faith tends to be a kind of diversion, a spiritual amusement, in which one gathers up accepted, conventional formulas and arranges them in the approved mental patterns, without bothering to investigate their meaning, or asking if they have any practical consequences in one's life.[30]

Probably no other artistic medium in our culture displays such an openness to spirituality as does film. One of the best examples of this is George Lucas's *Star Wars*. Whatever one might conclude of the *Star Wars* movies, few can dispute their remarkable impact on the American consciousness. A few years ago, the Smithsonian's Air and Space Museum mounted "Star Wars: The Magic of Myth," an exhibition that unabashedly pushed the metaphysical angle. On the religious overtones of Lucas's work, novelist Alexander Theroux, writing for the *Wall Street Journal,* wryly observes,

> For make no mistake, this is a religion, with Lucas as God, the multiplex as church, and rabid fans as fevered acolytes who can both "witness" the "truth" and later show their good faith by bringing their custom to outlying stores (open until 10 P.M.!), their essential parish.[31]

The film industry has even begun to attract some of the celebrated writers of our own day. And sometimes a Christian worldview turns up in some of the strangest of places—and films. Stephen King, the American master of the macabre, has displayed a rich appreciation for Christian themes in his novels, which are finding their way onto the screen. In his 1989 preface to *The Stand,* King summarized his epic apocalypse as a "long tale of dark Christianity."

His novel *Desperation* (1996) turns on the meaning of 1 John 4:8 ("The one who does not love does not know God, for God is love.") for a boy who has just been converted by a Methodist minister. In an interview on the Internet, King made these remarkable statements concerning *Desperation:*

> It seemed to me that most people who are writing novels of supernatural suspense are very interested in evil, and the evil side resonates for them. . . . And I wanted to see if I could create a strong force of good and desperation, as well. So it's a very Christian novel in that way, too. It's going to make some people uncomfortable, I think.[32]

While King's throng of admirers wondered how a recent serious accident might affect his work, the movie version of *The Green Mile* arrived at the theaters in late 1999. The movie stars Tom Hanks, David Morse, and Michael Clarke Duncan, and was directed by Frank Darabont, who also directed another film based on a King novel, *The Shawshank Redemption.* Although Darabont wrote the script for *The Green Mile,* he stayed close to the original, apparently adding only one scene. The rest of the movie (including the last line) is vintage Stephen King. In *The Green Mile,* King has written an imaginative and profound parable portraying the triumph of sacrificial love over genuine evil and wickedness. And no one has ever disputed that King has a remarkable grasp for what is truly evil. *The New Yorker* even went so far as to call *The Green Mile* a "Christian allegory."

It is at the very end of *The Green Mile* (part 6, "Coffey on the Mile") that the hero reflects on the providence of God. A fine preacher could not present a more accurate portrayal of Jesus Christ's substitutionary atonement and the impenetrable sovereignty of God.

> I think back to the sermons of my childhood, booming affirmations in the church of Praise Jesus, The Lord Is Mighty, and I recall how the preachers used to say that God's eye is on the sparrow, that He sees and marks even the least of His creations. Yet this same God sacrificed John Coffey, who tried only to do good in his blind way, as savagely as any Old Testament prophet ever sacrificed a defenseless lamb, as Abraham would have sacrificed his own son if actually called upon to do so. . . . If it happens, God *lets* it happen, and when we say "I don't understand," God replies, "I don't care."[33]

Films such as *The Green Mile* can have a profound effect in communicating to our secular culture a Christian worldview in a way that is powerful yet covert in its methodology. Some would even argue that film (as well as other art forms, such as paintings and plays) are quickly becoming a substitute religion that offers a dose of transcendence to modern worshipers who, having thrown off the tenets of orthodoxy, still yearn for meaning, purpose, and significance.

I can recall attending some years ago the mesmerizing play *Les Miserables,* based on the novel by Victor Hugo. At the end of the play, the audience stood in rapturous applause, many with tears streaming down their cheeks as they celebrated the impact of God's mercy and pardon in the life of Jean Valjean.

Intriguingly, Geoffrey Hill, author of *Illuminating Shadows: The Mythic Power of Film,* suggests that secular "worshipers" go to the temple of the cinema for the same transcendent purposes that the people in the Old Testament went to the religious temple. His provocative book begins:

As ironic modern worshipers we congregate at the cinematic temple. We pay our votive offerings at the box office. We buy our ritual corn. We hush in reverent anticipation as the lights go down and the celluloid magic begins. Throughout the filmic narrative we identify with the hero. We vilify the anti-hero. We vicariously exult in the victories of the drama. And we are spiritually inspired by the moral of the story, all while believing we are modern techno-secular people, devoid of religion. Yet the depth and intensity of our participation reveal a religious fervor that is not much different from that of religious zealots.[34]

As we sojourn in a culture where many have become "bloody sick of the old house of orthodoxy" (to use Walker Percy's phrase), the world of literature and film may provide an entrée to spiritual issues for our unbelieving culture. In an age where Enlightenment sentiment has disparaged Christian theism, the beauty and longings intimated through the arts may be a final, but abiding, intimation of Heaven.

Perhaps we who are Christians would do well to "leverage" the arts for the cause of Christianity. I am reminded of an interview with writer Philip Yancey conducted a few years ago. In the premier issue of *Mars Hill Review*, a journal that seeks to integrate Christianity with contemporary culture, Yancey recounted a discussion with a Christian who taught philosophy at a secular college in Virginia. The teacher described how he would take his students back to read Greek philosophy, starting with Aristotle and Plato, and they would all agree on the three verities: truth, goodness, and beauty. But the teacher reached an impasse with his students. As we attempt to impact our post-Christian culture — so like the world of the Greek Mars Hill — with the hope of Christianity, his friend's observations are instructive:

He said that in today's environment he could get nowhere trying to express truth. There is no absolute truth for these kids, they don't believe there is one, it's a hopeless search and they would just laugh at you if you held that up. Next is goodness. Where do you get morality? Unless you believe and accept a revelation like the Bible, the Koran or whatever, you have no basis for morality. Everybody does what is right in his own mind. That's exactly how these kids are. He said, "I've got no foothold in either one of these places to put my foot and stand firm, but in the realm of beauty they are open. . . . They don't have a pure ideal of truth, they don't have a pure ideal of goodness, but they do have a pure ideal of beauty. I think that this is a very significant starting point, if the church on "Mars Hill" is trying to reach modern people. I think we're wise to start where the cracks and openings are.[35]

CHAPTER 7

Our Experience of Pain and Suffering

Pain insists upon being attended to. God whispers to us in our pleasures, speaks in our conscience, but shouts in our pains. It is His megaphone to rouse a deaf world.

—C. S. Lewis

To know and to serve God, of course, is why we're here, a clear truth that, like the nose on your face, is near at hand and easily discernible but can make you dizzy if you try to focus on it hard. But a little faith will see you through. What else will do except faith in such a cynical, corrupt time? When the country goes temporarily to the dogs, cats must learn to be circumspect, walk on fences, sleep in trees, and have faith that all this woofing is not the last word.

—Garrison Keillor

"IF GOD WERE GOOD, HE WOULD WISH TO MAKE HIS CREATURES PER-fectly happy, and if God were almighty, He would be able to do what He wished. But the creatures are not happy. Therefore God lacks either goodness, or power, or both." This, states C. S. Lewis, is the problem of pain, in its simplest form.[1] In these few words, Lewis has laid out the dilemma we face when we consider human suffering and God. While a definitive treatment of this subject is beyond the scope of this chapter (and this book!), we will consider not only the real-ity of our painful existence and our grappling with God about suf-fering, but more importantly, how pain and suffering serve as another powerful signpost to Heaven.

Our Painful Existence

Confronting ultimate questions about suffering and evil is a daunt-ing task, and we rarely have any clues as to the "why" of our painful existence. In the film *Hannah and Her Sisters,* the character played by Woody Allen tries to tell his Jewish parents that he has difficulty believing in the God of their faith. His mother won't hear of such nonsense and locks herself in the bathroom. Confused, Allen's char-acter shouts into the bathroom, "Well, if there's a God, then why is there so much evil in the world? Just on a simplistic level, why were there Nazis?" At this, his mother calls out from behind the bathroom door to her husband in the kitchen, "Tell him, Max." The father replies, "How in the world do I know why there were Nazis? I don't even know how the can opener works!"

Whether or not one embraces such a cynicism about ultimate questions, one does not have to be an astute observer to realize that, despite its beauty and pleasures, our world is commonly character-ized by pain, suffering, and loss. The breakdown of the family in America has become widespread, which often leaves children disil-lusioned about life. Don Henley captures the heartache of a man who, as a boy, lost the love he was meant to know when his parents divorced. In the opening lines of his popular song "The End of the

Innocence," he speaks of when "happily ever after fails" because "we've been poisoned by these fairy tales."

And we know that pain and suffering are not confined to the American scene. Simply turn on your television to catch the local newscast or tune in to CNN, and you realize quickly that ours is a blighted planet. As you read this book, innocent blood is being shed throughout the world, tens of thousands of children are starving, many are being beaten by their parents, and millions of other people live with the squalor of disease, the promise of a long life only a faint hope. It is easy to become numbed to such tragedies, but when we experience suffering firsthand the questions come cascading like a waterfall. It was Loren Eiseley who said that we humans are the only Cosmic Orphans, because it is only we who ask the question, Why?

Rabbi Harold Kushner wrote the best-selling book *When Bad Things Happen to Good People* because he had to try to come to grips with tragedy in his own life. Why was it that his only son was struck with the rare disease progeria that made him age prematurely, so that he looked like an old man by the time he died in his teens? Why?

Annie Dillard, the Pulitzer Prize-winning author of *Pilgrim at Tinker Creek,* has spent much of her writing life musing over the issue of human suffering and attempting to reconcile this with her Christian belief in an all-powerful and benevolent God. Her recent book, *For the Time Being,* chronicles many of the horrors and tragedies of human life. In her earlier work *Holy the Firm,* she writes of seven-year-old Julie Norwich, whose burns from a plane accident so haunted Dillard that she questions deeply the presence, or rather the absence, of a loving God:

> Into this world falls a plane. . . . I heard it go. The cat looked up. There was no reason: the plane's engine simply stilled after takeoff, and the light plane failed to clear the firs . . . the fuel exploded; and Julie Norwich, seven years old, burnt off

her face. Little Julie mute in some room at St. Joe's now. . . .
Can you scream without lips? . . . Of faith I have nothing, only
of truth: that this one God is a brute and traitor, abandoning
us to time, to necessity and the engines of matter unhinged.
This is no leap; this is evidence of things seen. . . . Faith would
be, in short, that God has any willful connection with time
whatsoever, and with us. For I know it as given that God is all
good. And I take it also as given that whatever he touches has
meaning, if only in his mysterious terms. . . . The question is,
then, whether God touches anything. Is anything firm, or is
time on the loose?[2]

Another critically acclaimed writer who has addressed the difficult topic of suffering is Reynolds Price. In 1994 his published mem-
oir, *A Whole New Life*, recounted with remarkable precision the story
of his 1980s ordeal with spinal cancer. Price was to receive a most
haunting and troubling letter from an unknown reader, a gravely ill
young man and former medical student, whose colon and liver cancer (which, as it turns out, would take his life) had recently been diagnosed. *Letter to a Man in the Fire* is Price's hurried (time was of the
essence) and profound response to that man, and it passionately takes
up two of the most compelling human questions, which constitute
the subtitle of the book: *Does God Exist and Does He Care?*

Even the saints, though they may have a deep-rooted belief in a
loving and all-powerful God, struggle with understanding human
tragedy. Lewis, after the loss of his wife to cancer, wrote of his grief
and disillusionment with God. Published just before Lewis's death
in 1963, and originally penned under the pseudonym N. W. Clerk,
the book asks,

Meanwhile, where is God? . . . When you are . . . so happy that
you are tempted to feel His claims upon you as an interrup-
tion, if you remember yourself and turn to Him with

gratitude and praise, you will be—or so it feels—welcomed with open arms. But go to Him when your need is desperate, when all other help is vain, and what do you find? A door slammed in your face, and a sound of bolting and double bolting on the inside. . . . Why is He so present a commander in our time of prosperity and so very absent a help in time of trouble?[3]

Mark Twain once observed, "When somebody you love dies, it is like when your house burns down; it isn't for years that you realize the full extent of your loss." And many of us—who, like Lewis, have lost loved ones—can greatly empathize with his startling yet candid words. But Lewis was a realist. And although he was an able defender of Christian orthodoxy, he deeply realized the great demands upon those who write to defend the Christian position on suffering.[4]

It goes without saying that it is a part of our humanness to question suffering in this life, no matter how righteous we are. Saint Teresa of Avila, when thrown off her carriage, slammed rudely to the ground, and deposited in a mud puddle, questioned God. He answered her, "This is how I treat all my friends." She tartly replied, "Then, Lord, it is not surprising that you have so few."[5] Even saints do not smile sweetly when God throws them into mud puddles.

Grappling with God

As Lewis's quote at the beginning of this chapter suggests, the perennial question of evil and human suffering is a theological problem. God is always brought into the matter, and the theological conundrum generally attempts to make sense of four seemingly inconsistent propositions: God exists, God is all-powerful, God is all-good, and evil exists. As humanity grapples with these four propositions, the only options available are to deny evil itself (idealism); to deny or minimize His divine attributes of goodness and power (finitism); or to deny His very existence based on the ongoing reality of evil and suffering (atheism).

In recent years, Eastern mysticism, or pantheism, which to a large extent denies the reality of evil (and moral absolutes), has been embraced by a growing segment of American culture. Generally speaking, Eastern mysticism sees all of life as impersonal and everything that exists as part of a greater, transcendent Oneness. It is somewhat similar to Buddhism, as well as Christian Science, which we might call idealism because it denies any true evil. And yet when we consider this as a legitimate option, it is clear to any casual observer that life teaches us differently! G. K. Chesterton once observed that the challenge of philosophy is to understand "why little Johnny likes to torture cats." But to Eastern mysticism, there are no cats for little Johnny to torture!

The simplest response to Eastern mysticism is to look at the most obvious and external evil: physical suffering and death. There was once a little boy who was a Christian Scientist. (Christian Scientists are followers of Mary Baker Eddy, who taught that evil was an illusion. They believe that sickness, suffering, and even death are illusions of the "mortal mind," which people believe only because they lack faith or proper insight.) This little boy went up to his Christian Science preacher and asked him to please pray for his father, who was very sick. The preacher replied to the little boy, "Son, you don't understand. Your father only thinks he's sick. Go tell him that. Tell him to have faith." The boy obeyed and ran into the preacher the next day. "How's your father, son?" "Oh, he thinks he's dead." [6] So much for this unlivable philosophy of life. To use Chesterton's image, we cannot wish away cats.

While the view of idealism (a denial of evil) is simple to refute, the view of finitism, which minimizes the twin divine attributes of God's omnipotence and benevolence, is harder to argue. Although some would deny the benevolence of God (the French poet Baudelaire declared, "If there is a God, then He is the Devil!"), more often it is the divine attribute of omnipotence that people call into question. This, you will recall, is the worldview of filmmaker Woody Allen, as expressed in his film *Love and Death:* When God does not deliver, then the worst we can say is that He is an "underachiever."

The position of finitism, which basically embraces a naturalistic God devoid of the supernatural ability to remove evil and suffering, is a theological cousin to atheism. Atheism essentially denies God's existence *because* of all of the observable evil and suffering in the world. Atheism generally contends that if God were all-good (benevolent), He *would* destroy evil, and if He were all-powerful (omnipotent), He *could* destroy evil; but because evil and suffering are not destroyed, an all-good, all-powerful God must not exist.

Atheism has had many adherents over the centuries, and the philosophy has been expressed by many artists and poets who deeply feel the anguish and sufferings of this world. Science-fiction writer H. G. Wells once declared, "If I thought there was an omnipotent God who looked down on battles and deaths and all the waste and horror of war—able to prevent these things—doing them to amuse Himself, I would spit in His empty face."

Likely the most powerful argument ever marshaled in defense of atheism is contained in one of the most profound pieces of literature ever penned—and interestingly, written by a great Christian. I am referring to Fyodor Dostoyevsky's *The Brothers Karamazov.* In this passage, Ivan Karamazov, a self-proclaimed "believer," challenges his saintly brother, Alyosha, to defend the existence of God in the light of the atrocities and sufferings of innocent children:

> I want to see with my own eyes the lions lie down with the lamb and the murdered man rise up and embrace his murderer. I want to be there when everyone suddenly finds out what it has all been for. All religions on earth are based on this desire, and I am a believer. But then there are the children, and what am I to do with them? That is the question I cannot

answer. I repeat for the hundredth time—there are lots of questions, but I've only taken the children. . . . Listen: if all have to suffer so as to buy eternal harmony by their suffering, what have the children to do with it—tell me, please? . . . We cannot afford to pay so much for admission. And therefore I hasten to return my ticket of admission. And indeed, If I am an honest man, I'm bound to hand it back as soon as possible. This I am doing. It is not God that I do not accept, Alyosha. I merely most respectfully return him the ticket.[7]

Ivan's argument against God can be distilled down to this fundamental issue: How could a good and loving heavenly Father allow such human sufferings and pain if He *truly* cares for and is in control of His creation? But as powerful and convincing as Ivan's argument is against God, as strongly as we may feel about the atrocities and the innocent sufferings of this world, these still fail to disprove God's existence. Why? Because ultimately it assumes God to disprove Him. Lewis went through the same questioning as he examined Christianity yet realized the fallacy of his reasoning. In his important apologetic work, *Mere Christianity*, he observes,

If a good God made the world why has it gone wrong? And for many years I simply refused to listen to the Christian answers to this question. . . . My argument against God was that the universe seemed so cruel and unjust. But how had I got this idea of *just* and *unjust*? A man does not call a line crooked unless he has some idea of a straight line. What was I comparing this universe with when I called it unjust?[8]

All of us grow weary of human pain and suffering. If we did not feel an innate sense of injustice at the atrocities, injustices, and sufferings in our mortal existence, we would be less than human. But to question the existence of God is ultimately to question the very standard by which we measure right and wrong. Along the lines of Lewis's comments, author Frederick Buechner, in his book *Wishful Thinking: A Theological ABC,* describes the dilemma of the atheist:

> A true atheist is one who is willing to face the full conse-
> quences of what it means to say there is no God. To say there
> is no God means among other things that there are no
> Absolute Standards. . . . An atheist is about as likely as any-
> body else to walk into a newsstand someday and pick up a
> copy of the *National Enquirer* or some such. On the front
> page is a picture of a dead child. The bare back is covered
> with welts. The eyes are swollen shut. Both arms are broken.
> The full story is on page 3 if you have the stomach for it. To
> be consistent with his creed, an atheist can say no more than
> that to beat a child to death is wrong with a small *w.* . . . The
> atheist holds the tabloid in his hand and asks the question
> Why should such things happen? Atheism can reply only,
> Why *shouldn't* such things happen? But he keeps on asking.[9]

As angry as we may become at the evil and seemingly point-less sufferings that pervade our existence, the observations of both Lewis and Buechner suggest that our grappling with God is actually a sure indication of our righteous indignation with this fallen world, our sense of right and wrong. To use Lewis's image again, to call a line crooked we must have some innate idea of what a straight line looks like. Consequently, with atheism one can only state preferences and choices, not absolute right or wrong. In the world of atheism, life has no ultimate meaning or purpose, and we are only here for a few short years. To quote Shakespeare, life is "full of sound and fury, signifying nothing." To embrace atheism is like screwing down the manhole covers on the great deeps and flattening the sky to a low ceiling. And instead of seeing the world as a forest of spires and turrets, like the Gothic art that expressed an age of faith, we find our world to be nothing more than a ranch-style, flattened, one-story existence.[10]

Making Some Sense Out of Suffering

Humanity loves to ask the deep questions about life and existence. We are a curious bunch! I think it was Martin Luther who, when asked what God was doing before He created the world, responded, "He was cutting up switches to flog people who ask such silly questions!" But we still want to know the answers to the tough questions of our existence, and there is nothing greater that makes us ask "why?" than human suffering. And today we live in a superficial culture that wants the bottom-line answers *right now!* It was Søren Kierkegaard who said that Christians reminded him of schoolboys who want to look up the answers to their math problems in the back of the book rather than work them through. Unfortunately, many of us have these schoolboy tendencies, especially when it comes to human suffering.

The Limits of Human Understanding

What are we to make of all the pain and suffering? And how might it serve as a clue that another world awaits us? The first thing we must do is to admit the limitations of our human understanding. Our world is filled with awe and mystery and is not always predictable (see Ecclesiastes 7:13-15; 1 Corinthians 13:12; Deuteronomy 29:29).

In an effort to fathom human suffering, people sometimes refer to the Old Testament book of Job, which describes Job's personal travails and the "counsel" of his three friends as he protests his innocence. Toward the end of the book, God ends His silence, firing zingers at the suffering (and now speechless!) saint. This God whom Job encounters does not fit neatly into a package. He is not some nice, little, formulaic God, but rather a profound Mystery. He is the God of whom Rabbi Abraham Heschel once said, "God is not nice. God is not an uncle. God is an earthquake."

Job is never told *why* he suffers. If anything, through God's interrogation he discovers that God is the Author of the play and he is merely an actor. Hence, Job is a hero, not of understanding, but of *faith*. For Job, resolution to his suffering does not come through getting answers to his questions, but in believing that somehow, some way, his suffering has *ultimate* meaning. To this suffering saint, as throughout the rest of the Bible, the question is never whether or not God exists or whether He is all-powerful, but whether He is good and can be trusted.

Job comes to the realization that life is not a problem to be solved rationally, but rather a mystery to be affirmed by faith: "Hear, now, and I will speak; I will ask Thee, and do Thou instruct me. I have heard of Thee by the hearing of the ear; but now my eye sees Thee; therefore I retract, and I repent in dust and ashes"(Job 42:4-6). In truth, the book of Job contributes to our genuine understanding of life, as Kreeft observes:

> Job is mystery. A mystery satisfies something in us, but not our reason. The rationalist in us is repelled by Job. . . but something deeper in us is deeply satisfied by Job, and is nourished. Job is not like consommé, clear and bright, but like minestrone, dark and thick. It sticks to your ribs. When we read Job we are like a little child eating his spinach. "Open your mouth and close your eyes." Job, like spinach, is not sweet tasting. But it puts iron in our blood.[11]

The Good News of Brokenness

So then, if we are to make sense of suffering, not only must we confess the limits of our human understanding, but we must also come to realize, with some trepidation, that we really grow through our trials and pains. It was Hemingway who once said, "The world breaks everyone and afterward many are strong at the broken places."

Similarly, in the film *Steel Magnolias,* when the central character (played by Julia Roberts) dies, the women who have been lifelong friends in a small town lament their great loss with the words, "What doesn't kill us makes us strong."

Sheldon Vanauken, under the tutelage of Lewis at Oxford, received correspondence from Lewis after the loss to cancer of his soul mate and wife. Lewis's words of encouragement and consolation center on the idea that God had dealt Vanauken a "severe mercy" in that the loss of his wife (who was a devout Christian) would lead to his greater devotion to God. That correspondence is contained in the spiritual journey authored by Vanauken and appropriately titled *A Severe Mercy.* James, the New Testament writer, similarly told us to "consider it all joy . . . when you encounter various trials, knowing that the testing of your faith produces endurance. And let endurance have its perfect result, that you may be perfect and complete, lacking in nothing" (James 1:2-4).

If we are honest, we will admit that our greatest growth in life comes not amidst prosperity but in adversity. The Swiss physician Paul Tournier spent much of his professional life examining the dynamics of human suffering. On the value of suffering, he writes,

> There is that extraordinary joy which radiates from many a sufferer from serious infirmity, and which contrasts astonishingly with the moroseness of so many of the healthy people one sees on the bus. What is the explanation? Well, I think that it is because their lives demand permanent courage, a constant expenditure of courage; and since courage belongs to the spiritual economy, the more one spends it, the more one has. . . . Where does the pleasure in living come from? More from struggling than from possessing.[12]

Despite the fact that suffering helps us grow, we don't like trials, even if they are good for us! T. S. Eliot once observed, "Humanity cannot stand very much reality," and rarely is this axiom more true than when it comes to our suffering. Even if we do grow through our trials and afflictions, hard times are surely not something we naturally desire. In truth, we would love for God to shower us with happiness and delight all the days of our lives. As Lewis wrote,

> We want, in fact, not so much a Father in Heaven as a *grandfather* in heaven—a senile benevolence who, as they say, "likes to see young people enjoying themselves," and whose plan for the universe was simply that it might be truly said at the end of each day, "a good time was had by all." [13]

The Intolerable Compliment

It is difficult for us to overcome this "right of entitlement," especially in prosperous America, where it is a *given* that we deserve The Good Life. But if we humans are creatures loved by God, as the Scriptures proclaim, then God may have higher purposes and designs for our lives than we can now fathom. Truly, if we are being molded and fashioned for an eternal destiny—Heaven—who can imagine what measures God may use to prepare us for that magnificent destiny? We may, as Lewis reminds us, need to have our conception of love corrected:

> We are, not metaphorically but in very truth, a Divine work of art, something that God is making, and therefore something with which He will not be satisfied until it has a certain character. Here again we come up against what I have called the "intolerable compliment." Over a sketch made idly to amuse a child, an artist may not take much trouble: he may be content to let it go even though it is not exactly as he meant it to be. But over the great picture of his life—the work which he loves . . . he will take endless trouble. . . . In the same way, it is natural for us to wish that God had designed

for us a less glorious and less arduous destiny; but then we are wishing not for more love but for less.[14]

Looking Ahead to Lenten Lands

But let us not come with any naïve, patronizing talk about evil and suffering. This world is often a painful place, even for the saint, and we may never fully understand the reasons behind the tragedies and atrocities that confront us throughout life. If we go back to Lewis's argument in *Mere Christianity,* you will recall that he could only know a line was crooked because he knew what a straight line looked like. As Lewis found himself arguing with God because of the injustices in the world, so also our contempt for this fallen, unjust world argues covertly for our deeply cherished sense of justice and righteousness. Deep down, we know that this world is fallen. And we desire and expect that one day God will right all the wrongs.

While we may never fully fathom the mysterious unknowns in this life, we would do well to remind ourselves that God Himself can *personally* identify with pain and suffering. From the Christian perspective, His taking on of human flesh in the person of Jesus Christ and Christ's consequent crucifixion on the cross demonstrate God's entering into our own "godforsakenness." He understands our pains, tragedies, and disappointments in life because He Himself has participated fully in humanity through His Son. As Dorothy Sayers observes,

> For whatever reason God chose to make man as he is — limited and suffering and subject to sorrows and death — He had the honesty and courage to take His own medicine. Whatever the game He is playing with His creation, He has kept His own rules and played fair. He can exact nothing from man that He has not exacted from Himself. He has Himself gone through the whole of human experience, from the trivial irritations of family life and the cramping restrictions of hard

work and lack of money to the worst horrors of pain and humiliation, defeat, despair, and death. When He was a man, He played the man. He was born in poverty and died in disgrace and thought it well worthwhile.[15]

While the sufferings of this world cannot be trivialized, the historical event of the resurrection of Jesus Christ, signaling His triumph over sin and death, radically alters the Christian's perspective of life after death. If one focuses exclusively on this world's pain and death, the Christian hope of Easter seems like a make-believe story, a conjured-up fairy tale. But if one takes God's entering into this blighted planet, suffering the pain and ignominy of the human race—and the Resurrection—as the starting point, then human history becomes the contradiction, and Easter, a preview of ultimate reality.[16]

I am reminded of the story of the little boy who was reading late at night before going to bed. His father noticed that his room light was on and asked him to turn it out and go to sleep. As the father passed his son's room, he heard his son saying softly, "If you only knew what I knew. If you only knew what I knew." In the morning over breakfast, the father asked his son what he meant by the phrase. The young boy responded, "Dad, I was really frightened by the story I was reading. The bad guys were winning. So I turned back to the end of the book to see how the story ended. And you know what? The good guys won! So when I went back to where I was in the book, every time I came to a scary part I just repeated the phrase, 'If you only knew what I knew.'"

This story captures the essence of the Christian hope. As the apostle John writes, one day God "shall wipe away every tear from their eyes; and there shall no longer be any death; there shall no longer be any mourning, or crying, or pain" (Revelation 21:4).

The biblical hope in a righteous world to come is often mirrored by our artists and musicians, who poignantly express a desire for a better place—Heaven. In 1991, songwriter and performer Eric Clapton lost his only son, Conor, when the little boy plunged forty-nine stories to his death from a Manhattan apartment. Amidst overwhelming grief, Clapton penned one of his most memorable songs, "Tears in Heaven," in which he poignantly asks whether his son would know his name "if I saw you in Heaven."

Amidst our deep grief and sorrows, to be human is to hope for the good, for a happy ending to our sufferings in this life. Isn't it interesting that even in our scientific age the highest-grossing movies tend to be ones rooted in the genre of the fairy tale? We are drawn to such movies as *Star Wars, Aladdin,* and *The Lion King,* movies that have happy endings. And at a very deep level, we *want* a happy ending to this Sacred Drama. Like much of life, fairy tales have that intrinsic quality of struggle and pain, that resolution at the end that replaces pain with joy, tears with laughter and smiles.

At the conclusion of Lewis's *The Last Battle,* Aslan reminds the Pevensie children that, despite the pain of this world—the Shadow-Lands—the holidays have begun.

> "Your father and mother and all of you are—as you used to call it in the Shadow-Lands—dead. The term is over; the holidays have begun. The dream is ended; this is the morning." . . .

> All their life in this world and all their adventures in Narnia had only been the cover and the title page; now at last they were beginning Chapter One of the Great Story, which no one on earth has read, which goes on for ever, in which every chapter is better than the one before.[17]

CHAPTER 8

Our Experience of Pleasures and Joys

Our Creator would never have made such lovely days,
and given us the deep hearts to enjoy them, above and beyond
all thought, unless we were meant to be immortal.

—Nathaniel Hawthorne

I know we have won many a soul through pleasure. All the same,
it is His [God's] invention, not ours. He made the pleasures; all
our research so far has not enabled us to produce one. . . . And
now for your blunders . . . you first of all allowed the patient to
read a book he really enjoyed, because he enjoyed it and not in
order to make clever remarks about it to his new friends. In the
second place, you allowed him to walk down to the old mill and
have tea there—a walk through country he really likes, and
taken alone. In other words you allowed him two real positive
Pleasures. Were you so ignorant as not to see the danger of this?
The characteristic of . . . pleasures is that they are unmistakably
real, and therefore, as far as they go, give the man who feels them
a touchstone of reality.

—C. S. Lewis

IF THERE IS ONE WORD THAT SEEMS TO CAPTURE THE ESSENCE OF AMERican life, it is the word "pleasure." For many Americans, a land of plenty and pleasure is perceived as our given birthright. *Harper's* magazine, well known for its monthly Index, has amassed over the years a dazzling array of trivia about our lifestyle. Consider a few of these statistics of minutia, which underscore our preoccupation with pleasure:[1]

- Percentage of U.S. households that contained at least three TV sets in 1990: 24

- Percentage that did in 1998: 40

- Percentage by which the cost of producing *Titanic* exceeded the 1997 budget of the National Endowment for the Arts: 100

- Rank of Disney World among the country's largest single-site employers: 1

- Number of shades of white offered in Ralph Lauren's 1996 paint collection: 35

- Ratio of Americans who said in 1996 that they "could not live without a blow-dryer" to those who felt the same way about personal computers: 1:1

- Estimated number of days each year during which no major-league sports event takes place in the U.S.: 5

- Number of TV sets owned by Martha Stewart: 16

- Number of phone lines connected to her five car phones: 7

These statistics, as arcane as they are, illustrate that the prevailing philosophy of American culture today is hedonism. Fundamentally, hedonism exalts pleasure as the beginning and end of our life's meaning and purpose.[2] Yet the pursuit of pleasure as a philosophy of life is fraught with danger and ultimately proves unsatisfying. In an earlier chapter we looked at the book of Ecclesiastes, where the vain pursuits of Solomon were sadly chronicled. Solomon's decadent lifestyle reminds us that no matter how much worldly success one achieves, in the end life is a futile chase, a "vanity of vanities" (1:2), a "striving after wind" (1:14), because death trumps even the most prosperous life. Consequently, our pursuit of ultimate pleasure and happiness is a wild goose chase, but there is no goose! You'll recall that Pascal once observed, "Anyone who does not see the vanity of life is vain indeed!" Qoheleth's legacy reminds us that to live life with wanton abandon leads ultimately to utter despair.

Such a hedonistic lifestyle is common in the entertainment industry. In *Wired,* the biography of the late comedian and actor John Belushi, journalist Bob Woodward recounts how those dependent on Belushi's continual popular success supplied him with cocaine and other drugs to keep him on his drug-induced frenzy.

> Giving or selling drugs to John was a kind of game, like feeding popcorn to the seals at the zoo; give him a little and he would perform, be crazy and outrageous; a little more and he'd stay up all night, outdancing, outdoing, outlasting everyone around him. . . . John needed psychiatric help, and [a Chicago psychiatrist] offered to see him professionally. "You've got to get him off drugs," he said deliberately [to Belushi's producer]. "If you don't, get as many movies out of him as possible, because he has only two or three years to live." [3]

Belushi's life and more recently that of Chris Farley, another *Saturday Night Live* comedian who died of a drug overdose, epitomize the *paradox* of hedonism. The more we seek fulfillment through sheer sensual abandonment, the more elusive happiness becomes.

But hedonism is not just found among Hollywood celebrities. In many ways hedonism accurately describes our current culture at large. In Western society we have largely turned toward pleasure and entertainment to fill—and ultimately give meaning to—our lives. When ultimate meaning and purpose are lacking, when the transcendent dimension of life is ignored (namely, God), culture increasingly turns toward external and superficial means to fill the void of the human heart. We increasingly devote more of our lives to leisure and recreation, to amusements and diversions. Theaters, music, entertainment, and sports now dominate our leisure landscape. In his critically acclaimed book *Amusing Ourselves to Death: Public Discourse in the Age of Show Business,* Neil Postman suggests that, contrary to common belief (even among the educated), Aldous Huxley and George Orwell did not prophesy the same thing. In his ominous foreword, Postman writes,

> What Orwell [in his book, *1984*] feared were those who would ban books. What Huxley [in *Brave New World*] feared was that there would be no reason to ban a book, for there would be no one who wanted to read one. Orwell feared those who would deprive us of information. Huxley feared those who would give us so much that we would be reduced to passivity and egoism. . . . Orwell feared we would become a captive culture. Huxley feared we would become a trivial culture, preoccupied with some equivalent of the feelies, the orgy porgy, and the centrifugal bumblepuppy. . . . In short, Orwell feared that what we hate will ruin us. Huxley feared that what we love will ruin us. This book is about the possibility that Huxley, not Orwell, was right.[4]

Huxley's prophecy has an eerie ring of truth. And while in an earlier age the gratitude for temporal blessings might have been evidenced by some degree of self-restraint, today the abiding mindset is "Encore!" G. K. Chesterton expressed the correct sentiment when he observed that "the proper form of thanks for God's good gifts is some form of humility and restraint: we should thank God for beer and Burgundy by not drinking too much of them."[5] While some of us may not approve of Chesterton's use of beer and Burgundy as illustrations, the principle of restraint still applies.

The Origin of Pleasure

Unlike pain, pleasure is rarely considered a problem to be explained. Yet the origin of pleasure poses the same dilemma for the atheist as the problem of pain for the Christian. As the Christian must soberly deal with the dilemma of how a good and all-powerful God allows pain in the world, so also the atheist or materialist (who denies a transcendent world to come) is under the equal obligation to explain the origin of pleasure in the world. In an atheistic world devoid of transcendent meaning and significance, how can we account for pleasure?

Take the matter of sexuality. On this subject our culture is obsessed. The question is often asked as to whether the Christian virtue of chastity is antiquated or relevant in our day? In *Mere Christianity*, C. S. Lewis addresses this issue of chastity being the most unpopular of the Christian virtues. In Lewis's opinion, because this virtue is so difficult, either Christianity is wrong or our sexual instinct has gone wrong. In an amusing passage, Lewis reminds us that while we can get a large audience together for a strip-tease act, would we not think it strange if we went to a country

> where you could fill a theatre by simply bringing a covered plate on to the stage and then slowly lifting the cover so as to let every one see, just before the lights went out, that it contained a mutton chop or a bit of bacon, would you not think that in that country something had gone wrong with the appetite for food?[6]

While the sexual instinct may very well have gone awry, the subject of human sexuality has always elicited interesting responses from literary curmudgeons. Lord Chesterfield declared, "The pleasure is momentary, the position ridiculous, and the expense damnable." Quentin Crisp observed, "Nothing in our culture, not even home computers, is more overrated than the epidermal felicity of two featherless bipeds in desperate congress." George Bernard Shaw asked, "Why should we take advice on sex from the Pope? If he knows anything about it, he shouldn't!" H. L. Mencken mused, "If a man and woman, entering a room together, close the door behind them, the man will come out sadder and the woman wiser." Evelyn Waugh opined, "All this fuss about sleeping together. For physical pleasure, I'd sooner go to my dentist any day." Artist Andy Warhol concluded, "Sex is the biggest nothing of all time."

Despite such cynical observations, most would agree that great pleasure attends the sexual experience. Garrison Keillor made these observations about the joys of sex:

> Somewhere, when I was young, I got the idea that the average American couple had sex twice a week, and I've carried this figure in my head for more than thirty years, as a benchmark, like the .300 batting average or the idea of three square meals a day . . . so it's a surprise to learn that according to the new survey, once a week is more like it. . . . Despite the low numbers, though, almost half the adult population claims to be *extremely pleased and satisfied,* which is a lot of pleasure in a country this big. . . . Despite jobs and careers that eat away at their evenings and weekends and nasty whiny children who dog their footsteps and despite the need to fix meals and vacuum the carpet and pay bills, these couples still manage to encounter each other regularly. . . . It is almost worth all the misery of dealing with real estate people, bankers, lawyers, and contractors—to have a home that has a bedroom where the two of you can go sometimes and do this. It is worth growing up and becoming middle-aged to be able to enjoy it utterly.[7]

Keillor's humorous comments underscore the fact that sexuality is one of the most pleasurable of human experiences. But *why* in the world is sex fun? Other animals may simply split in two when they want to reproduce, but the human species involves pleasure in the procreative process. But how do we explain the joys of sex?

Or let's consider food. Why is eating so much fun? One would be hard-pressed to rival the joyful celebrations we have with family and friends centered around food. Many of us could probably write memoirs of our lives based on the fellowship and community we experience with food as its centerpiece. It is a communal experience that heightens our sense of pleasure with those around us. Obviously, we could receive our nutrition by other means, without the benefit of taste and variety, as do many of the lower animals, but it would not be nearly as delightful. On the immense joy of eating, Robert Farrar Capon observes,

> Food these days is often identified as the enemy. Butter, salt, sugar, eggs are all out to get you. And yet at our best we know better. Butter is . . . well, butter: it glorifies almost everything it touches. Salt is the sovereign of all flavors. Eggs are, pure and simple, one of the wonders of the world. And if you put them all together, you get not sudden death, but hollandaise — which in its own way is not one less bit a marvel than the Gothic arch, the computer chip, or a Bach fugue. Food, like all the other triumphs of human nature, is evidence of civilization — of the priestly gift by which we lift the whole world into the exchanges of the Ultimate City which even God himself longs to see it become.[8]

The pleasure that comes from fine dining is beautifully portrayed in *Babette's Feast*, a film based on the play by Isak Dinesen. In the play, a French woman, Babette, enters the lives of two sisters, who are members of a small, ascetic religious community. After acquiring a sizable sum of money, Babette, an exile from Paris where she served as a master chef, decides to prepare a lavish feast for them and their fellow parishioners. Before the meal begins, they all take a vow not to speak a word about it, however delicious and exquisite the food may taste. Having an ascetic view of life, they believe that pleasures are somehow beneath the dignity of their Christian faith, and they believe they should always "cleanse [their] tongues of all taste and purify them of all delight or disgust of the senses, keeping and preserving them for the higher things of praise and thanksgiving."[9]

Yet despite their earnest resolve, as they taste of the magnificent feast they cannot keep themselves from speaking of the sumptuous meal they have been privileged to experience. Afterward, in candid conversations, forgiveness is extended and old jealousies and rivalries are buried. Through their eating, they "taste and see" that the Lord is good and that He gives good gifts, like food, to be enjoyed with one another (Psalm 34:8; see also Ecclesiastes 2:24-25). The meal reestablishes their bonds of community.

There is a God-given joy—yes, even a transcendence—that occurs in eating. Qoheleth declares in Ecclesiastes, "There is nothing better for a man than to eat and drink and tell himself that his labor is good. This also I have seen, that it is from the hand of God. For who can eat and who can have enjoyment without Him?" (Ecclesiastes 2:24-25).

And how do we explain other pleasures and joys that play such an important part in our human existence? Why is it that we have such delightful experiences as art, film, and music? Do they really contribute to our biological existence? Is there any wonder that music, such a powerful earthly haunting, was ascribed to the gods (the Muses) and not human beings? And could we not physically function just as well if we did not have movies, museums, and artwork to admire and to entertain us?

And why do we have colors in our world? Is it really necessary to see in color to comprehend the world? And what about the seasons of the year, which display such magnificent colors? How do we account for these pleasures that we so often take for granted? Have you ever noticed how we often walk through life without any real sense of appreciation for the joys and pleasures of life? Listen to these reflections of an anonymous Nebraskan friar:

If I had my life to live over again, I'd try to make more mistakes next time.

I would relax, I would limber up, I would be sillier than I have been this trip.

I know of very few things I would take seriously.

I would take more trips. I would be crazier.

I would climb more mountains, swim more rivers, and watch more sunsets.

I would do more walking and looking.

I would eat more ice cream and less beans.

I would have more actual troubles, and fewer imaginary ones.

You see, I'm one of those people who lives life prophylactically and sensibly hour after hour, day after day. Oh, I've had my moments, and if I had to do it over again I'd have more of them.

In fact, I'd try to have nothing else, just moments, one after another, instead of living so many years ahead each day. I've been one of those people who never go anywhere without a thermometer, a hot-water bottle, a gargle, a raincoat, aspirin, and a parachute.

If I had to do it over again I would go places, do things, and travel lighter than I have.

If I had my life to live over I would start barefooted earlier in the spring and stay that way later in the fall.

I would play hookey more.

I wouldn't make such good grades, except by accident.

I would ride on more merry-go-rounds.

I'd pick more daisies.[10]

Pleasures: Hints of Heaven

As we are reminded of the daily pleasures and joys that accompany our existence, we must ask ourselves the question, What do these pleasures tell us about this world? And what do these pleasures suggest about life?

In his most formidable book, *Orthodoxy,* Chesterton deals with the origin of pleasure and how it played a significant role in his spiritual pilgrimage from atheism to Christian orthodoxy. Essentially, he believed that materialism was too thin a veneer to adequately account for this world of wonder and delight. In his thinking, only a *romantic* world effused with mystery and awe—like the story of Robinson Crusoe saving goods from his shipwreck—could account for our sense of gratitude and delight in the world. In Chesterton's thinking, the ordinary blessings of life intimate a mysterious world: "I felt in my bones; first, that this world does not explain itself. . . . There was something personal in the world, as in a work of art. . . . I thought this purpose beautiful in its old design."[11]

In these few words, he has powerfully set forth the problem of pleasure for the atheist or materialist. For Chesterton, who was not looking to defend Christian orthodoxy, only Christianity provides a cogent explanation for the existence of pleasure in the world. In his experience and ours, pleasures are Edenic remnants, bits of paradise washed ashore from our ancestral shipwreck.

How are we to account for the existence of pleasures and joys in this life? As Chesterton intimated, only a Christian theology can adequately account for pleasures—they come from the very hand of God. And while the world at large seeks from this life pleasures and happiness as the *summum bonum* of existence, it is the saint who properly recognizes that "every good thing bestowed and every perfect gift is from above, coming down from the Father of lights, with whom there is no variation, or shifting shadow" (James 1:17).

In one of his most inviting books, *Letters to Malcolm: Chiefly on Prayer,* Lewis discusses the interplay between the adoration of God and our daily pleasures. In the form of warm and relaxed letters to a fictional friend, Malcolm, Lewis addresses his meditations on many of the puzzling questions surrounding the intimate dialogue between mankind and God. In the seventeenth chapter, he recounts the invigorating experience of his friend turning to a brook and splashing his burning face and hands in a waterfall, no doubt reminiscent of the many hikes Lewis and his Oxford friends, the Inklings, took together. Lewis observes that the cushiony moss, the cold water, the sound of the waterfall, along with the dancing light, while being very minor blessings compared with "the means of grace and the hope of glory," still serve as an exposition of the glory itself. These blessings are "shafts of the glory" that point to Heaven:

> I was learning the far more secret doctrine that pleasures are shafts of the glory as it strikes our sensibility. . . . Gratitude exclaims, very properly, "How good of God to give me this." Adoration says, "What must be the quality of that Being whose far-off and momentary coruscations are like this!" One's mind runs back up the sunbeam to the sun. . . . Any patch of sunlight on a wood will show you something about the sun which you could never get from reading books on astronomy. These pure and spontaneous pleasures are "patches of Godlight" in the woods of our experience.[12]

CHAPTER 9

CELEBRATING THE DAILY HUMDRUM

Either all of life is sacred, or none of it is sacred.

—Malcolm Muggeridge

Do not forget that the value and interest of life is not so much to do conspicuous things . . . as to do ordinary things with the perception of their enormous value.

—Teilhard de Chardin

WHETHER THROUGH OUR UNIVERSAL UNHAPPINESS, OUR ALIENATION AND discord, our encounter of transcendence through literature and film, or even our pains and pleasures, our hearts tell us that we are destined for more than this world. We are creatures being fashioned for eternity.

But if we are not careful, we will make the terrible mistake of overlooking perhaps the most profound of all the hints of transcendence. I am referring to our experience of the daily humdrum, the living out of the ordinary and most mundane things in our lives. Such a view of life sees everything that we do — literally, everything "under the sun" — as having a sacramental perspective. What do we mean by sacramental? *Webster's New Collegiate Dictionary* suggests that "sacrament" derives from the Latin verb *sacrare,* meaning "to consecrate," and the noun form suggests something that is a sign or symbol of a spiritual reality.[1] It also is closely akin to the Old Testament idea of "holy," which means to be set apart or consecrated.

So to say that all of life has a sacramental perspective is to envision all our affairs — our eating and drinking, our working and playing, our loving and serving — as being holy reminders of divine mysteries. Granted, these ordinary routines have their appointed functions, but a sacramental perspective infuses the daily humdrum with deep meaning. In addition to their immediate function, these activities ultimately look to Heaven. There is a holy splendor in the ordinary.

A sacramental view of life is suggested by the apostle Paul when he encourages the Corinthian believers: "Whether, then, you eat or drink or whatever you do, do all to the glory of God" (1 Corinthians 10:31). From the Christian perspective, even our most mundane activities — when done with excellence — are tokens of gratitude; they are unglamorous acts of worship, but no less genuine.

Such a sacramental perspective is immediately at odds with the prevailing secular notion of life, which delights in leeching any remote idea of transcendence — or God — from our existence. This mindset is largely the result of the scientific New Myth, looked at earlier, which embraces the belief that there are no divine mysteries in life and that everything can be exhaustively explained according to function. In contrast, the Christian's sacramental outlook is in many respects closer to the ancients than to most twenty-first-century people. The Christian believes that we live and walk in the presence of the Unseen. He or she believes that this world is a sign of the divine mysteries.

Yet we modern Christians often find it daunting to keep before us this notion of mystery, this idea of the sacred and hallowed, except as some sort of cloud or inner witness that should inform our thinking and imagination in worship and prayer. We struggle with truly seeing ourselves as walking daily among the hallowed — that is, seeing ourselves as living in the presence of divine mysteries as we carry out the commonplace routines of daily living. We fall prey to making the unbiblical distinction between the secular and the sacred. We constantly put the supposed Big Things in life (like worship, sacrifice, and mystery) into the religious arena (which is dutifully discharged in church life) and relegate the bulk of our lives (like eating, meeting with others, and driving) into the secular arena. But when we embrace a sacramental perspective of life, everything matters. All is holy. To use Malcolm Muggeridge's phrase, "Either all of life is sacred, or none of it is sacred."

The Mystery of Manners

One aspect of the daily humdrum charged with transcendent overtones is the practice of courtesy and manners. Why do we have manners? What is the basis of our showing courtesy to one another? What is the origin of the belief that we are to treat others with dignity and respect?

C. S. Lewis began *Mere Christianity* with the observation that there is a "moral oughtness" that informs our human existence. We know the right thing to do, Lewis argues, and we know that we are supposed to treat others with dignity and respect. But there is a second universal, namely, that *none* of us are really keeping this Law of Nature:

> This year, or this month, or, more likely, this very day, we have failed to practice ourselves the kind of behavior we expect from other people. There may be all sorts of excuses for us. . . . The question at the moment is not whether they are good excuses. The point is that they are one more proof of how deeply, whether we like it or not, we believe in the Law of Nature. . . . For you notice that it is only for our bad behavior that we find all these explanations. It is only our bad temper that we put down to being tired or worried or hungry; we put our good temper down to ourselves.[2]

As Lewis suggests, it almost goes without saying that we often find ourselves coming up short—transgressors of this moral oughtness—when it comes to treating people with the respect they deserve. One of the most memorable put-downs of all time involved the inimitable Winston Churchill and took place at a dinner party toward the conclusion of a heated exchange between Churchill and Lady Astor. The woman chided Sir Winston, "Mr. Churchill, you are drunk," to which he replied, "And you, madam, are ugly. But I shall be sober tomorrow." Ouch!

Let's examine this idea of manners and courtesy in more detail. What is the origin of manners? Take the word "courtesy," which comes from the word "court." The court carries with it the idea of the residence or establishment of a sovereign, and to be "courteous" means to be "marked by polished manners, gallantry, or ceremonial usage of a court . . . marked by respect and consideration of others."[3] Therefore, to treat others courteously is to show them the dignity and respect that is appropriate for the court. In other words, when we treat others with dignity and respect, we are treating them like royalty.

Our manners stem from a royal and transcendent worldview, namely, that we inhabit a world under the dominion of the one true Sovereign. And at the very heart of our courtesy and respect for others is the deep-seated belief that people deserve this respect, not necessarily because they have earned it, but because they are fellow human beings. Interestingly, all the major religions of the world attach a certain sacredness and dignity to human life. We extend courtesy and respect to one another because people are important. People matter. They bear the image of God; they carry the imprimatur of the Divine King.

Civility: Taking a Turn for the Worse

In recent days civility and manners have taken a turn for the worse and have become a hot topic in our national conversation. With the hectic pace of American life, some would argue that it is becoming more difficult to show courtesy to others. Did you know that in a lifetime, the average American will spend six months sitting at stop lights, eight months opening junk mail, one year looking for misplaced objects, two years unsuccessfully returning phone calls, and five years waiting in lines? Whew! It is little wonder that no one believes he or she has time to be courteous!

A recent article in *USA Today* dealt with this issue of poor manners in our society. Entitled "Excuse Me, But . . . Whatever Happened to Manners?" the story discussed how difficult it is "to ignore the growing rudeness, even harshness, of American life. . . . An overwhelming majority of Americans — 89% in a *U.S. News & World Report* poll — think incivility is a serious problem. More than three in four said it's gotten worse in the past 10 years."[4]

In his thought-provoking book *A Short History of Rudeness: Manners, Morals, and Misbehavior in Modern America,* social critic Mark Caldwell gives a history of the demise of manners and the triumphant "progress" of rudeness in America.[5] What is it that makes a U. S. representative stand on the floor of the House and urge Congress to "tell the president to shove his veto pen up his deficit." On the Internet, angry Americans constantly spew forth invectives and obscenities in chat rooms. And a student in Massachusetts shows up for class wearing a T-shirt that reads, "COED NAKED BAND; DO IT TO THE RHYTHM."

Predictably, as the breakdown of civility has become a national obsession, it has led to the rise of etiquette watchdogs like Miss Manners and Martha Stewart to deliver us from this onslaught of nastiness. In his witty and engaging book *Say Please, Say Thank You,*[6] Donald McCullough gives us gentle reminders of how to make this world a better place by taking advantage of simple opportunities to treat others with dignity and respect. The simple things—like saying "please" and "thank you," picking up the check for dinner, not being late for appointments, dressing appropriately for occasions, and writing notes of appreciation—demonstrate respect and honor to the people in our lives.[7]

Civility and Clothes: Is There a Connection?

One of the most interesting and subtle ways that manners have run amok is revealed in our clothing. In recent years we have witnessed a more casual approach to dressing for the workplace, to say the least. This has evolved to the point that we now even use the adage "Dress-Down Friday." While many embrace this new casualness in the workplace, casual dress may subtly convey to others and ourselves that what we are doing can also be taken casually. There appears to be an erosion of symbols that once lent a certain dignity to the person. In years gone by, specific types of clothing *meant something.* But now casual clothes are deemed appropriate for all occasions.

In an article in the *Wall Street Journal,* "Dress to Regress," writer Ned Crabb laments the contemporary emphasis on casualness. It is Crabb's contention that if clothes make the man—or woman—then we are all in a lot of trouble! His essay is prefaced by an advertisement that appeared in the *New York Times* on April 25, 1999:

After 40 years on Madison Avenue near 43d Street, Worth & Worth, the venerable hatter, will be moving or closing for good at the end of May.

When I was a boy, ... a youngster began the slow metamorphosis from childhood to manhood when ... he hung up the baseball cap for the night and sported a fedora, a smaller version of the one dad wore. ... The point is that hats were once prominent among those garments that symbolized a transition from looking like a child to looking like an adult.

A complete ensemble of such adult clothing gave the wearer an appearance and a sense of dignity. ...

We have lost much of the personal dignity once inherent in our clothes. ... More and more adults are now dressing like children. ... Grandfathers and fathers, once figures of veneration in tweed coats and cardigan sweaters, and grandmothers and mothers ... are now seen disporting themselves in public in sweatpants and jean jackets. Sweatpants are one of the ugliest pieces of clothing ever conceived, looking, even when laundered, like toddlers' dirty pajamas. They are useful to athletes, but they never should have left the locker room.[8]

Crabb is suggesting that in a bygone era clothes were symbolic of a certain dignity and propriety that fit the occasion, whether it was work, athletics, weddings, or funerals. In that world, the Old Myth prevailed. Things mattered, so we dressed appropriately for the occasion. But with the advent of the New Myth, these symbols are being dismissed as being old-fashioned and out-of-date. To modernity, they smack too much of hierarchy for our educated sensibilities. The modern world prefers to be "flattened out," removing all distinctions between people.

Crabb is revealing something important about our culture.

Clothes *do* matter. The way we dress for different occasions reveals not only our attitude about whatever we are doing (work, worship, play), but also our respect (or lack, thereof) for others.

The story is told of Cecil Rhodes, the South African statesman and financier (for whom the Rhodes Scholarship is named), who was known for being a stickler for proper dress. As he was hosting a formal dinner one evening and about to welcome his guests (who were all wearing full evening dress), he was told about one of his guests, a young man who had arrived by train without the opportunity to change from his travel-stained clothes. Rhodes disappeared, leaving the guests to wonder what had happened to him. He eventually returned to the dinner party wearing a shabby old blue suit so his young guest would not feel uncomfortable. Rhodes' gesture demonstrates that the clothes we wear can actually be a means of showing grace, favor, and hospitality to the people around us.

Clothes often reflect the demeanor of the wearer. They signify something. A well-meaning customer of the famed Neiman Marcus department store was prompted to send founder Stanley Marcus the following letter:

Dear Mr. Marcus:

I have been receiving beautiful and expensive brochures from you at regular intervals. It occurs to me that you might divert a little of the fortune you must be spending for this advertising matter to raise the salaries of your more faithful employees. For instance, there's an unassuming, plainly dressed little man on the second floor who always treats me with extreme courtesy when I visit your store and generally persuades me to buy something I don't really want. Why don't you pay him a little more? He looks as though he could use it.

Yours truly, Mrs. WS

By return mail came Marcus's reply:

Dear Madam:

Your letter impressed us so deeply that we called a directors'
meeting immediately, and thanks solely to your own solici-
tude, voted my father a $20-a-week raise.

Yours truly, Stanley Marcus.

While such displays of humility often go unnoticed, we are still
reminded that our deportment—the way we dress—says a lot about
the kind of people we are and what we think of others. And while
civility, manners, and common courtesy may continue to deterio-
rate, their abiding presence in our lives signifies that people are
important. And because they are important, we do well to treat others with the dignity and honor they are entitled to, not because they
have earned it, but because they are *human*. We are all playing out
this sacred drama in the court of the sovereign King.

The Hallowed Home

In addition to the daily rituals of civility and manners, another aspect
that bears the scent of transcendence is found in the home. It is in
the home, where ordinary daily living transpires, that the celebration of these mysteries occurs and is to be offered up in sacrificial
service to God. It is in the family household—with all its eating and
drinking, working and playing, serving and loving—that these hints
of the divine are observable. The home, which represents the family—with the corresponding themes of men and women, children,
sex, and marriage—is a central element in the vision of G. K.
Chesterton. Amidst the moral problems that our society faces, his
writings in defense of the home as a transcendent institution continue to provide a needful remedy to a confused world.

Alvaro de Silva offers the following observation on Chesterton's
defense of the family in his introduction to a collection of Chesterton's writings on the family:

Gilbert K. Chesterton (1874-1936) thought that the Victorians had lost "the sense of the sacredness of the home." The succeeding generation tried to get rid of the home altogether. Now we hunger and search for it everywhere. For some, a cat will do, or a dog or an expensive fur or a cheap affair with a stranger. . . . We are spiritual barbarians and emotional nomads. In our despair, we put two broken umbrellas together and call it home sweet home. . . . Thus our expectations of a home have become one of the most important decoys in advertising. Every conceivable commercial product is supposed to remind buyers about the delights and offerings of "family." Respect, caring, understanding, sharing, loyalty, freedom, love, joy and a smile or two are now being offered as readily available outside, at the bank or at the hardware store, because these commodities are found less and less at home. Despite the efforts to find one, there is no alternative to the family.[9]

Few have written as passionately or as provocatively on the importance and sacredness of the family as Chesterton. To him, the family mirrors what is truly important in life. The family images the things that really matter, because "the business done in the home is nothing less than the shaping of the bodies and souls of humanity. The family is the factory that manufactures mankind."[10] For him, the family carries this sacramental aspect, and consequently, marriage is one of the greatest contributions of orthodox Christianity to civilization, while divorce serves as one of civilization's greatest perils.

Ironically, our society looks at divorce as the very *entitlement* of marriage, parading it as the means to progress and liberty—and not to be taken too seriously. Aldous Huxley envisions such a perspective on marriage in the preface to *Brave New World*, when he declares, "Marriage licenses will be sold like dog licenses, good for a period of twelve months, with no law against changing dogs or keeping more than one animal at a time."[11]

But Chesterton saw divorce as a sentimental superstition, a flight from reality, an unwanted paradox in that for many men and women the happy ending of their love is divorce. To him, divorce is a barbarous act of "dividing the tune from the words of a song," and he found himself in good company with Charles Williams, who declared that "adultery is bad morals, but divorce is bad metaphysics."[12] In reality, a civilization's survival depends more on proper metaphysics than proper morals. The consequences of false thinking are more far-reaching than those of bad morals.

So then, Chesterton sees the marriage relationship between husband and wife as the foundation of the family, and this family is a picture of the spiritual drama being played out in our world:

> When we defend the family we do not mean it is always a peaceful family; when we maintain the thesis of marriage we do not mean that it is always a happy marriage. We mean that *it is the theatre of the spiritual drama,* the place where things happen, especially the things that matter. It is not so much the place where a man kills his wife as the place where he can take the equally sensational step of not killing his wife.[13]

Different Rooms in the Sacred House

While we are indebted to Chesterton for his contributions to our understanding of the sacredness of the family, we might even go further to reflect on how the house represents the transcendent dimensions of life. As we carry out normal and routine affairs of daily living, the ordinary gives way to the mystery. When we discharge our daily, menial tasks, they are fraught with spiritual overtones.

The architecture of a house, with its various rooms associated with their functions, gives us a picture of the diversity that we observe in all of life. And while it is true that "either all of life is sacred or none of it is sacred" (as Muggeridge said), when we observe distinctions between rooms according to their various functions, we are granting them the appropriate dignity and honor befitting them.[14] Thomas Howard provides an excellent study of the sacramental aspect of the different rooms of a house in his book *Hallowed Be This House*.[15] Let's examine the rooms more closely.

The Entryway

Consider the entryway, or front door, of a house. It is simply a place for passing through, as we are always en route when we are in the entryway. Yet today our coming and going is rarely through the front door of a house, but rather through the garage with its maze of garden equipment, lawn mowers, washing machines, and winter jackets. We even greet many of our guests by this route, with the casual remark, "Well, they're just family, anyway." In another era, the entryway served as a reminder that before you could "let down," you had to get farther into the house. So then, the entryway of a house suggests that the home ought to be a place of order and grace.

Another idea is at work in the entrance hall. For the guest, this hallway serves as a welcome, the place where we greet and bid farewell. Rarely do we see this in society today—only in old movies! But by making this area as beautiful as possible, someone is in essence saying, "You are welcome; we honor you with the best we have." As discussed earlier, we are dealing fundamentally with the matter of honoring one another, extending courtesy to others, treating all that come to our home as though they were kings and queens. And these acts of courtesy and generosity toward others are born out of a sacramental perspective, which says that this person is created in the image of God and this is a holy and glorious thing. He or she deserves to be greeted and bid farewell in an appropriate manner.

The Living Room

What about the living room? While no particular activity is specifically attached to it, when we think of the living room we generally think of families gathering to be together for conversation or entertaining. The living room portrays what families are all about, the glorious enterprise of husband and wife committing themselves to the daunting task of raising children to be upstanding and dedicated members of society. Certainly, raising children is no simple task. Listen to how Garrison Keillor portrays the challenge of raising a daughter:

> The father of a daughter, for example, is nothing but a high-class hostage. A father turns a stony face to his sons, berates them, shakes his antlers, paws the ground, snorts, runs them off into the underbrush, but when his daughter puts her arm over his shoulder and says, "Daddy, I need to ask you something," he is a pat of butter in a hot frying pan. The butter thinks to itself, "This time I really am going to remain rectangular," and then it feels very relaxed, and then it smells smoke.[16]

For those of us who have sons and daughters, we can definitely appreciate Keillor's insights, which address the challenges we face in the living room. The living room images what family members, bound by flesh and blood, have the opportunity to begin learning together. It is the lesson that is applicable to the entire human race—the lesson of love, or charity. It is in the family that husbands and wives, sons and daughters, begin to learn about genuine love—that self-giving, freedom, and joy are part of a sacred dance that portrays what our lives are to be all about. By our becoming accustomed to acknowledging our debts to one another, by our helping each other, by our giving and receiving, we see a microcosm of what Heaven (and Hell) may be like. As Howard says,

> For is not Charity the name given to that final, perfect, gloriously free and blissful state where all the lessons have been so mastered that the rules ("Pick up your paper dolls," or "Thou shalt not steal") have withered, and all of us have won through

to the capacity to experience as joy the thing that was hinted at in all our early lessons; namely, that My Life For Yours is the principle at the bottom of everything, to embrace which is to live and to refuse which is to die? Heaven or hell. This is carrying it high indeed—heaven and hell lurking in the living room. But if it is not this, what is it? . . . Heaven is the place where these mutual acknowledgments are forms of joy; hell is the place where no such indebtedness is acknowledged at all.[17]

The Dining Room

The dining room speaks of greater things than the mere consumption of food. And while eating may occur in any room of the house, clearly much more is going on in our meals than the mere function of getting physical nourishment for our bodies. From a utilitarian perspective, our nourishment might be achieved with pills or liquids or needles (as is done when people are sick and unable to eat for themselves), but such arrangements normally will simply not do.

No, we humans prefer to ceremonialize our eating. Take the simple meal, not just the fancy rehearsal dinner for a wedding that you may have in mind. We mark this three-times-repeated daily ritual with certain formalities, no matter how seemingly insignificant. We lay out colorful place mats on our table and put the fork on the left by the napkin (even though most of us will use it with our right hand!) and not by the knife, even though there is no functional advantage. We prefer our food to be neatly arranged on our plate and not simply jumbled together (unless it is a soup or stew!), and we consider it proper that everyone wait until the others are served before we begin. We enjoy a bit of color in the presentment of the meal, perhaps some red tomatoes along with the green vegetables, and we find a bouquet of flowers on the table aesthetically pleasing.

Needless to say, the advent of fast food and the hectic pace in our culture have seriously undermined our attempts to make eating more than the mere transfer of food to the body. We see people eating standing up in the food courts at malls, eating in their cars driving down the expressway, and eating at their desks in the workplace. Yet we often still find ourselves attempting to eat our meals with some amount of dignity and decorum. Chances are, even when we are by ourselves we will not stand over the stove and shovel the food out of the skillet directly into our mouths! If someone objects to this ceremonializing of even our ordinary, "non-special-occasion" meals, preferring a utilitarian approach, Howard provides a fitting response:

> The objection to this line of thought will come, of course, from someone who will say, "Oh, but I *do* do it that way. I do leave milk cartons about, and I love stand-up meals. . . . The only answer to this objection is: very well, you may be the busy career girl or board chairman who has a glass of Metrecal or a pastrami sandwich at your desk. But whatever else it is that overrides, in your mind, the usual pattern of pause and formality with which we mark this business of eating, I'll bet you don't see this as the ideal meal. . . . If you do, of course, and await the day when mealtime will mean a quick stop by the coin machine for an intravenous shot of some elixir from a syringe, then your paradise is my hell and you will have to write your own book.[18]

Eating expresses something profound, and when we adorn it with ritual we give it dignity. It is a signal that things matter, that they are worth something, that they are *significant*. We are intimating that this commonplace activity is more than the thing itself.

Perhaps behind the activity of eating is the picture of community and fellowship with one another. When we set apart the business of eating from the rest of the household functions and approach it (particularly the evening meal) as the occasion when men, women, and children gather together, is this not a gathering together to enact our common humanness?

When we think about those most joyful occasions of our lives, were they not frequently attended by the breaking of bread with close friends and relatives? Is there not an almost sacred aspect to these gatherings? Is there any surprise that most of the major religions of the world include eating as a central element in their faith? Do these gatherings not in fact resemble holy feasts?

Dining is indeed a noble business when men and women, made in the image of God, face each other around a table and break bread together. It is little wonder that in the Christian faith, eating is nothing less than a communal meal that is an indispensable aspect of the covenant relationship between God and His people. It is a sacred banquet. And certainly a Christian's dependence on "daily bread" for physical sustenance is a symbol for the greater Bread of Life, the life of the Lamb of God, who has laid down His life that we might live.

The Kitchen

As lifestyles have grown more casual and gadgets and appliances have grown more high-tech, the kitchen has not been one of the rooms we parade before our friends. It tends to be "behind the scenes," where the preparation and cleanup are performed, but rarely is it center-stage. We prepare a meal for the occasion and when the meal begins, the work of preparation is put out of sight. The same is true of the cleaning of the kitchen and the utensils employed. The cleaning up looks in retrospect to the meal just finished and is not the thing itself.

The kitchen may best image the dignity and role of *service*, because service's whole reason for existence is to prepare *for* something, and it is never an end in itself. Service finds itself waiting in relative obscurity for the next job. And when we carry out our daily routines of service around the household, we are playing out the drama of charity. While most of us strive after power, glory, and prestige as being the most important things of life, it is service that perhaps lies closest to the heart of what really matters in the Sacred

Drama. Service may in fact tell us a lot about life in Heaven.

> The splendid mysteries are there, acknowledged and cele-
> brated in commonplace routines. The supposition at work all
> the time is that these routines are like the tips of icebergs, say,
> or peepholes through which we may glimpse huge vistas of
> joy. The man following the plow along thousands of miles of
> furrow year after year or sitting in endless committee meet-
> ings, or the woman cooking ten thousand meals and washing
> a hundred thousand dishes . . . And do Christians not believe
> that, fully revealed, this Charity will turn out to be ecstatic,
> hilarious, and splendid beyond imaging? Otherwise, what is
> all the imagery of heaven about? It is either a lot of whistling
> in the dark . . . or it is True.[19]

The Bathroom

And what in the world are we to make of the bathroom? Certainly if
we say almost anything about the bathroom it will make us anxious!
How can we say anything "spiritual" or "holy" about such private
goings-on? Oh dear! And it is not just the Victorians who sought to
go behind closed doors for such private activities. Throughout
human civilization, there has been a perpetual need for privacy. It
may be worth asking *where* this tradition — this human preoccupation with concealment — came from?

As unpopular and antiquated a notion as it may seem, could
this need for "covering" not in fact be our innate sense of shame?
Could it be that this desire for privacy is nothing other than a desire
to keep veiled what in fact ought to be veiled? Do our attitude and
behavior not serve as a litmus test of how seriously we take this sense
of shame?

Our society revels in a laissez-faire attitude that seeks to make
nothing private, nothing veiled. Everything, we are told, is to be open

before the watching world. In the moral arena, this viewpoint invariably leads to open marriages, pornography, and a desire for openness and candor about even the most private of affairs. One only has to tune in to an episode of the *Jerry Springer Show* to see how our culture has embraced this "cult of frankness."

Such open discourse on sexuality has historically been considered taboo. This worldview of frankness suggests that the only way to transcend the Victorian priggishness and to liberate society to its truly "natural and free" expression is to fight anything that smacks of censorship or fidelity. In his brilliant analysis of the history of Western culture, the national bestseller, *Forbidden Knowledge,* Roger Shattuck raises serious concerns about our quest for knowledge amidst the explosion of scientific knowledge and the increasing problem of pornography:

> Are there things we should not know? Can anyone or any institution, in this culture of unfettered enterprise and growth, seriously propose limits on knowledge? Have we lost the capacity to perceive and honor the moral dimensions of such questions? . . . What has happened to the venerable notion of forbidden knowledge? In the practicalities of daily living, we accept constraints ranging from environmental regulations to truancy laws to traffic lights. In matters of the mind and its representations, Western thinkers and institutions increasingly reject limits of any kind as unfounded and stultifying. . . . Both scientific research and the worlds of art and entertainment rely on an unspoken assumption that total freedom in exchanging symbolic products of mind need not adversely affect the domain of daily living and may well enhance it.[20]

While such an "enlightened" worldview sees no proper limits to knowledge and no need for privacy, an idea of old says otherwise.

Not everyone is warranted in seeing everything or going everywhere. Behind every closed door, behind every taboo, behind every veil, behind every prohibitive "Thou shall not," there is something at work that tells me that I am not allowed in. There are limits. We are sometimes excluded, discriminated against, because we don't have the right to "go in."

So let us reflect on this most embarrassing of all rooms, the bathroom. Although it is far from the smoke and holiness of religious sanctuaries, this place is still "private" from a Christian perspective. In leaving behind our Edenic innocence and our unashamed nakedness, we want "coverings" for our bodies because we do not want to be seen "uncovered." And while many believe that we can return to that Eden-like existence by taking off our clothes and being "free and natural," the fact of the matter is that we are presently exiles from Eden. We are no longer at home there.

In his commentary on the book of Genesis, Derek Kidner observes that in the story of the Fall in Genesis 3, the serpent's promise of "eyes opened" was in fact a grotesque anticlimax to their dream of enlightenment and carried with it the necessary symbol of shame:

> The fig leaves were pathetic enough, as human expedients tend to be, but the instinct was sound and God confirmed it (v. 21), for sin's proper fruit is shame. The couple, now ill at ease together, experienced a foretaste of fallen human relations in general. There is no road back, as the nudists and those who make a cult of frankness, the spiritual nudists, suppose.[21]

No, such superficial frankness will not do. Our shame about the nakedness of our bodies is symbolic in that it tells us we cannot, in our present state, sustain openness with one another. Behind the closing of the bathroom door is the story, in cameo, of Paradise lost.

The need for privacy displays our mortality and vulnerability. When we close the bathroom door, we show our membership card in the club universal, the exiled Adamic race.

Besides symbolizing the shame that accompanies our humanity, the bathroom also serves appropriately for what needs to happen behind closed doors—*cleansing*. All that goes on behind those doors has to do with the removal of impurities (could the porcelain fixtures perhaps represent lavers, which are basins used for ceremonial cleansing?)—dealing with the teeth, skin, digestive system, hair—that are continually collecting on us. Even this perpetual ritual of cleaning our bodies speaks of higher things.

It seems as though our experience mirrors that of Adam, for just as he had to till the soil, so we are forced to tend our bodies in sorrow. It is an old idea that the body is a walled garden, and so our uncleanness and decay image a life of mortality, reminding us of our frailty and shame. Our impurity and decay can perhaps even be seen as subtle reminders of our guilt. Howard observes,

> Just as the greatest of saints have to return daily to their spiritual ablutions, so even the healthiest among us have to be daily at our physical ablutions. Ablution needs to be taken care of in private, as it were, since our sins and our impurities unfit us to hold concourse with others. We have to wash and purge ourselves and *then* go forth to greet our brothers and sisters and fathers and mothers, the idea being that human intercourse is such a high and holy thing that we must be as pure as we can for it. . . . We must at least *try* to be arrayed in purity when we approach other selves made in the awe-full image of God. They are most holy creatures. We are most holy creatures. Our intercourse is holy. Dirt and dandruff and sweat and sin mar that intercourse.[22]

The Bedroom

In celebrating the humdrum, our human sexuality provides yet another clue that suggests a deeper meaning than simply the physical act. It is in the bedroom that the goings-on are laden with transcendent significance and meaning. The bedroom is generally the room of our beginnings and our end. It is here where we are conceived and born, as well as where we sleep, and ultimately where we die. The fact that the home has now largely abdicated its role in birth and death to the hospitals is a concession to modern life. And while this is convenient, effective, and generally accepted, deep down we probably have the sentiment that it is not as it should be.

In recent decades a new myth has emerged: the sexual revolution. This new myth suggests that sexuality is a normal and natural function of healthy people, contributing to the general happiness of humanity, and that we can make up our *own* minds about how we will understand and utilize this pleasurable activity.

To modernity, sexuality has no transcendent dimension, but is only a physiological need of the human species. In the thinking of much of contemporary culture, we must "get over" the oppressive Victorian prudery that has created a deep sense of false guilt and shame for what is in fact a normal part of the human experience. Let us cast off the shackles of earlier generations, the new myth suggests, which have surrounded our sexual appetites with such deep suspicion and taboos.

Yet when people say that sex is "nothing to be ashamed of," what exactly do they mean? They may mean one of two things. They may mean that there is nothing to be ashamed of in the fact that the human race produces itself in a certain way nor in the fact that it is a pleasurable experience. And if they mean that, they are on safe ground because Christianity says that the sexual act was designed by God not only for the procreation of the human race but also to give pleasure. Contrary to the popular sentiment of our culture, the sin of our ancestors in the Garden was not sexual, but prideful rebellion against God's will in their lives. In fact, some Christians teach that if man had never fallen, sexual pleasure would actually have been greater than it is now. Pleasure is not the problem. As Lewis writes,

> When people say, "Sex is nothing to be ashamed of," . . . I think they are wrong. I think it is everything to be ashamed of. There is nothing to be ashamed of in enjoying your food: there would be everything to be ashamed of if half the world made food the main interest of their lives and spent time looking at pictures of food and dribbling and smacking their lips.[23]

While the world revels in advocating no restraints on sexual desires, Christianity suggests that the sexual instinct has gone awry. It has become perverted. Sexuality is not just another physiological phenomenon, to be experienced at every whim and fancy. Rather, when human sexuality is properly understood, we realize that it is an act that is charged with transcendent meaning and purpose. When a man and woman come together as "one flesh," the juncture of their bodies represents something holy and profound. We humans know deep down that this kind of joining of flesh is much more serious than, say, shaking hands!

In fact, when engaged in by a man and woman who have covenanted themselves in marriage, this sexual rite is a playing out of their desire "to know" the other, a knowledge that is the most sacred and intimate in the world. The Bible suggests that, in some mystical sense, this knowledge is akin to the intimate knowledge of personally *knowing* God.

That is why promiscuity actually devalues the full design of sexuality, because it focuses on the experience of sexuality as an object and minimizes the God-designed intent of "knowing" the other person. In actuality, the sexual rite is a sacramental activity that carries with it transcendent dimensions. While the sexual act can obviously be entered into casually by those who are not married, by people who do not seem malicious or even evil and who look at the activity as a perfectly simple way to assuage an appetite, it is in fact a parody of the real thing, according to Howard:

> It is like a Black Mass. For both involve all the equipment, movement, and pantomime of the real thing, and both promise a reward of the real thing (orgasm; supernatural food). But they are not addressed to the object which the ritual was designed to address. . . . In sexual intercourse . . . there is a communion under the specious of human anatomy. . . . The human body . . . when it is taken into the service of the sexual rite, a universe of significance comes upon it. . . . Taken into the rite, it is transformed. . . . The human body is the epiphany of personhood.[24]

Hence, when we are dealing with the sexual act, we cannot characterize it simply as a physical experience, for it is latent with spiritual overtones. And when we think of sexuality, we are dealing not only with conception—the beginning of life—but also with the consummation of love. Here the man and woman come together to "flesh out" their marital bonds to which they have been moving from the inception of their love. Their small tokens of generosity toward one another, their sharing of dreams, and their commitment to one another are all expressions of charity that find their ultimate consummation in their truly "becoming one flesh."

And yet the coming together of these two individuals represents a kind of death, if you will, a death of their own individual rights to be autonomous and independent creatures. For when a man and woman become one flesh, they display the charity that is observable in other rooms of the house. Self-giving becomes the entrée to self-discovery, and the life laid down leads to new life. Jesus declares, "Truly, truly, I say to you, unless a grain of wheat falls into the earth and dies, it remains by itself alone; but if it dies, it bears much fruit.

He who loves his life loses it; and he who hates his life in this world shall keep it to life eternal" (John 12:24-25). My Life for yours.

> And in the rite of conception, we can see . . . the whole story in one little act. Here life is "laid down" quite dramatically, in order that the life of love may be born anew, and that literal new life may come into being. The exactness of the picture is astonishing, not to say amusing: both bodies lay down, like the corn of wheat; both laid open, like the corn of wheat. Vulnerability, defenselessness, giving and receiving—nay, giving and receiving wholly indistinguishable from each other, for who will keep tally in these blissful exchanges to make sure the score is even?[25]

As we conclude this chapter, we have observed how there is a sacredness in the ordinary. The daily humdrum—our courtesy and manners, the family, daily living in the home—means something more, something greater, than mere function. We celebrate the ordinary because all of life is sacred, even the most ordinary and mundane of our affairs. They carry the scent of Heaven.

> Holy things, for the Christian . . . aren't some remote category of things—mumbo jumbos, arcane regalia, or basalt meteorites from the sky. Holy things are ordinary things perceived in their true light, that is, as bearers of the divine mysteries and glory to us. Looked at this way, eating becomes eucharistic, and working becomes the *opus dei,* and loving becomes an image of the City of God.[26]

CHAPTER 10

TRANSCENDENCE IN OUR WORK

And the wind shall say: here were a decent, godless people,
Their only monument, an asphalt road and a thousand lost golf
balls.

—T. S. Eliot

Men lust, but they know not what for;
They wander, and lose track of the goal;
They chase power and glory, but miss the meaning of life.

—George Gilder

Work is not, primarily, a thing one does to live, but the thing one
lives to do.

—Dorothy Sayers

MARK TWAIN ONCE DECLARED, "I DO NOT LIKE WORK EVEN WHEN SOME-one else does it." Robert Frost opined, "By working faithfully eight hours a day, you may eventually get to be a boss and work twelve hours a day." Charles Baudelaire mused, "Everything considered, work is less boring than amusing oneself." Paul Valery observed, "A businessman is a hybrid between a dancer and a calculator."

Work. We love it and hate it, but we can't do without it. These writers' sentiments express the ambivalence that we often have about work. Despite the vast number of waking hours that we devote to work, work's *purpose*—and what it signifies—is rarely considered. Observing the alienation that pervades many contemporary, affluent, industrialized societies, noted psychologist Victor Frankl pondered the plight of those who "have enough to live by, but not enough to live for," who seemed to have "the means, but no meaning."

In this chapter, as we seek to understand work as yet another signal of transcendence pointing toward Heaven, we need to first understand the confusion over the meaning and purpose of work that pervades modern-day culture. To understand this confusion, let's first consider our expectations about work, which have gone through significant changes in recent years.

As Frankl suggested, our secular age is one where we often have the *means*, but little or no *meaning*. Fundamentally, that is because we have abdicated the transcendent dimension of work. The truth of the matter is that we work for more than money and for far more profound reasons than we might imagine.

Crisis in the Workplace

Certainly in our day we have witnessed monumental changes in the workplace. With the general movement from an industrial to more of an informational and technological economy, and the consequent rise of entrepreneurial businesses, the measure of success, as well as *why* we work, is being discussed more than in perhaps any other time in American history.

The workplace is no longer the relatively safe, secure haven it once was. Just as Freud made the famous cry of resignation, "Women, what do they want?" men, who have traditionally defined themselves by the ability to bring home the paycheck, are now often asking the question, What do *men* really want?

And because the workplace has seen a great influx of women, coupled with downsizing and reorganization, instability has become the accepted norm of corporate America. Men in particular no longer look at work—or life—in the same light. The contemporary man lacks a firm self-identity, and even manhood now finds itself under assault. In *The Book of Guys,* Garrison Keillor laments man's current state of affairs, especially as it relates to how he is perceived by women.

> Years ago, manhood was an opportunity for achievement, and now it is a problem to overcome. Plato, St. Francis, Michelangelo, Mozart, Leonardo da Vinci, Vince Lombardi, Van Gogh—you don't find guys of that caliber today. . . . They are trying to be Mr. O.K. All-Rite, the man who can bake a cherry pie, go play basketball, come home, make melon balls and whip up a great souffle, converse easily about intimate matters, participate in recreational weeping, laugh, hug, be vulnerable, be passionate in a skillful way, and the next day go off and lift them bales into that barge and tote it. A guy who women consider Acceptable. Being all-rite is a dismal way to spend your life, and guys are not equipped for it anyway. . . . A man is like a bear riding a bicycle: he can be trained to do it but he would rather be in the woods, doing what bears do.[1]

Even the meaning of success is being evaluated in a different light. Sociologist Michael Kimmel, writing in the *Harvard Business Review,* addresses this new paradigm of work when he notes that the contemporary man's view of success is quite different from his predecessors'. More specifically, "Few men today fit the traditional picture of the distant father, patriarchal husband, and work-obsessed breadwinner. Yet neither have many dropped out of the working world to participate in full-time daddydom."[2]

Rather, today's corporate man carries a briefcase while pushing a baby carriage. And while he considers his career important, he doesn't want to sacrifice time with his family. His wife may have a demanding job, which he supports; but he may wonder if she thinks he's less of a man than her father, and he may resent her for the time she spends away from home.[3]

Historically, a man's identity was a reflection of how he saw himself in the workplace. Kimmel provides an excellent discussion of how American manhood has changed over the past several centuries in his significant work, *Manhood in America: A Cultural History*. He argues that while at the turn of the nineteenth century American manhood was rooted in land ownership or in being an independent artisan or farmer, the Industrial Revolution changed all that. And while the volatile marketplace was a far less stable venue for one's self-identity, it was certainly more exciting and potentially rewarding. Yet, as Kimmel notes, it did not deliver a peaceful existence:

> The Self-Made Man of American mythology was born anxious and insecure, uncoupled from the more stable anchors of landownership or workplace autonomy. Now manhood had to be proved. . . . This book is a history of the Self-Made Man—ambitious and anxious, creatively resourceful and chronically restive, the builder of culture and among the casualties of his own handiwork, a man who is, as the great French thinker Alexis de Tocqueville wrote in 1832, "restless in the midst of abundance."[4]

Kimmel suggests that the American male's idea of success has historically been tied to his financial success in the workplace. The

Self-Made Man in America has gloried in his autonomy and accomplishments, with his self-esteem and identity being rooted in his ability to provide financially for his family. But even if the modern man (and this now applies to women professionals in the workplace as well) finds himself financially successful, he is still "restless in the midst of abundance." Today's professional loves the deal, the chase, the game. This heady, stimulating approach to work Douglas LaBier describes as *careerism*.

> Careerism has become the main work ethic of our times. At root, careerism is an attitude, a life orientation in which a person views [his or her] career as the primary and most important aim of life. An extreme but not uncommon expression of this is found in the comment of a man who told me that he feared dying mainly because it would mean the end of his career.[5]

LaBier's observation suggests that the modern worker does not fear death, but neither does he envision any overarching purpose as to *why* he works. His greatest fear of dying lies not with the traditional religious sentiments of guilt or possible judgment, but simply that when he dies he can no longer experience the euphoric experience of "making the deal"! If pursued to its logical end, the mindset of careerism often carries with it a certain malaise. Why? Because the business professional senses that nothing he or she does will have lasting significance.

Work: Secular or Sacred?
This sense of insignificance in work is the Achilles heel of modernity. I can be successful, but what is the *significance* of my work? Do these business meetings and unending business trips really make a difference? Does anything truly have an enduring value? Does anything really matter? Am I truly valued? In *The Male Ego*, psychiatrist Willard Gaylin accurately captures the ambivalence and frustration

of men, as illustrated by his observation that "I have never met a man—among my patients or friends—who in his heart of hearts considers himself a success." He satirizes the executive's need for "little pink roses," those pink message slips that tell a man that he's wanted. But when that chairman of the board or CEO finally retires, he suddenly learns he's lost all value. "He becomes a non-person," in Gaylin's words, shocked and overwhelmed by the fact that "he never was someone to be cherished for his own sake but only as an instrument of power and a conduit of goods."[6]

It is because work has been divorced from its transcendent perspective that we face such a crisis concerning our individual identity and significance. But someone may well ask, "What do you mean, transcendent dimension of work? How does my work have *anything* to do with God or transcendent matters like Heaven?"

This question underscores the fact that modern culture sees little or no correlation between work and the issues of meaning and purpose in one's life. "How can the Christian faith have anything to do with my work?" they ask, believing that a religious perspective has no place in the workplace. "Let us simply be about the business of making a living." Such a narrow perspective of work is captured in a few lines from T. S. Eliot's "Choruses from 'The Rock,'" that speak of London's haughty attitude:

> ... Men do not need the Church
> In the place where they work, but where they spend
> their Sundays.[7]

Eliot's words have an eerie, contemporary feel to them, reflecting our culture's belief that Christianity has little to do with business life. Yet when the transcendent purpose of work is abdicated and we see work only through the lens of *this* life, it leads ultimately to despair. Leonard Woolf, the well-known British politician, made these candid observations:

Looking back at the age of eighty-eight over the fifty-seven years of my political work in England, knowing what I aimed at and the results . . . I see clearly that I achieved practically nothing. The world today and the history of the human ant hill during the last fifty-seven years would be exactly the same as it is if I had played ping pong instead of sitting on committees and writing books and memoranda. I have therefore to make the rather ignominious confession to myself and to anyone who may read this book that I must have in a long life ground through between 150,000 and 200,000 hours of perfectly useless work.[8]

Woolf's words aptly describe the dichotomy between the sacred and the secular. Perhaps there was a time back at the beginning of history when life was Eden-like, when we sensed a relationship between our work and our Maker. It was a time when we could still see that our daily work had something to do with the whole rhythm of life, and in some way we understood that our labors were offered up as a sacrifice to God. But sadly, such an appreciation of work has long ago disappeared. Now we make our offerings in church when the plate comes past.[9]

The mindset that dominates the workplace today is not unlike the worldview we previously considered in the Old Testament book of Ecclesiastes. No longer is the modern man or woman, even at the height of his or her work achievements, truly satisfied. There's always something more to pursue—another advancement to accept, another deal to close, another company to start. One is reminded of John Cheever's observation, "The main emotion of the adult American who has had all the advantages of wealth, education, and culture is disappointment."[10]

Cheever, like a modern-day Qoheleth, has put his finger on the pulse of the contemporary workplace. Even amidst great financial and personal success in our work, we remain ultimately unsatisfied and disappointed. We want *more.* We even become bored and unfazed with great success, because it has come to be expected. And when work is divorced from a transcendent perspective, it can only be seen as futile, meaningless, vain, and yes, ultimately boring. Playwright Arthur Miller, a great observer of our culture, called our boredom "the hallmark of society as a whole," a society in which people merely exist and move among "a string of near-experiences marked off by periods of stupefying spiritual and psychological stasis, and the good life is basically an amazed one."[11]

Work: Success or Significance?

Ultimate significance and satisfaction in work can only be recognized as we embrace what was earlier referred to as a sacramental perspective of life. From a Christian worldview, our work matters and is significant because it is part of our life—and *all* of life is sacred. We celebrate our work, like the daily humdrum, because it signifies transcendent matters.

A secular perspective of life, divorced from a transcendent dimension, does not truly satisfy the human soul. We may gain fame, fortune, prestige, and power, but these measures of success will grow hollow and tinny if our work does not satisfy the deepest longings of our heart. We want to know *why* we were placed on this earth. Our deepest passion is to know that we are fulfilling the purpose for which we were created. We need to have a sense of calling, to have a reason for our existence, to have a purpose, as Kierkegaard put it, "for which I can live and die."

In an early draft of Fyodor Dostoyevsky's *The Brothers Karamazov*, the Inquisitor gives a terrifying account of what happens to the human soul when it doubts its purpose: "For the secret of man's being is not only to live . . . but to live for something definite. Without a firm notion of what he is living for, man will not accept life and will rather destroy himself than remain on earth."[12] Without such an understanding, life is, as Shakespeare described it, "full of sound and fury, signifying nothing."

In his book *The Call: Finding and Fulfilling the Central Purpose of Your Life,* Os Guinness contends that we cannot divorce purpose and meaning in our work from a fundamentally religious view of life. Guinness observes that people are looking not simply for success, but also for significance in life. This is the premise of Bob Buford's best-selling book, *Halftime,* which contends that people spend the first half of their lives looking for success and the latter half looking for significance.

While some are turning to the East to find purpose in their lives, others take the Western route, a kind of Nietzschean Superman approach, where the goal in life is to conquer. Guinness suggests that, in contrast to these two worldviews, the deepest and most profound answer to our individual longing for purpose is to rise to the call of our Creator. Guinness defines "calling" as "the truth that God calls us to himself so decisively that everything we are, everything we do, and everything we have is invested with a special devotion, dynamism, and direction lived out as a response to his summons and service." [13]

In this definition Guinness makes the proper distinction between an individual's primary calling to God and the secondary calling to vocation or work. Guinness suggests that historically there have been two great distortions about work in the history of the church. One is the "Catholic" distortion, which is a form of spiritual dualism that elevates the spiritual at the expense of the so-called "secular" or mundane. He observes that evangelical Christians have been guilty of this same distortion when they refer to "full-time Christian service," a phrase that separates clergy and other professional Christian workers from the laity.

The other distortion is the "Protestant" distortion, a secular form of dualism that elevates the secular or mundane at the expense of the spiritual. The Protestant distortion makes work sacred and calling exclusively secular. Guinness traces this distortion back to the Puritans, who magnificently championed the spiritual aspect of calling but allowed an imbalance to grow into a full-grown distortion. Thus one's "calling" became synonymous with one's "vocation," as seen by the interchange of the terms "work" and "employment" with "calling" and "vocation." This would blossom in the late nineteenth and early twentieth centuries into the Protestant work ethic, where work was made virtually sacred. This worship of work was epitomized by the declaration of President Calvin Coolidge, who believed that "the man who builds a factory builds a temple, and the man who works there worships there." Automobile magnate Henry Ford once said work is "the salvation of the human race."

Recovering the Dignity of Work

The Christian position never demeans daily, ordinary work in favor of the "spiritual" (the Catholic distortion), nor does it make work "sacred," minimizing the transcendent dimension that infuses a proper perspective on work (the Protestant distortion).

While some may embrace an optimistic perspective of work, believing it to be inherently sacred, others subscribe to a pessimistic view. They believe work to be the result (in the Christian understanding) of the curse due to mankind's rebellion against God, as described in the early chapters of Genesis. This is a popular view of work put forth frequently by well-intentioned people yet lacking in biblical support. The Scriptures suggest that work, however tainted and marred after the curse of Genesis 3, was still a part of God's original design. Man was placed in the garden before the curse to "cultivate it and keep it" (Genesis 2:15). However we may understand it in this earliest of human history, work was originally designed by God for His creatures as a form of spiritual service to be rendered to Him.[14]

Because God Himself is the Worker and because humans are, according to the Christian understanding, created in His image, all work has inherent dignity. We humans work as "subcreators" because we are made in the image of God, the Worker par excellence (see Genesis 1:26-28; 2:2).

Hence, the sacramental perspective on work suggests that there is no such thing as "sacred" or "secular" work, because all work bears the imprimatur of the divine King. All work, like all of life, has inherent dignity. Almost five hundred years ago, Martin Luther, writing as an Augustinian monk, recommended the abolition of all orders and abstention from all vows because it engendered conceit and contempt for the "common" Christian life. In *The Babylonian Captivity*, written in 1520, Luther declared,

> The works of monks and priests, however holy and arduous they be, do not differ one whit in the sight of God from the works of the rustic laborer in the field or the woman going about her household tasks, but that all works are measured before God by faith alone. . . . Indeed, the menial housework of a manservant or maidservant is often more acceptable to God than all the fastings and other works of a monk or priest, because the monk or priest lacks faith.[15]

More recently, writer and Christian apologist Dorothy Sayers chided the church on its neglect in formulating and communicating a truly sacramental perspective on work. Sayers, a gifted mystery writer, playwright, and medievalist who translated Dante's works, was one of the most celebrated Christian apologists of the twentieth century, a woman who passionately embraced her work as well as all of life.[16]

But despite Sayers' passion for living and her commitment to the Christian faith, she found it difficult to stick to her calling as a writer. Clergy often besieged her, requesting her to open garden fetes, which would take her away from her writing. She was also uncomfortable when fame thrust her into the role of Christian apologist as church leaders sought to capitalize on her name for the Christian faith. Yet she believed that her vocation as a writer was deeply spiritual, and that to be involved in anything less would have been to compromise her own integrity and calling. She wrote passionately of the church's dire need for a Christian theology of work that truly embraces a sacramental view of all of life. In an address she delivered at Eastbourne, England, entitled "Why Work?" she laments this failure of the church:

> In nothing has the Church so lost her hold on reality as in her failure to understand and respect the secular vocation. She has allowed work and religion to become separate departments, and is astonished to find that, as a result, the secular work of the world is turned to purely selfish and destructive ends, and that the greater part of the world's intelligent workers have become irreligious, or at least, uninterested in religion. But is it astonishing? How can any one remain interested in a religion which seems to have no concern with nine-tenths of his life?[17]

Sayers rightly understood that work cannot and should not be divorced from the spiritual life, because work is inherently spiritual.

Pursuing Excellence in Work

What is it that makes us pursue excellence in our work? The book of Genesis tells us that when God finished His work of creation, He saw that it was "very good" (Genesis 1:31). Because we are made in the image of God, there is something quite fulfilling when we seek to perform our work with quality and excellence. While our work may not always be the very best, we still experience deep pleasure when we do the best we can, when we are commended for a job well done (see Matthew 25:21,23). And when we perform work with excellence, we are fulfilling our God-given identity as workers made in His image.

Interestingly, the philosophy of the Shakers in their furniture-making demonstrates this concern for excellence. Each Shaker chair, it was said, was to be of high enough quality for an angel to sit on.

Shakers were to make every product better than it had been made before, not only the parts one could see but also the parts one couldn't. They were to use only the best materials, even for the most everyday items, and were advised to give the same attention to the smallest of details. Everything was to be designed and made as if it would last forever.[18] The Shakers had a glimpse of what it means to see one's work as an offering and sacrifice to God.

The challenge to pursue excellence should be uppermost in our thinking, especially among Christians. C. S. Lewis reminds us that, unfortunately, the work of the saint sometimes lacks the standard of excellence with which we have been provided. In his essay "Good Work and Good Works" he writes,

> "Good works" in the plural is an expression much more familiar to modern Christendom than "good work."...
>
> And good works need not be good work, as anyone can see by inspecting some of the objects made to be sold at bazaars for charitable purposes. This is not according to our example. When our Lord provided a poor wedding party with an extra glass of wine all round, he was doing good works. But also good work; it was a wine really worth drinking. . . . Let choirs sing well or not at all.[19]

Because work has a God-given dignity to it, we are most satisfied when we do a good job at our tasks. Intuitively, we pursue excellence in our work because it brings us pleasure, and the God in whose image we are fashioned is our Audience.

Furthermore, in a way we can hardly fathom, our work is nothing less than an offering to God. The essence of this quest for excellence is captured by the plaque beside the gravesite of Sayers, which summarizes her philosophy of living: "The only Christian work is a good work well done."

Work matters, because God is the One for whom we ultimately work. This principle is commanded by the apostle Paul when he declares to the Colossian believers, "Whatever you do, do your work heartily, as for the Lord rather than for men.... It is the *Lord Christ* whom you serve" (Colossians 3:23-24, italics mine). When we come to grips with the sacramental aspect of work and pursue excellence, we sense a deep, abiding pleasure. Why? Because reminiscent of our Edenic existence, we begin to see our work for what it really is—an offering to God. When we understand that our work is for Christ rather than for men, we are reminded of Heaven.

What Brings Us Fulfillment in Work?

In his best-selling book, *If Aristotle Ran General Motors,* Tom Morris, a former philosophy professor at Notre Dame, draws on the wisdom of history's wisest thinkers to demonstrate their contribution to the contemporary workplace. Addressing the present challenges in the workplace environment, Morris observes that for quite some time American business leaders have been talking about rediscovering the vital importance of product and service quality in our highly competitive world. In recent years, nearly everyone has been talking about reengineering the corporation and redesigning the processes by which work is done to attain greater efficiencies and new forms of business excellence. While management strategies have multiplied, we've become inundated with new techniques and find ourselves almost drowning in information. For all the ballyhooed talk about excellence in the workplace, something very important has been forgotten, as Morris observes:

> Behind the products, services, and processes of modern business, behind all the strategies and techniques and data, are the people who do the work. And too often ... the employees of modern businesses feel themselves more the victims than the beneficiaries of the new corporate strategies for success....

Too many people feel insecure, threatened, and unappreciated in their jobs. . . . People at work are the only true foundation for lasting excellence, and so I think the time has come to focus on the deeply human issues of happiness, satisfaction, meaning, and fulfillment in the workplace.[20]

Morris contends that any company serious about attaining true excellence in business must adhere to four timeless virtues first identified by Aristotle more than two thousand years ago: truth, beauty, goodness, and unity.[21]

One of the most important contributions of Morris's book is his belief that we have inherited essentially three basic views of finding true happiness in life. And the approach we take to life—and our work in particular—has tremendous bearing on whether or not we sense genuine happiness and significance. These three basic views are happiness as *pleasure,* happiness as *personal peace,* and happiness as *participation* in something fulfilling.[22]

The first view of how we achieve happiness—through pleasure—is essentially the philosophy of hedonism. Although it comes from the distant past, it still dominates contemporary society. As we chase money and work with the aspiration of ever-increasing incomes to get other things, we embrace the illusion that having more will bring us happiness. Yet in the century just ended, Albert Einstein echoed Aristotle when he made this bold declaration about any worldview that puts happiness (viewed as pleasure) at the center of our lives: "In this sense I have never looked upon ease and happiness as ends in themselves—such an ethical basis I call more appropriate for a herd of swine."[23]

Second, others seek happiness in life and the workplace through personal peace. Tranquility. Calm. Repose. Clearly, we could all use a little more relaxation in our lives, with anxiety reaching epidemic proportions in America. We are a stressed-out bunch, worrying about our jobs, our children, our marriages. Our lives mirror Charlie

Brown's when he says to Lucy in a *Peanuts* cartoon, "My anxieties have anxieties!"

And while we need something like inner psychic shock absorbers as we hit the potholes of life, the very pace of modern life militates against calmness. With life having shifted into fast-forward, a happy life utterly devoid of personal peace is virtually impossible. While we may sometimes resent the demands placed on us in the business world, the truth is that we humans don't really grow amid tranquility. We need problems to solve. We need—believe it or not—a healthy amount of tension in our lives. Human happiness is not the emotional equivalent of taking one gigantic nap!

Because complete quietude occurs only at death, we come to understand that life and business is the activity of the living. Mary Ann Evans, who wrote more than a hundred years ago under the pen name George Eliot, once remarked, "It is vain to say that human beings ought to be satisfied with tranquility: they must have *action;* and they will make it if they cannot find it."

A third and ultimately more satisfactory venue for happiness is through our significant participation with a task that is fulfilling and meaningful. The essence of this view of happiness in the workplace is simply that we are at our best and feel our best when we are engaged in a worthy task. Writing with sage advice, Frederick Buechner suggests, "The place God calls you to is the place where your deep gladness and the world's deep hunger meet." [24]

No, happiness is not synonymous with pleasure, nor is it the same thing as personal peace. True happiness rarely exists in passivity. Writer E. B. White observed, "I arise in the morning torn between a desire to improve (or save) the world and a desire to enjoy (or savor) the world. This makes it hard to plan the day." Genuine, fulfilling happiness is experienced when we are significantly involved in something we deem important. Even Walt Disney realized that happiness in life was more than the accumulation of wealth:

I've always been bored with just making money. I've wanted to do things, I wanted to build things. Get something going.... I'm not like some people who worship money as something you've got to have piled up in a big pile somewhere. I've only thought of money in one way, and that is to do something with it.... I don't think there is a thing that I own that I will ever get the benefit of, except through doing things with it.[25]

Disney's words and approach to living suggest happiness is a dynamic phenomenon of participation in something that brings fulfillment. This was beautifully portrayed in the film *Chariots of Fire* when Eric Liddell proclaims that God has made him to run fast, "and when I run, I feel His pleasure."

In reality, happiness never exists in passivity. And while happiness is most often accompanied by pleasure and a good measure of inner peace, one of the highest forms of peace is that which accompanies satisfying engagement in a job worth doing. Likewise, one of the greatest pleasures in life comes from participation in a job worth doing. Thus happiness is connected with peace as well as with pleasure, but ultimately it is to be found in the activity. It is in the work.[26]

Splendor in the Ordinary

We have suggested in this chapter that there is a dignity and worth to all work and that when we are participants in a worthwhile task, it often results in genuine fulfillment and happiness. We know that exclusively pursuing pleasure—the mere accumulation of wealth, fame, and fortune—does not bring genuine happiness. Deep down we want more than money and recognition.

Nor are we happy simply by "checking out" of society—the way of passivity. We enjoy our times of rest and relaxation, but work is part of our living and we crave the hustle and bustle. We want activity and we want to work. When we stop working, we lose touch with an important God-given aspect of our humanity. Have you noticed how bored wealthy or retired people become when they have stopped working, even though they may have ample financial resources?

When we begin to understand the transcendent nature of work and sense its true spiritual nature, we can begin to see it in a new light. It in fact points beyond ourselves and our world to an earlier time. In such an Edenic world, work had inherent dignity because it was part of our mandate of being God's vice-regents over creation.

Work understood from a sacramental perspective serves as a clue to Heaven. And because we humans are created in the image of God, our work matters. Whatever our vocation, whatever our job, it matters because there is dignity and splendor in the common and the ordinary. There is no such thing as a "higher" calling for the minister, the priest, or the paid religious professional. Rather, every job, every task, however seemingly secular or mundane, is imbued with dignity and worth. We are workers who serve in the court of the King, and only such a worldview brings significance and meaning to life. A few lines from George Herbert's poem "The Elixir" express the sentiment well:

> Teach me, my God and King,
> In all things Thee to see,
> And what I do in anything,
> To do it as for Thee.[27]

CHAPTER 11

TRANSCENDENCE IN OUR PLAY

Baseball is our religion. The stadium's our temple.
The beer and peanuts, our sacrament.

— *USA Today* advertisement,
Fastball.com

Faith has lost its joy. . . . Where everything must be useful and
used, faith tends to regard its own freedom as good for nothing.
It tries to make itself "useful" and in doing so often gambles
away its freedom. Where freedom of play has been lost, the
world turns into a desert.

—Jurgen Moltmann

As we saw in the last chapter, we Americans are passionate about our work. As part of our celebrated Puritan work ethic, work continues to have a prominent place in the American psyche. And while progress was formerly measured more or less by the continuous fall in the number of work hours per week, the clock has been turned back with the new millennium's advent. Despite the movement from the minimum sixty-hour week decades ago to the classic forty-hour week, we're now working longer hours—208 more hours a year than two decades ago. And the number of workers putting in fifty or more hours a week has jumped from 24 to 37 percent. Americans work more hours than inhabitants of any other country in the advanced industrial world, passing even the fabled Japan, and we work the equivalent of an amazing eight weeks a year longer than the average Western European.[1]

What lies behind our feverish working? What's the purpose? Sure, the standard of living is generally higher for most Americans. But many are beginning to wonder whether it's worth it, whether all the material possessions, amusements, and fattened retirement accounts are worth the loss of time and vitality that used to exist outside of work.

It goes without saying that rampant careerism, which has spread to a significant segment of the American workforce, has exacted a tremendous toll upon our personal lives. Because work is exalted in our culture, it costs us dearly, both relationally and spiritually. In his book *Work, Play, and Worship in a Leisure-Oriented Society,* sociologist Gordon Dahl profoundly captures the dilemma created in our society by the work-leisure-worship triangle:

> Most middle-class Americans tend to worship their work, to work at their play, and to play at their worship. As a result, their meanings and values are distorted. Their relationships disintegrate faster than they can keep them in repair, and their lifestyles resemble a cast of characters in search of a plot.[2]

We Americans have largely bought into Nike's slogan, "Life is short, play hard," yet many of us are seeking to restore balance between our work and leisure time. We are discovering the importance of creating lasting memories with our families and friends. But an underlying question remains that is rarely addressed: What exactly is leisure, anyway? What is the true meaning and purpose of leisure? What are we supposed to do with this leisure time? And more germane to our consideration in this chapter, How do leisure and play give us clues about Heaven? But first things first. What do we even mean by "leisure"?

What Is Leisure?

To most of us, leisure has an ethereal feel to it, like smoke through our fingers. The concept of leisure may create hazy, if not boring, associations. And while postcards and glossy advertisements lure us to some faraway place for "R & R," the nature and essence of true leisure still eludes us. In truth, we often come back from vacations worn out, in need of rest.

Part of our dilemma stems from the various synonyms used to describe leisure, such as "play," "game," and "recreation." Further complicating our understanding, some define leisure as an *activity,* while others describe it as a *state of mind.* While modern culture tends to conceive of leisure as our "free time" — that time not devoted to our paid vocations — the older, classical tradition conceives of leisure as the cultivation of the self and a preoccupation with the higher virtues of life. For this classical understanding of leisure, we are largely indebted to Aristotle, who believed that the cultivation of the self was an integral part of living the virtuous life.

Let's for a moment consider the background of our English word "leisure." It comes from the Latin *licere,* which means "to be permitted." Interestingly, the Latin word for work was *negotium,* or "non-leisure." The Greeks also stressed the primacy of leisure; their word for leisure was *schole* (which relates to the English words "school" and "scholarship"), while their word for work was *ascholia,* which meant essentially "absence of leisure." Work was thus seen as secondary to leisure. To the ancients, leisure was about contemplation, character formation, and spiritual growth.

How different our idea of leisure is today amidst a compulsively utilitarian culture, which measures virtually everything we do through the lens of work. We even say that we play, work out, or go on vacation so that we can come back refreshed and ready to be more productive in our jobs! Is the idea of a "working vacation" not in fact a contradiction in terms?

Leisure: A Celebration of Life

The true sense of genuine leisure and play, while certainly being set apart from our "work" lives, includes much more. It involves a break from the tedium and monotony of the everyday, yet it also carries with it the idea of contemplation and celebration of the world we inhabit. Commenting on the distinctiveness of leisure, Josef Pieper observes,

> Leisure does not mean the same as a "break." . . . Leisure is something entirely different. The essence of leisure is not to assure that we may function smoothly but rather to assure that we, embedded in our social function, are enabled to remain fully human. . . . That we may . . . contemplate and celebrate the world as such, to become and be that person who is essentially oriented toward the whole of reality.[3]

Hence, true leisure is self-reflective in nature and helps us to better understand the world and ourselves. Leisure leads us to ask ourselves some deep and penetrating questions about who we are, what we are doing, where we are going. And perhaps more than any other time in our history, we need to learn anew how to give ourselves permission to reflect on our lives as well as to relax and enjoy life. We also need time to reflect on the goodness of God, who has provided such richness in our human experience. Qoheleth sees such times as from the very hand of God:

> Go then, eat your bread in happiness, and drink your wine with a cheerful heart; for God has already approved your works. . . . Enjoy life with the woman whom you love all the days of your fleeting life which He has given to you under the sun; for this is your reward in life, and in your toil in which you have labored under the sun. (Ecclesiastes 9:7,9)

To live life with gaiety and frivolity is certainly not frivolous! It is in fact a celebration of our humanness. When we live a life of celebration, we are proclaiming our approval of the world as it is and are fundamentally asserting that the world is "good" and in the right order. Thus leisure depends on the necessity of our finding the world and ourselves somewhat agreeable. Furthermore, this concept of gaiety and festivity, the idea of having a good time, should be inconceivable without a sense of contemplation.

Architect Frank Lloyd Wright once told of an incident that perhaps seemed insignificant at the time, but had a profound influence on the rest of his life. The winter he was nine years old, he went walking across a snow-covered field with his reserved, no-nonsense uncle. As the two of them reached the far end of the field, his uncle stopped him and pointed out his own tracks in the snow, straight and true as an arrow's flight. He then pointed out young Frank's tracks, which meandered all over the field. "Notice how your tracks wander aimlessly from the fence to the cattle to the woods and back again," his uncle said. "And see how my tracks aim directly to my goal. There is an important lesson in that." Years later, the world-famous architect liked to tell how this experience had greatly contributed to his philosophy of life. "I determined right then," he said with a twinkle in his eye, "not to miss most things in life, as my uncle had."

I think Wright's meandering across that snow-covered field,

curiously looking at everything in his path, comes very close to this notion of contemplation and genuine leisure. In our times of festivity and leisure, we sense the grandeur and beauty of the world.

What is more, when we make time for leisure and play, such rest becomes not simply a break in the monotony of daily living, but rather a celebration of God's goodness and provision. As we seek to balance our lives between work and leisure, we are imitating the behavior of God, whose image and likeness we bear and who as Genesis 2:3 tells us, "rested from all His work." Pieper observes,

> The day of rest is not just a neutral interval inserted as a link in the chain of workaday life. It entails a loss of utilitarian profit. In voluntarily keeping the holiday, men renounce the yield of a day's labor. . . . The day of rest, then, meant not only that no work was done, but also that an offering was being made of the yield of labor . . . A festival is essentially a phenomenon of wealth; not, to be sure, the wealth of money, but of existential richness.[4]

Throughout history, philosophers have sensed this transcendent, spiritual dimension of leisure and sport as they observed humans absorbed in the act of playing or of being spectators in a human drama to see how a game "plays out." As already mentioned, Aristotle was a key contributor to this mindset and believed that in play, mankind perhaps comes closest to the idea of genuine contemplation. What is more, in some of our most cherished sports, primarily those that extol the contemplative life, there are (in the apt phrase of sociologist Peter Berger) "signals of transcendence."

Three Contemplative Sports
In times of playful contemplation amidst our leisure activities, we sense that they are pregnant with spiritual overtones. These truly

leisure sports challenge us to listen with our hearts, to examine our individual lives and life in general, because they not only teach us about this life, but also beckon us to another. They hint at much more than the sport itself, and therein is their sublime appeal. We will look at three leisure sports that are awash with spiritual overtones: fishing (especially fly-fishing), golf, and baseball.

The Virtues of Fly-Fishing

Amidst the hectic pace of daily life, fishing—and particularly fly-fishing—can provide a necessary venue to help us understand our personal lives and life in general. A number of articles have appeared in recent years that show the similarities between religion and fly-fishing.

A more eloquent spokesman cannot be found for describing these similarities than Norman Maclean, author of *A River Runs Through It*. Maclean, who grew up in the western Rocky Mountains and served as a distinguished professor of English at the University of Chicago, weaves an enchanting story of a lifetime of fishing with his father and brother. Maclean's writing displays an uncanny blending of fly-fishing with the affections of the heart as he recounts his memories from the Big Blackfoot River, as well as the lessons of growing up with a wayward brother and a strict Presbyterian minister for a father. It is the touching story of an older man telling about his life, but beneath the veneer is a spiritual wisdom with tremendous lessons about life and faith. Listen to the first lines of his winsome book:

> In our family, there was no clear line between religion and fly-fishing. We lived at the junction of great trout rivers in western Montana, and our father was a Presbyterian minister and a fly fisherman who tied his own flies and taught others. He told us about Christ's disciples being fishermen, and we were left to assume, as my brother and I did, that all first-class

fishermen on the Sea of Galilee were fly fishermen and that John, the favorite, was a dry-fly fisherman.[5]

Throughout *A River Runs Through It*, in addition to the lessons about life's hardships and challenges, there is something contemplative, relaxing, comforting, and yes, instructive, about fly-fishing. For when one fly-fishes, he or she is throwing the line, and not a weight at the end of the line as do bait fisherman. The power of a fly rod comes as one learns to move the rod back and forth like the movements of a clock hand between ten and two. There is demanded of the fisherman a certain rhythm, patience, and focus so that power comes at the end of the fishing rod. The finer the rod, the more patient and attentive one must be in allowing it to release its power and throw that tiny yet intricate fly out over the turbulent water before wary trout. Force the action, get careless and forget about where to put the power, and the line collapses in a tangled mess. Listen to Maclean's memories of what his father taught him about the art of fly-fishing—and life:

> Until a man is redeemed he will always take a fly rod too far back . . . and lose all his power somewhere in the air. . . . Power comes not from power everywhere, but from knowing where to put it on. . . . My father was very sure about certain matters pertaining to the universe. To him, all good things—trout as well as eternal salvation—come by grace and grace comes by art and art does not come easy.[6]

In many ways, fly-fishing is remarkably similar to the life of faith. Both demand certain qualities from us, like patience, rhythm, wisdom, and grace. We cannot manipulate or be coercive, because living, like fly-fishing, is an art. It does not reward those who seek to make something happen, but those who know the source of their power and when to use it. The sport transcends the activity itself and serves as a metaphor for beauty, power, and splendor, attesting to another world.

> As a Scot and a Presbyterian, my father believed that man by nature was a mess and had fallen from an original state of grace. . . . As for my father, I never knew whether he believed God was a mathematician but he certainly believed God could count and that only by picking up God's rhythms were we able to regain power and beauty. Unlike many Presbyterians, he often used the word "beautiful." [7]

Golf: A Good Walk Spoiled?

Golf nowadays is gaining tremendous popularity, though all who have played the game would probably admit it is the most frustrating sport they have ever attempted. Most would agree that there are days when Mark Twain's famous quip is too true: "Golf is a good walk spoiled."

Those who play golf and periodically vent their frustrations are often met with the puzzled question from spouses and friends, "If you love golf so much, then why are you so upset after playing a round?" John Feinstein, the award-winning sports writer, begins his enjoyable book *A Good Walk Spoiled: Days and Nights on the PGA Tour* with this mysterious conundrum about golf.[8] Along similar lines, celebrated psychiatrist M. Scott Peck, author of *The Road Less Traveled*, declares in his book *Golf and the Spirit* that golf is "probably the most nonlinear pastime in the face of the earth."[9] Consequently, he sees an important lesson imaged in the game of golf: most of the time life and reality do not behave the way we want them to.

The mutual joys and frustrations of golf are difficult, if not impossible, to answer. In many ways, golf is the least precise game in the world; golfers rarely are able to determine with any precision exactly why they are playing well or poorly. Without fail, even when he or she is playing well, or in "the zone," the golfer waits with trepidation for the "wheels to come off." He knows that it is just a matter of time before he will lose that rhythm and confidence that has allowed him to master the past few holes. Even among the best golf professionals, there are no sure-fire answers for improving one's game. Just take a look at all of the bulging instructional sections in the golf magazines; golfers are all looking for the "secret" that doesn't exist. On the severity of the game, Feinstein observes,

> No one has the answers. . . . Hard work can make you better but it won't always make you better. Sometimes, it will make you worse. Golf has no guarantees. And what makes it even more difficult, there are no excuses. . . . No one ever gets a bad call in golf. No one strikes you out or tackles you or blocks your shot or hits a forehand so hard you can't get to it. The ball doesn't move and neither does the hole. You either get the ball into the hole quickly or not quickly enough. Period. . . . There is no sport as solitary as golf. No sport humanizes you like golf.[10]

Golf keeps track of every mistake. Unlike many sports where one can make a comeback to get back in the game, there are no second chances with golf. In tennis, which is frequently compared to golf because both are individual sports, you can fall behind two sets, then rally to win. In golf, every shot counts. Every mistake is deftly recorded on a scorecard—and in ink. PGA professional Billy Andrade, a friend to many major league baseball players, enjoys telling them, "You can strike out your first three times up and still be a hero by hitting a homer your fourth time up. In golf, you make three errors and you're dead." Or as the legendary Sam Snead once chided Hall of Famer Ted Williams, "In golf, you have to play your foul balls."[11]

In golf, we learn a lot about ourselves and who we really are. Novelist Walker Percy often uses the golf course as a setting reminiscent of his childhood memories of growing up in a Birmingham, Alabama, suburb. To Percy, golf is the contemplative conduit that fosters self-understanding, how we perceive this world, and our understanding of others. In his novel *The Second Coming*, the central character is Will Barrett, a successful, middle-aged attorney, who is nevertheless despairing and bored with life. Barrett firmly believes that someone can learn more about a man from playing a round of golf with him than could be learned from spending a year of sessions on a psychiatrist's couch. In his excellent biography of Percy, *Pilgrim in the Ruins*, writer Jay Tolson makes this interesting observation about him and his penchant for including golf in his works:

> The triumph of golf in the South is itself a curious fact of cultural history. It is, as anyone who has ever played it knows, a penitential little game, as much a trial of character and bearing as of skill. (Walker Percy . . . would later explore the peculiar moral dimensions of the game in almost as much depth as his northern fellow-in-letters, John Updike.) Fittingly, golf was invented by a Scotsman, for only a Calvinist could have found pleasure in a pursuit that required so much restraint for so delayed a reward.[12]

If golf teaches us anything, it mercilessly shows us our failures and shortcomings in life. While in many avenues of life we may attempt to fool ourselves into thinking that we are doing magnificently, golf is not nearly so kind and forgiving. It gives us a glimpse of our inner souls. Listen to John Updike's profound observations about the brutal honesty of the game, from his essay, "Moral Exercise":

> Most of us don't really know how well we're doing, in real life, and imagine we're doing not so bad. The world conspires to

flatter us; only golf trusts us with a cruelly honest report on our performance. Only on the golf course is the feedback instantaneous and unrelenting. . . . In the sound of the hit and the flight of the ball it tells us unflinchingly how we are doing, and we are rarely doing well.[13]

Golf testifies that we are imperfect creatures. A similar case is also made in Michael Murphy's best-selling book, *Golf in the Kingdom*. It is the imaginary story of a young man en route to India, who stops in Scotland to play the legendary Burningbush golf club, where his life is transformed. The young man is paired with a mysterious club professional named Shivas Irons, who leads him through a phenomenal round of golf. Although Murphy's book is laden with a superficial Eastern mysticism, it still provides some interesting insight into the game, particularly in the provocative chapter entitled "A Hamartiology of Golf." The chapter describes how a faulty golf swing reflects the soul and, more particularly, our "coming up short" in our moral character:

> Peter McNaughton had remarked that nowhere does a man go so naked as he does before a discerning eye all dressed for golf. Shivas recalled the remark and asked me if I knew the word "hamartia." "It originally meant bein' off the target, in archery or some such," he said, " and then it came to mean bein' off the taraget in general in all yer life — it got to mean a flaw in the character . . . when a man swings he tells us all about himself." . . . "Yes, a man's style o' play and his swing certainly reflect the state of his soul," he resumed his description of golfing hamartiology, "Ye take the one who always underclub. The man who wants to think he's stronger than he is. D' ye ken anybody like that?" He raised one quizzical eyebrow. "Think about the rest of his habits. Is he always short o' the hole?" [14]

Despite abysmal failures on the course, golfers will often go to extreme measures to correct flawed, aggressive swings, and wayward putting strokes. In how many other sports do you see professional athletes going out to practice for hours *after* they have played for the day? Most golfers love working at their game and realize that they will fail more often than they succeed. Citing this curious aspect of golf, Greg Norman observed, "The failure is what makes succeeding so sweet . . . in golf, failure is a great thing—an absolutely necessary thing." [15] As Norman observes, failure teaches us a lot about life and a lot about ourselves. It reveals our deeply flawed character.

Golf is the ultimate head and heart game. To play golf is a spiritual exercise, because it deflates our ego and shows us how far we have to go. In response to the question of why he persists in playing golf even though he is regularly confronted with his shortcomings, Peck candidly remarks,

> I play golf precisely because it is humiliating. While I don't enjoy being humiliated, I do need it. There's another word for what golfers go through that's even stronger than *humiliation*: *mortification*. It is derived from *mors*, the Latin word for "death," as is the term *mortician* for "undertaker." To be mortified is to feel so humiliated that you would rather bury yourself deep in the nearest sand trap than ever show your face on a golf course again. . . . In doing battle on the golf course against my own personality—against my ego, if you will—I am attempting to practice kenosis: getting myself out of my own way. It is what spiritual growth is all about. . . . Among other reasons, I play golf because it is for me a highly useful spiritual discipline. [16]

But golf does more than simply show us our moral flaws and shortcomings. We are also asked, if you will, to "trust, have faith," to discover that the game is played not so much by might as it is by feeling that appropriate rhythm where grace and freedom abound. The transcendent dimensions of the game are present, and we will see them if we care to look for them. Hopefully, we can occasionally relax and enjoy that saintly *letting go* that golf asks of its devotees, and in the process gain a bit more insight into what it means to live by faith. Updike says it so well:

> Unconstituted Adam wants to kill the ball, and to watch it fly. ... The correct golf swing is a web of small articles of faith, all of which strain common sense.... Taking a light grip goes dead against our furious determination to hammer the course into submission.... Golf is a study in our greed as well as our lack of faith. In remembering a round, we write off the missed two-foot putt and the approach shot that just barely drifted into the trap as not us, as not legitimately part of the round, but incorporate without gratitude the skulled wedge that somehow wound up on the green.[17]

Baseball: The Great American Pastime

A few years ago, the nine-month professional baseball strike, by many accounts, exacted a substantial toll on the psyche of even the most ardent fans. People became disillusioned that many of these well-compensated athletes—earning more in one season than most workers would realize in a lifetime—could turn "America's Pastime" into such an ugly display of selfishness. Nor was the ire reserved for the players alone. Anger and dismay were also directed toward wealthy team owners. To register their disenchantment, a number of baseball fans refuse to attend major league games to this day.

For many of us, baseball matters, and it signifies something more than the game itself. Baseball resonates deeply within us, probably more than any other sport in the American culture. Ken Burns, the producer and director of the popular 1994 PBS series *Baseball*, expressed this sentiment in a speech before the National Press Club in Washington, D.C., a few years ago: "Baseball is a Rosetta Stone upon which you can see writ quite plainly the soul of the country."[18] Baseball is frequently used as a metaphor for life, as witnessed by the various T-shirts with messages emblazoned across them, like "Baseball Is Life … All the Rest Is Details." Annie Dillard captures our youthful exuberance for the game when she beautifully describes what many of us have experienced:

> A baseball weighted your hand just so, and fit it. Its red stitches, its good leather and hardness like skin over bone, seemed to call forth a skill both easy and precise. On the catch—a grounder, the fly, the line drive—you could snag a baseball in your mitt, where it stayed, snap, like a mouse locked in its trap, not like some pumpkin of a softball you merely halted, with a terrible sound like a splat. You could curl your fingers around a baseball, and throw it in a straight line. When you hit it with a bat it cracked—and your heart cracked, too, at the sound. It took a grass stain nicely, stayed round, smelled good, and lived lashed in your mitt all winter, hibernating.[19]

Despite America's deep love for the game, many people look at all sports (including baseball) as mere escapism. To such people, sports are like a mild drug akin to double-strength Tylenol—harmless enough perhaps, but certainly distracting us from the *real* issues of life. Yet in the classical perspective, sports were not viewed as an elixir for escapism, but rather dealt with the contemplation of the higher values of life. George Will, in his critically acclaimed book *Men at Work: The Craft of Baseball*, comments on the classic understanding of sports as it relates to baseball:

> Proof of the genius of ancient Greece is that it understood baseball's future importance. . . . Sport, they said, is morally

serious because mankind's noblest aim is the loving contemplation of worthy things, such as beauty and courage. . . . Seeing people compete courageously and fairly helps emancipate the individual by educating his passions.[20]

And in baseball, whether as a participant or a spectator, we gain a greater appreciation of beauty, courage, and what it means to be human. James Schall recounts a letter he received from a friend that underscores the importance of true play:

I find this interesting. Not one person in the family has ever played a video game. They will not buy one for their kids and will not play one themselves. A curious reason for this, with which I agree, surfaced. This is not a human game played on a machine. Reason? Because there is no chance to cheat! One big choice is removed. . . . This is not my idea of playing a game. As you say, our ability to make the wrong choice is proof of our glory.[21]

While Schall is certainly not promoting cheating, he is suggesting that there is no game if there is no possibility of cheating. Games are played by people, who are free moral agents. Therefore they can either win or lose, play fair or cheat, and this is why we yell, "Murder the bum!" at referees. Even with instant replay, there is high drama!

Not only do we experience the high drama of winning or losing in baseball, which is a signature of our glory as free agents, we also yearn for what is best in ourselves. We become spectators, not for any selfish reasons such as fame or fortune (maybe this is the reason for the public's disdain for selfish players and owners), but simply because the game is there and we lose ourselves in its playing. Years ago songwriter and longtime Yankees fan Paul Simon was asked to explain the lyric from the song "Mrs. Robinson": "Where have you gone, Joe DiMaggio, a nation turns its lonely eyes to you."

He replied, "It has something to do with heroes . . . people who are all good with no bad in them. That's the way I always saw Joe DiMaggio."

Baseball also serves as a metaphor for justice and righteousness. It appeals to our deep moral sense of how things *ought* to be. Baseball attempts to provide a "level playing field" of what life should be like. Through baseball we seek to ensure the predictable outcome that is lacking in the drama of real life. (What else could account for the insatiable keeping of baseball statistics?) Our deep longing for fairness is poignantly expressed in the words of Thomas Boswell, the renowned writer for the *Washington Post*, in his classic on baseball, *Why Time Begins on Opening Day:*

> In contrast to the unwieldy world which we hold in common, baseball offers a kingdom built to human scale. Its problems and questions are exactly our size. Here we come when we feel a need for a rooted point of reference. . . . Baseball isn't necessarily an escape from reality, though it can be; it's merely one of our many refuges *within* the real where we try to create a sense of order on our own terms. Born to an age where horror has become commonplace, where tragedy has, by its monotonous repetition, become a parody of sorrow, we need to fence off a few parks where humans try to be fair, where skill has some hope of reward, where absurdity has a harder time than usual getting a ticket.[22]

In addition to our desire for justice and fairness on the playing field, the baseball diamond deeply images our aspirations for paradise, namely, Heaven. Each spring, baseball ushers in a season of promise and hope—not just on the field but beyond the fence—in lives going into the "late innings."

A. Bartlett Giamatti, who taught Renaissance literature at Yale and served as baseball's seventh commissioner until his untimely death, was fond of pointing out the similarities between the contemporary and ancient worlds. Giamatti noted that the etymological root for the word "paradise" is an ancient Persian word meaning "enclosed park or green." Baseball, Giamatti suggests, inspires us toward deep and resonant hopes and reminds us of another time in our Edenic past.

> So much does our game tell us about what we wanted to be, about what we are. Our character and our culture are reflected in this grand game. It would be foolish to think that all of our national experience is reflected in any single institution, even our loftiest, but it would not be wrong to claim for baseball a capacity to cherish individuality and inspire cohesion in a way which is a hallmark of our loftiest free institutions. Nor would it be misguided to think that, however vestigial the remnants of our best hopes, we can still find, if we wish to, a moment called a game when those best hopes, those memories for the future, have life; when each of us, those who are in and those out, has a chance to gather, in a green place around home.[23]

Holy Play

As we have seen regarding these three contemplative sports, we not only enjoy them for providing a break from the hurried pace of life, but also for providing a window to our souls. Fly-fishing teaches us about the inability of brute power to achieve things by sheer force and about entering into the rhythms of life and grace. Golf provides a case study of what kind of people we really are and serves as a spiritual exercise in humility and mortification. Our golf swing shows us unapologetically how far we "fall short" of perfection. And in baseball we experience the high drama of winning or losing, and we look for fairness and justice on the playing field, something we cannot count on in the game of life. In baseball we look beyond the "enclosed park or green," to the true paradise, Heaven, where our deepest dreams and aspirations will one day be realized.

Amidst the trials and pains that we experience in this life, leisure — especially as seen in contemplative sports — provides a respite from this world. While some may see sports as frivolous activities amidst the seriousness of life, sports actually suggest the abiding joy that will be the "serious business" of Heaven. In one of the most glorious passages from his last book, *Letters to Malcolm: Chiefly on Prayer*, C. S. Lewis wrote,

> I do *not* think that the life of Heaven bears any analogy to play or dance in respect of frivolity. I do think that while we are in this "valley of tears," . . . certain qualities that must belong to the celestial condition have no chance to get through . . . except in activities which, for us here and now, are frivolous. . . . No, Malcolm. It is only in our "hours-off," only in our moments of permitted festivity, that we find an analogy. Dance and game *are* frivolous, unimportant down here; for "down here" is not their natural place. Here, they are a moment's rest from the life we were placed here to live. But in this world everything is upside down. That which, if it could be prolonged here, would be a truancy, is likest that which in a better country is the End of ends. Joy is the serious business of Heaven.[24]

Part III

The Implications of Heaven

We are very shy nowadays of even mentioning heaven. We are afraid of the jeer about "pie in the sky," and of being told that we are trying to "escape" from the duty of making a happy world here and now into dreams of a happy world elsewhere. But either there is "pie in the sky" or there is not. If there is not, then Christianity is false, for this doctrine is woven into its whole fabric. If there is, then this truth, like any other, must be faced, whether it is useful at political meetings or no.

—C. S. Lewis

In part 1 we observed how our culture has imitated the true concept of Heaven by secularization and trivialization. Culture has lost its sense of transcendence and consequently has abdicated the transcendent dimension of life that provides meaning, purpose, and significance. And when society dismisses its belief in God, this results in the trivialization of the serious matters of life, like faith, death, and life beyond the grave. Better to joke about such matters, society reasons, than to seriously reflect upon them. As such, when society jettisons its belief in God, only a parody remains.

In part 2 we saw how much of this world, in an effort to recapture a sense of awe and transcendence in life, *intimates* that another life awaits us. In this section we examined various "clues along the way" of another world that lies before us. These intimations of Heaven include our universal unhappiness; our sense of alienation in this world; the transcendent dimension of literature and the cinema; our pain and suffering; our pleasures and joy; the humdrum of the ordinary; our desire for significance in our work; and the contemplative nature of some of our sports. All of these aspects of daily living provide us with hints, glimmers of a transcendent world beyond the present one.

With these things in mind, let us now turn to consider "The Implications of Heaven." This section will cover three major facets dealing with Heaven. First, how can we have *certainty* about our belief in Heaven? Upon what basis do we believe that Heaven is real? Is Christianity a reliable guide about Heaven? Second, we will look at the *choice* of Heaven. Is it possible to believe that *everyone* gets to Heaven? More specifically, what are we to make of the Christian doctrine of Hell? Is it plausible in our modern world? And third, what will be the *character* of Heaven? Where is Heaven? Will we have bodies in Heaven? Is there time in Heaven? What in the world will we do in Heaven? Will we know everything and recognize others in Heaven? Will we all be equal in Heaven?

CHAPTER 12

THE CERTAINTY OF HEAVEN

It's humiliating to belong to a race that can make anything as exciting as truth dull!

—Josiah Royce

Make no mistake: if He rose at all it was as His body; if the cell's dissolution did not reverse, the Church will fall.

—John Updike

Can we know for certain that Heaven is real? Is Christianity a reliable guide to inform us about Heaven? Journalist H. L. Mencken, certainly no friend of Christianity, once chided religious faith as "the illogical belief in the occurrence of the improbable." Mark Twain gave the definition most beloved by critics when he quipped, "Faith is believing what you know ain't so." A floundering minister in a John Updike novel confesses, "Something's gone wrong. I have no faith. Or rather, I have faith, but it doesn't seem to apply." In the film *Leap of Faith*, Steve Martin plays a charlatan television-evangelist that preys on humble, religious folk, who desperately want to believe in God for miracles of healing and prosperity. In these and numerous other instances, faith is caricatured as irrational belief, something that is against the hard evidence and contrary to what we know to be so. Therefore, when we speak of the intimations of Heaven, the criticism predictably comes: "You can speak of these hints of Heaven, but you have no certainty that this is *really* the way things are. It's only by a blind leap of faith. You can't *prove* it!" Such cynicism and disbelief cajole those who embrace a belief in Heaven.

The Road to Unbelief

Dietrich Bonhoeffer's words—uttered in the early part of the 1900s—that the world had "come of age" have a prophetic ring to them. He was suggesting that people no longer considered it necessary to believe in God to account for man and our world. In essence, God became expedient, a non-player in the cosmos and in the game of life.

My, how far we have come! Only a few centuries ago it would have been unthinkable for humanity to believe that God was unimportant in our understanding of the world. Peter Kreeft describes what modernity has lost in its concept of the afterlife over the past few centuries:

> To medieval Christendom, it was the world beyond the world that made all the difference in the world to this world. The

Heaven beyond the sun made the earth "under the sun" something more than "vanity of vanities" (Ecclesiastes 1:3; 2). Earth was Heaven's womb, Heaven's nursery, Heaven's dress rehearsal. Heaven was the meaning of the earth. . . . Medieval man was still his Father's child, however prodigal, and his world was meaningful because it was "my Father's world" and he believed his Father's promise to take him home after death. This confidence towards death gave him a confidence towards life, for life's road led somewhere. The Heavenly mansion at the end of the earthly pilgrimage made a tremendous difference to the road itself. . . . The glory has departed. We moderns have lost much of medieval Christendom's *faith* in Heaven because we have lost its *hope* of Heaven.[1]

Fundamentally, our uncertainty does not deal exclusively with what lies beyond the grave, but is tied to the very notion of God. The root issue, then, is whether God exists. Writing at the beginning of the twentieth century, English novelist Thomas Hardy expressed this disdain for religious belief when he smugly declared, "I have been looking for God for fifty years, and I think if he had existed I should have found him."

To better understand the cynicism about God and the afterlife that permeates our society today, let's briefly consider the various worldviews that the Christian faith has encountered over the past few centuries. Historically speaking, orthodox Christianity has embraced a number of tenets considered authoritative over roughly the first seventeen centuries of the Christian era. Most people assumed that God is real and must be taken into account. It was understood that good is in conflict with evil and that human beings, while sinful, still have an inherent dignity and are the objects of God's salvation. Nature was seen as God's creation, but there was believed to be a reality beyond nature—the realm of the spirit, the fundamental source of all values and the ultimate destiny of human beings. Furthermore, Christianity has held that humanity, society, and nature are not autonomous; all are utterly dependent on the sovereign and benevolent God.

While Christian theism was the dominant position for approximately the first eighteen centuries, Christianity has found itself at odds with other worldviews over the past few hundred years. It first faced modernity, which was rooted in the Enlightenment, beginning in the 1700s. The worldview of modernism, which birthed the Age of Reason, placed much emphasis on scientific discovery and human autonomy and believed that science could explain virtually everything. Yet the Enlightenment, with its assumption that reason is the most important human faculty, sparked the reaction of Romanticism, which assumed that emotion is the essential ingredient of our humanness. Similarly, materialism as a worldview began to take center stage at the beginning of the twentieth century, and it sparked the reaction of an agnostic or atheistic existentialism, which fundamentally sees no inherent meaning or purpose in life.

The World of Postmodernism

According to existentialism, the objective realm is absurd—void of any significance—and meaning cannot be found in the objective world. Rather, meaning is a purely human-fabricated phenomenon, and while there is no inherent meaning in life, individuals can create meaning and order for themselves through their deliberate choices and actions. With existentialism, the meaning that individuals create for themselves has no validity for anyone else, because everyone must determine his or her own meaning, which remains private, personal, and unrelated to any sort of objective truth.

It is this worldview of existentialism, which began in the nineteenth century and which by the middle of the twentieth century had become a major philosophical movement, that provides the rationale for contemporary relativism. And since, according to existentialism, everyone creates his or her own meaning, *every* meaning is equally valid. Consequently, religion becomes a purely private affair that cannot be "proved" to anyone else, much less imposed on others! And because everyone creates and inhabits his or her own "virtual reality," the content of one's meaning makes little difference. Consequently, "what's true for you may not be true for me."

Does this sound familiar? The seeds of existential ideology form the basis for the worldview known as "postmodernism," a term first employed by historian Sir Arnold Toynbee. According to postmodernism, the problem with modernism is not its uncritical dependence on human reason alone, but its assumption that there is such a thing as *objective* truth. In his excellent book *Postmodern Times: A Christian Guide to Contemporary Thought and Culture*, Gene Edward Veith Jr. distinguishes between the two ideologies of modernity and postmodernity:

> Modernists believe in determinacy; postmodernists believe in indeterminacy. Whereas modernism emphasizes purpose and design, postmodernism emphasizes play and chance. Modernism establishes a hierarchy; postmodernism cultivates anarchy. Modernism values the type; postmodernism values the mutant. Modernism seeks the *logos*, the underlying meaning of the universe expressed in language. Postmodernism, on the other hand, embraces silence, rejecting both meaning and the Word.[2]

As one can easily surmise, we live in a culture where belief in absolute truth is met with derision. Such ideas as meaning, purpose, and significance are not considered inherent values of our world, but are seen as created through our experience.

Yet, as we discussed in an earlier chapter concerning the trivialization of Heaven, Christianity holds that we do not *create* Heaven because we desperately want it to be true, but that Heaven exists because it is a part of ultimate reality. Belief in Heaven is not escapism from a painful world, but realism, for our beliefs conform to the way

things really are. That is why C. S. Lewis makes the seemingly audacious statement that "it is more important that heaven should exist
than that any of us should reach it." [3]

The Quest for Meaning and Purpose in Life

If we are truthful with ourselves, we will admit that something within
us yearns to know the truth about reality and our world. Granted,
we cannot empirically "prove" that God exists, any more than we can
prove the reality of Heaven, but we want to know. Truth about reality is the mind's food. And if we distill the matter of God, Heaven,
and the afterlife down to its very essence, it comes down to a matter
of faith. Yet this idea of faith is not to be understood as "an illogical
belief in the occurrence of the improbable," as Mencken defined it.
Rather, faith or belief means fundamentally affirming the view of life
that most reasonably accounts for our world.

In *Mere Christianity*, Lewis sets forth the reasonableness of belief
in the Christian understanding of our world. He suggests that there
are only two alternatives that lie behind the Law of Human Nature,
or the Law of Right and Wrong:

> Ever since men were able to think, they have been wondering
> what this universe really is and how it came to be there. And,
> very roughly, two views have been held. First, there is what is
> called the materialist view. People who take that view think
> that matter and space just happen to exist, and always have
> existed, nobody knows why. . . . The other view is the religious
> view. According to it, what is behind the universe is more like
> a mind than it is like anything else we know. That is to say, it
> is conscious, and has purposes, and prefers one thing to
> another. . . . You cannot find out which view is the right one
> by science in the ordinary sense. Science works by experi-
> ments. It watches how things behave. . . . But why anything
> comes to be there at all . . . this is not a scientific question. [4]

Lewis goes on to say that in the long run a religious view of life is a reasonable position and best helps us explain the world and ourselves. While a defense of Christian theism is beyond the scope of our discussion, the shortcomings of atheism and agnosticism are apparent. In their excellent book that deals with objections to the Christian faith, *I'm Glad You Asked,* authors Kenneth Boa and Larry Moody write concerning this issue:

> It is completely unreasonable to say, "I *know* that God does not exist." A person would have to know everything before that statement could be confirmed . . . a person may deny the existence of God, but he must be omniscient to logically do so. Ironically, one would have to be God to be sure that God does not exist . . . it is sometimes good to help (someone) think his way through the implications of a universe with no God. The human heart cries out for meaning, value, and purpose, but these are precisely the things that are denied in an atheistic cosmos . . . without God, we have no basis for morality, meaning that values such as right and wrong and good and bad are totally relative and have no absolute mooring. . . . Man is also stripped of purpose in a godless reality. . . . All of us act as though human existence has meaning, as though moral values are real, and as though human life has purpose and dignity. But all these things presuppose an infinite-personal Creator, so if God is dead, man is also as good as dead.[5]

So then, while hard, empirical proof is impossible when it comes to matters of faith about God and the afterlife, we nevertheless must come to some personal decision. While agnosticism is not as unreasonable as atheism, it still fails to take into account the circumstantial evidence that strongly favors theism.[6]

What we must do is consider what *kind* of evidence is necessary for believing in God and how we are to come to a decision about the important issues of life. In reality, none of us live our lives and base our daily decisions on 100 percent proof! In courts of law, civil cases are determined based on what is considered to be "proof," the preponderance of the credible evidence. Even in criminal cases, the jury must render a decision that is "beyond a reasonable doubt." So when it comes to religious faith, proof cannot be empirically determined, but rather one's confidence is based on the credible evidence at hand. And as we have suggested, much of our life powerfully suggests that God exists. The stuff of life, the basis of our morality, our concept of right and wrong, our desire for meaning, purpose, and dignity, all strongly suggest that Christianity is not only plausible, but also true.

Human history is filled with men and women who spent much of their lives asking the deep questions about meaning and purpose in life. One of the most famous midlife crises in history was experienced by the great novelist Leo Tolstoy. After becoming rich and celebrated, having written such classics as *War and Peace* and *Anna Karenina*, Tolstoy found himself questioning the meaning and purpose of it all. In his *Confession*, written in 1882, he describes how he began to question the life of celebrity, wealth, and fame that had come to him:

> But five years ago something very strange began to happen to me. At first I began having moments of bewilderment, when my life would come to a halt, as if I did not know how to live or what to do; I would lose my presence of mind and fall into a state of depression. But this passed, and I continued to live as before. Then the moments of bewilderment recurred more frequently, and they always took the same form. Whenever my life would come to a halt, the questions would arise: Why? And what next?[7]

Like a modern-day Tolstoy, Woody Allen raises the question of meaning and purpose in life in many of his films. In *Hannah and Her Sisters*, Mickey (played by Allen) is worried that he has cancer.

Even after celebrating the doctor's report that he is fine, he is struck by the realization of the brevity of life and of his need for answers to the puzzle of meaning and purpose. Deciding to quit his job and search for answers, he explains to an associate, "Do you realize what a thread we're all hanging by?" Reflecting on the certainty of death as the ultimate trump card in the game of life, he is reminiscent of Tolstoy as he muses, "Can you understand how meaningless everything is? Everything. I gotta get some answers."

Allen, like Tolstoy, knows deep down that only a transcendent purpose can truly explain life and deliver ultimate meaning. If there is no God, then Dostoyevsky was right: "All things are permitted."

Signposts of the Truth

As we seek to determine the answers to life's daunting questions, many reliable guides have come before us. Blaise Pascal, the seventeenth-century scientist and Christian apologist cited earlier, made significant contributions regarding the reasonableness of the Christian faith through his *Pensées.* He believed that the Christian faith has much to commend itself to someone who genuinely seeks to know the truth about life and God. Yet he was aware that we often see and believe only what we want to believe. Consequently, Pascal believed that it is important to present the supreme attractiveness of the promises offered by Christianity, so that one might then genuinely consider the truth claims of the Christian faith. Toward the beginning of the *Pensées,* Pascal wrote this note to himself:

> *Order.* Men despise religion. They hate it and are afraid it may be true. The cure for this is first to show that religion is not contrary to reason, but worthy of reverence and respect. Next, make it attractive, make good men wish it were true, and then show that it is. Worthy of reverence because it really understands human nature. Attractive because it promises true good.[8]

To Pascal, religious conviction need not be perceived as contrary to reason, but rather as in deep harmony with it. Further, it was his belief that God had not left Himself without a legitimate witness in the world and that only Christianity offered the true ultimate good for man: the hope of Heaven. Although Pascal wrote over 350 years ago, many strands of evidence for Christianity that Pascal used are quite powerful, even in our contemporary culture. Let's now look at a number of these marks of the truth that Pascal urges us to consider carefully.[9]

The Enigmatic Human Condition

Pascal believed that one important sign of the truth of the Christian faith is its account of human nature and its diagnosis of the human condition. We are a puzzle to ourselves, and our enigmatic nature cries out for an explanation. Pascal believed that only Christianity adequately explains both our greatness and our wretchedness. He was convinced that this in itself is an important mark of the truth of the Christian faith. To Pascal, no secular view of the human race can account for both diagnosing our ills and explaining our strengths.

> Man's greatness comes from knowing he is wretched: a tree does not know it is wretched. Thus it is wretched to know that one is wretched, but there is greatness in knowing one is wretched. . . . If he exalts himself, I [God] humble him. If he humbles himself, I exalt him And I go on contradicting him until he understands that he is a monster that passes all understanding.[10]

Pascal felt that our perennial dissatisfaction with life is another telling indicator. In reality, our lives largely comprise ungrounded hopes, daily frustrations, and insatiable desires. We are dissatisfied with life, we yearn for change, and we are always on the prowl for something new to make life exciting and appealing. And to add insult to injury, when our elusive dreams are sometimes met — when we get that car, home, or job promotion — horror of horrors, we are still not satisfied! When we acquire that much-sought-after possession, that position of prominence or prestige, that thing that we believe will make all the difference in the world, surprise! We are terribly let down and disillusioned. According to Pascal,

> *Man's condition.* Inconstancy, boredom, anxiety . . . Anyone who does not see the vanity of the world is very vain himself. So who does not see it, apart from young people whose lives are all noise, diversions, and thoughts for the future? But take away their diversion and you will see them bored to extinction. . . . What causes inconstancy is the realization that present pleasures are false, together with the failure to realize that absent pleasures are vain.[11]

Pascal, like Qoheleth in the book of Ecclesiastes, has us pegged. We are a restless and unhappy bunch. And if we live our lives exclusively within the confines of what this world has to offer, we are living within a cocoon of illusion.

In Pascal's opinion, Christianity is in touch with reality because it gives us an adequate account of mankind's true state of affairs. Our greatness is seen in that we have been created in the image of God, just a little lower than the angels, crowned with glory and majesty as God's vice-regents over creation (see Genesis 1:26-28; Psalm 8:5). Yet we have fallen from our high estate, and the human race is now dispossessed kings and queens, because of our rebellion — our "foul revolt" against our Sovereign, as Milton described it (see Genesis 3; Romans 3:23). We, along with the apostle Paul, recognize that even the saint struggles with sin and temptation in this life, discovering that "evil is present in . . . the one who wishes to do good" (Romans 7:21) and that the natural and spiritual life are at enmity with one another (see Galatians 5:16 and following).

Because of our enigmatic human nature—our greatness and our wretchedness, as well as our universal unhappiness—Christianity gives us a picture of reality and is at least plausible. And though we seek happiness in this world, often through vain pursuits and temporal pleasures, our true and only good is God Himself. Because the Christian faith gives us an account of the way life really is, it is revelatory. Consequently, Pascal saw this as an important signpost of its authenticity.

The Definitive Divine Revelation

Another strand of truth that Pascal believed strongly argued for Christianity is that it offers the most complete revelation of God to humanity. It further claims another important exclusivity: that God the Father, the God of Jesus Christ, is the only God there is and that only by virtue of a proper relationship to Christ is one's proper relationship to God assured. These are obviously strong exclusivist claims, which in our world of religious pluralism are met with animosity.

While a defense of the exclusivity of Christianity is beyond the scope of our discussion, it is important to consider briefly these objections. Critics often like to point out that these Christian truth claims are not entirely unique among the world religions and thus infer that Christianity has no right to make a distinctive claim upon the truth. For example, they argue that a number of Old Testament stories are similar to other ancient Near Eastern traditions. We know of Mesopotamian fertility religions where there was a numinous relationship between the ancient worshiper and the pantheon of the gods, and there is a recurrent theme of a dying and rising vegetation god. We also know that other religious traditions besides the Christian faith are founded on moral principles (such as the Golden Rule) that affirm the dignity and sanctity of human life. Because of this commonality with other world religions, critics reason that Christianity should not be considered utterly unique, despite its claims. They suggest that if Christianity shares some similar ideas and beliefs with other religious traditions (many of which grew up independent of the influence of

Christianity), then either Christianity has borrowed some of its ideas from these other traditions or those ideas arose independently within Christianity and the other religions. Whatever the case, they dismiss the claim of Christianity being the one true religion.

Let's now follow the critics' reasoning to its natural conclusion. They suggest that if Christianity has borrowed its ideas from other religions, then the ideas came not from God but from men and women. And if these ideas developed independently in Christianity and the other religions, they say this is evidence that the source is not divine revelation but human inspiration. If Christian theology is sheer human fabrication—a pastiche of ruminations about ultimate issues, as critics suggest—then there is no reason to believe that it, above other religions, captures the truth. But Pascal turns the tables on such flawed reasoning. In a cryptic note dealing with the Christian revelation, he suggests that while the Christian religion is not entirely unique, "far from being a reason for believing it not to be the true religion, it is on the contrary what proves it to be so." [12]

Pascal believed that if there is a God who created all human beings for eternal fellowship with Him, then we should not be surprised that He would have created them with some capacity or ability to come to know about Him. Further, because God is loving, perfect, good, and wise, and desires to have this fellowship with His creatures, neither should we be surprised that He would make Himself available to them, both in obvious and covert ways. And if there is one—and only one—way of attaining this eternal fellowship with God amidst our present fallen state, then we should expect various hints of truth to be available to the entire human race. If in the Christian faith we have the most complete revelation of God's divine plan of salvation, then we would naturally *expect* the Christian faith to elucidate and clarify elements of the divine truth present in a number of world religions. Lewis reasons in *Mere Christianity* that if he had to deny the existence of truth in all the other great world religions, he would never have been able to embrace the Christian faith:

If you are a Christian you do not have to believe that all the other religions are simply wrong all through. If you are an atheist you do not have to believe that the main point in all the religions of the whole world is simply one huge mistake. . . . But, of course, being a Christian does mean thinking that where Christianity differs from other religions, Christianity is right and they are wrong. As in arithmetic—there is only one right answer to a sum, and all other answers are wrong; but some of the wrong answers are much nearer being right than others.[13]

So then, the fact that the Christian faith is not utterly unique is not problematic, but rather to be expected from a God who loves and seeks to save all the lost. Further, it is not a Christian claim that no revelation exists outside the Bible. On the contrary, the Scriptures make it abundantly clear that God has not left Himself without witness. King David exults, "The heavens are telling of the glory of God; and their expanse is declaring the work of His hands" (Psalm 19:1); the apostle Paul declares that creation evidences proof for God:

That which is known about God is evident within [men]; for God made it evident to them. For since the creation of the world His invisible attributes, His eternal power and divine nature, have been clearly seen, being understood through what has been made. (Romans 1:19-20)

Paul tells the Athenians in his sermon at Mars Hill that the God who made the world wants to have fellowship with them, because He desires "that they should seek God, if perhaps they might grope for Him and find Him, though He is not far from each one of us" (Acts 17:27).

So while we should not be surprised that other religions of the world contain at least vestiges of the truth, there is no sidestepping the fact that Christianity, certainly from Pascal's and Lewis's perspectives, claims to be the purest and most comprehensive revelation from God to mankind. As such, the Christian faith is the only world religion that can be judged to be true as a whole.

The Jewish Preservation

Another significant signpost to Pascal for the truth of Christianity concerns the preservation of the Jews. Pascal believed that if any atheist or agnostic truly searched the different world religions to determine which was true, he would be led to conclude that, if there is a God, it is the God of the Christians. And naturally, because the Christian faith is rooted in the Old Testament and God's covenant with the Jewish people, he saw this covenantal continuity between Judaism and Christianity as another mark of the authenticity of the Christian faith. He was captivated by the Jewish faith:

> I find then this great and numerous people, descended from one man, worshipping one God, and living according to a law which they claim to have received from his hand. They maintain that they are the only people in the world to whom God has revealed his mysteries; that all men are corrupt and in disgrace with God . . . that a Redeemer will come, for all; that they are in the world to proclaim him to men. . . . My encounter with this people amazes me and seems worthy of attention.[14]

What is remarkable about the Jews, Pascal argued, is that they have gone to great pains to preserve a book that is hardly flattering to them! Let's just say they have not presented to the world a sacred history that portrays them in the most favorable light. Rather, they have preserved and transmitted their ancient history with Yahweh, their covenant God, and this is a history that cannot be explained in purely human terms. Pascal suggests that because the portrayal is not flattering, they must have preserved and transmitted their history because it is true and because it is of divine origin.

This peculiarity of the Jews and this authentication of the Christian faith are subtly portrayed as a proof for God's existence by Walker Percy in his national best-seller *The Thanatos Syndrome*. The story features Dr. Tom More, a psychiatrist who has been away serving several years in prison for selling prescription drugs to truckers on Interstate 12. When he returns home, he discovers that certain clinical changes have taken place among some of his former patients, and his wife is acting strange, as is his old friend Father Rinaldo Smith. Father Smith's hospice is not doing well, and the priest has gone to the top of a fire tower in the forest and won't come down. He is angry at the people below for living in wickedness and falling away from the Christian faith. (In many ways, Father Smith is reminiscent of early Christian ascetics, such as St. Simeon Stylites, who railed against the excesses of the institutional church.) When Tom visits Father Smith in his fire tower a hundred feet above the forest, the priest confides that he can no longer preach, because his words of faith do not "signify." Percy's point is that in the late-twentieth-century setting, words are deprived of their meaning. The only "sign" of God's presence that has not been "evacuated" of meaning is the Jews. To Father Smith—and to Percy—the Jews remain an abiding sign of God's presence in the world:

> "That's the only sign of God which has not been evacuated by an evacuator," he says, moving his shoulders. "What sign is that?" "Jews." "Jews?" "You got it, Doc." He sits, gives the azimuth a spin like a croupier who has raked in all the chips. "Got what?" "You see the point." "What's the point?" He leans close, eyes alight, "The Jews—cannot—be—subsumed." "Can't be what?" "Subsumed." "I see." "Since the Jews were the original chosen people of God, a tribe of people who are still here, they are a sign of God's presence which cannot be evacuated. Try to find a hole in that proof!" [15]

The Messianic Predictions

In addition to the special place that the Jews maintained in the authentication of the Christian message, Pascal also placed much weight on the Old Testament prophecies, especially those that centered on the coming of the Redeemer, the long-awaited Messiah. As remarkable as the events of the New Testament were in themselves, Pascal rightly recognized that these events were predicted hundreds of years before they came to pass. While contemporary biblical scholarship often embraces an *a priori* anti-supernaturalistic bias against the possibility of prophecy (which also serves to undermine the possibility of divine inspiration), Pascal rightly took a saner, more reasonable approach. He kept an open mind concerning the possibility of divine influence on the authors of the biblical documents. Furthermore, he saw prophecy as an important and credible basis for the truth of Christianity. In many passages of *Pensées,* he simply reproduced passages from the Old Testament prophets.[16]

Why exactly did Pascal believe that the biblical prophecies had anything to do with the credibility of the Christian faith? Basically, he posited that some can occasionally make a lucky guess about predicting the future, but when many predictions are later confirmed to be accurate, which is the case with the biblical testimony, one has a harder time simply ascribing it all to luck or chance. Sooner or later, reason suggests that such prophecies most likely should be accounted for by some special power or ability. Pascal insightfully suggested that if a single man had written a book that foretold of the time and manner of Jesus' coming and it proved true, it would carry a tremendous amount of credibility. But Pascal noted that there is much more credible evidence from a succession of men over a period of four thousand years "coming consistently and invariably one after the other, to foretell the same coming. . . . This is of quite a different order of importance." [17]

Even allowing for a somewhat exaggerated zeal on Pascal's part, the fact remains that for such a great number of prophecies to be uttered by so many people over such a vast time span and for them to find their convergence in the person and life of Jesus Christ demands a significant explanation.[18] And according to Pascal, the most weighty proofs for Jesus Christ were the prophecies, for it is only reasonable and logical to conclude that God was involved in the process and fulfillment of these messianic predictions. To Pascal, the fulfillment of prophecy gave greater credence for accepting Jesus Christ as the ultimate fulfillment of God's divine revelation.

The Existence of the Miraculous

Yet another mark of the authenticity of the Christian faith for Pascal was the miracles that Jesus Christ performed. We have some thirty-five recorded miracles in the four Gospel accounts, which served to validate His claims of deity. The apostle John even writes that He did "many other signs" (John 20:30). And while for centuries the miracles of Jesus have served as an important confirmation of His deity, they have come under greater scrutiny in recent years.

The modern world, taking some of its cues from the Scottish philosopher David Hume, has gone so far as to call miracles "impossible." It was Hume who defined a miracle as a violation of the laws of nature and who concluded that it is always more probable that a miracle story is false than that a law of nature has actually been violated.

While a defense of miracles is far beyond our purview, it is sufficient to say that from an objective basis Hume, as well as contemporary anti-supernaturalists, has come to an erroneous conclusion. Pascal and a host of serious Christian thinkers understand miracles to be not the violation of the laws of nature but rather events that *transcend* the normal laws of nature.

In one of his brilliant essays, "Religion and Science," Lewis shows the narrow-mindedness of those who ascribe to an anti-supernatural worldview. In it, he carries on an imaginary conversation (perhaps not so imaginary!) with a friend who believes that science is "inviolable," and has therefore proven that miracles are impossible. When Lewis suggests that "something outside" of nature could possibly alter the fixed laws, his friend replies:

> "Look here . . . Could this 'something outside' that you talk about make two and two five?"
>
> "Well, no," said I.
>
> "All right," said he. "Well, I think the laws of Nature are really like two and two making four. The idea of their being altered is as absurd as the idea of altering the laws of arithmetic."
>
> "Half a moment," said I. "Suppose you put sixpence into a drawer today, and sixpence into the same drawer tomorrow. Do the laws of arithmetic make it certain you'll find a shilling's worth there the day after?"
>
> "Of course," said he, "provided no one's been tampering with your drawer."
>
> "Ah, but that's the whole point," said I. "The laws of arithmetic can tell you what you'll find, with absolute certainty, *provided that* there's no interference. If a thief has been at the drawer of course you'll get a different result. But the thief won't have broken the laws of arithmetic — only the laws of England. Now, aren't the laws of Nature much in the same boat? Don't they all tell you what will happen *provided* there's no interference?" [19]

No, we cannot discount the reality of the miraculous unless we believe that interference from the outside is an impossibility, that no one has "been tampering with the drawer." The issue that Lewis was addressing with his friend was not science, which is limited to natural and observable phenomena, but a naturalistic "scientism," which embraces *a priori* that the miraculous is impossible.

Sometimes even the saints are surprised at God's interventions. Fred Craddock tells the amazing story about a pastor visiting a hospitalized old lady who was near death. "Mrs. Jones," he said, "before I leave, is there anything you would like me to say or do?" "I'd like you to pray for my healing, of course," she answered. He thought to himself, *Oh God*, but prayed, "Father, if it's Your will, please heal our dear sister, and if not, help everyone to adjust to the situation. Amen."

With that, Mrs. Jones sat up in bed, threw her feet over the side, stood up, and flexed her muscles. "This is unbelievable! I feel wonderful!" Then she headed down the hall toward the nurses' station shouting, "I think I'm well! I think I'm well!" But as the pastor left the hospital, he remarked to God, "Don't You ever do that to me again!"

If there is a God, then we cannot rule out the miraculous, even when it is least expected! For once one grants the existence of God, then miracles are at least possible. The issue of the veracity of the miraculous lies outside the realm of true science. While scientists generally agree that the universe had a beginning, what remains a mystery is what existed, if anything, before our universe came into being. The scientist's pursuit of the past ends in the moment of creation. In his book *God and the Astronomers*, scientist Robert Jastrow succinctly expresses the fact that for all the advancements of science, its attempt to answer the ultimate question of origins lies not in the realm of science, but of religion:

> For the scientist who has lived by his faith in the power of reason, the story ends like a bad dream. He has scaled the mountains of ignorance; he is about to conquer the highest peak: as he pulls himself over the final rock, he is greeted by a band of theologians who have been sitting there for centuries.[20]

For Pascal, a scientist as well as a committed Christian, the miracle stories of the New Testament provide a serious and compelling basis for the truth of Christianity. And as for the charge that there are many false stories of miracles, which tends to make the whole enterprise of the miraculous suspect, he argues convincingly that false accounts of the miraculous actually serve to authenticate the genuinely miraculous:

> It is the same with prophecies, miracles, divination by dreams, spells, etc., for, if none of this had ever been genuine, none of it would ever have been believed. Thus instead of concluding that there are no true miracles because there are so many false ones, we must on the contrary say that there certainly are true miracles since there are so many false ones, and that false ones are only there because true ones exist.[21]

Hence, Pascal believed that despite the reality of false stories of miracles, the New Testament presents a strong case for the authenticity of the miracles reported. Furthermore, the documents of the New Testament present the miracles of Jesus Christ as phenomena not anticipated or expected by His disciples. And when we consider the miraculous stories that comprise the New Testament's validation of Jesus' identity, certainly the most profound and extraordinary is the bodily resurrection of Jesus Christ from the dead.

The Grand Miracle

The account of Christ's resurrection is told in various ways and by different writers, but the central thread in every case is that it took His followers totally by surprise. They were as shaken as the rest of the world by this astounding event!

Over the centuries, various explanations for Jesus' empty tomb have been set forth in an attempt to deny the fact of the Resurrection as well as to explain away Christ's post-resurrection appearances. Yet the most reasonable conclusion is that He was bodily and miraculously raised from the dead and appeared to His disciples and other followers, albeit with a resurrection body.[22]

Even in our current day, the debate rages as to whether the physical, bodily resurrection of Jesus Christ has any true *relevance* to the Christian faith. From the vantage point of many liberal scholars, the bodily resurrection of Christ is an embarrassment to the modern, sophisticated mind. Marcus J. Borg, a leading theologian of the Jesus Seminar, a liberal think tank that disputes the imbedded supernaturalism of the Bible, revealingly shows how his understanding of the Resurrection and its importance to the Christian faith have changed:

> Easter is utterly central to Christianity. "God raised Jesus from the dead" is the foundational affirmation of the New Testament. . . . My understanding of Easter has changed over the course of my lifetime. Not just deepened (I trust), but changed. . . . As a child, I took it for granted that Easter meant that Jesus literally rose from the dead. I now see Easter very differently. For me, it is irrelevant whether or not the tomb was empty. Whether Easter involved something remarkable happening to the physical body of Jesus is irrelevant.[23]

Borg has no problem divorcing the bodily resurrection from the meaning and story of Christianity. To him, whether or not God has acted supernaturally some two thousand years ago is totally irrelevant to his faith. He cares little whether the events of the New Testament have any historical veracity. But when we turn to the straightforward testimony of the Scriptures, we see that the bodily resurrection of Christ in space-time history is essential to the Christian message of hope, salvation, and life beyond the grave. The apostle Paul declares to the Corinthian believers that if the historical, bodily resurrection is denied, then Christianity is little more than a lot of wishful thinking:

But if there is no resurrection of the dead, not even Christ has been raised; and if Christ has not been raised, then our preaching is vain, your faith also is vain. Moreover, we are even found to be false witnesses ... against God that He raised Christ, whom He did not raise, if in fact the dead are not raised. ... And if Christ has not been raised, your faith is worthless; you are still in your sins. Then those also who have fallen asleep in Christ have perished. If we have hoped in Christ in this life only, we are of all men most to be pitied. (1 Corinthians 15:13-15,17-19)

N.T. Wright, an Oxford don and former dean of Lichfield Cathedral in England, has co-authored with Borg *The Meaning of Jesus: Two Visions.* Wright, a noted theologian and historian, seems more intent on taking the biblical text seriously and provides us with a perspective on the Resurrection that better relates it to the truth claims of Christianity. Speaking of the evidence of the resurrection, Wright observes,

Turning to the gospels, we find all the puzzles of which readers have been aware for centuries. The stories of Easter morning in Matthew 28, Mark 16, Luke 24, and John 20 are notoriously difficult to harmonize. ... But, as many have pointed out, it is precisely this imprecision, coupled with the breathless quality of the narratives, that gives them not only their unique flavor but also their particular value. Despite the scorn of some, lawyers and judges have regularly declared that this is precisely the state of the evidence they find in a great many cases: this is what eyewitness testimony looks and sounds like. ... It is as though the writers are saying, all through, "I know this sounds ridiculous and extraordinary, but this is actually what happened." [24]

While Wright rightly believes that the historian cannot compel anyone to believe the biblical testimony, he does think that one can clearly set forth what the options are: either solve the historical puzzle by agreeing that Jesus' body was transformed into a new sort of life or disregard the data, coming up with provocative flights of fancy that create even greater problems. Wright believes that if we are honest with the data at hand, the most straightforward solution to this profound issue is that God has entered into space-time history to raise Jesus from the grave and has transformed His body into a new resurrection body.[25]

With many world religions one can remove the miraculous and the religion remains essentially intact, but with Christianity the miraculous, and specifically the resurrection of Jesus, is the cornerstone of its authenticity. A naturalistic Christianity, stripped of its miraculous element, essentially denigrates all that is specifically "Christian." Even irreligious H. L. Mencken realized the centrality of the Resurrection in Christianity when he made this startling admission: "There is no possibility whatsoever of reconciling science and theology, at least in Christendom. Either Jesus rose from the dead or he didn't. If he did, then Christianity becomes plausible; if he did not, it is sheer nonsense!"[26]

One thing we can say about Mencken is that he at least took the biblical testimony seriously! Whether or not someone chooses to follow an understanding of the biblical documents to their logical outcome, there is at least a sense of integrity when he or she takes them at face value—as reported historical narratives.

Understanding the critical historicity for the Christian faith had a major impact on Lewis in his own spiritual pilgrimage. He recounts in his autobiography, *Surprised by Joy: The Shape of My Early Life*, how the "Hound of Heaven" used a most unlikely person to penetrate his own spiritual apathy:

Early in 1926 the hardest boiled of all the atheists I ever knew sat in my room on the other side of the fire and remarked that the evidence for the historicity of the Gospels was really surprisingly good. "Rum thing," he went on. "All that stuff of Frazier's about the Dying God. Rum thing. It almost looks as if it had really happened once." To understand the shattering impact of it, you would need to know the man (who has certainly never shown any interest in Christianity). If he, the cynic of cynics, the toughest of the toughs, were not—as I would still have put it—"safe," where could I turn? Was there then no escape?[27]

To Lewis, Pascal, and many others down through the centuries, the historicity of the New Testament documents and their compelling veracity concerning the Resurrection have led many to make a personal commitment to Jesus Christ.[28]

Trustworthy Testimony of the Disciples

One of the key elements that has influenced many who have considered the circumstantial evidence for the Christian faith is the remarkably bold testimony of those first-century eyewitnesses, the apostles. These followers of Jesus, who were not expecting Jesus' resurrection (see Mark 16:1-4; John 20:19–21:14), were only a short time later fearlessly proclaiming that God had raised him from the dead. Further, they claimed that He had appeared to them over a period of weeks, had walked among them and eaten with them, and had given them instructions for the continuation of His work and mission in the world (see 1 Corinthians 15:1-8; John 20:10–21:14; Acts 1:1-8).

Pascal wanted people to understand that to reject the apostles' testimony is to be confronted with an unsatisfying dilemma. To suppose that their testimony is false, one would have to conclude that the apostles were either deceived or deceivers. While Jesus was with them He could sustain them, Pascal reasoned, but afterward, if He did not appear to them, who made them act?[29]

As to the first possibility—that these followers were themselves deceived—Pascal rightly reasoned that it would have been too difficult to imagine that a man has risen from the dead. Such speculation that these followers were somehow deluded and would have made such a glaring mistake is, in Pascal's thinking, too incredible to believe.

The other possibility—that the apostles' testimony was false—is also problematic. While spurious stories would have been hard work for the disciples to continually fabricate and a conspiracy of lies would have been even more difficult to manage, there is a more fundamental problem. Essentially, it is that the biblical authors were willing to lay down their lives for what they understood to have actually occurred with Jesus. More specifically, the biblical account and Christian tradition relate that all but one of the apostles died a martyr's death. Understandably, the fact that those who reported and wrote of these miraculous accounts were willing to be put to death for their belief had a profound impact on Pascal's thinking. His thoughts are summed up in a brief but powerful sentence: "I only believe histories whose witnesses are ready to be put to death." [30]

The Claims of Jesus Christ

Pascal further believed that when we take the New Testament portrayal of Jesus seriously, we discover His unique identity and status. While many think they are being gracious toward the Christian faith when they say that Jesus was a "great moral teacher," they are in fact dismissing the central Christian claim that He was God Incarnate, God in the flesh. Throughout the pages of the New Testament, Jesus presents Himself as standing in a unique relationship to God the Father, and His actions and words are easily construed as having divine prerogatives—He forgives sins, performs miracles, and makes some seemingly audacious statements, especially to Jewish ears, such as when He declares that "before Abraham was born, I am" (John 8:58).[31]

Reflecting the logic of Pascal's argument for the reliability of the apostolic witness, Lewis presented the claims of Jesus Christ in a manner that puts the critical issue of Jesus' identity at the center-piece of Christianity's claims. Wearied by his fellow intellectuals at Oxford University who referred to Jesus as a great moral teacher but who cavalierly dismissed Christianity's claim that He was truly God Incarnate, Lewis presented the claims of Jesus Christ in his famous "trilemma" argument.

> I am trying here to prevent anyone saying the really foolish thing that people often say about Him: "I'm ready to accept Jesus as a great moral teacher, but I don't accept His claim to be God." That is the one thing we must not say. A man who was merely a man and said the sort of things Jesus said would not be a great moral teacher. He would either be a lunatic— on a level with the man who says he is a poached egg—or else he would be the Devil of Hell. You must make your choice. Either this man was, and is, the Son of God: or else a madman or something worse. You can shut Him up for a fool, you can spit at Him and kill Him as a demon; or you can fall at His feet and call Him Lord and God. But let us not come with any patronizing nonsense about His being a great human teacher. He has not left that open to us. He did not intend to.[32]

In some of his most memorable lines ever, Lewis shows how Jesus' words and deeds do not allow us to accept Him simply as a great moral teacher. If He was not God and knew He was not, yet presented Himself as such, then He was a liar and deceiver of the worst sort. Yet this is hardly plausible, seeing that Jesus Christ is acknowledged as one of the greatest moral teachers the world has ever known.

A second possibility, Lewis reasons, is based on the assumption that Christ sincerely believed this falsehood that He was God but was mistaken in His own identity. Yet such a portrayal of Jesus is grossly out of character with the powerful picture that we have of Him in the New Testament, where He is described serving His own disciples, ministering to the downtrodden, and teaching profound truths about human happiness and joy, as in the Sermon on the Mount.

Thus the conclusion that Lewis was driven to, and which has led many people since to embrace the Christian faith, is that Jesus was indeed the Messiah, the Lord, the Savior of the world.

Lewis powerfully portrayed this trilemma argument about Jesus Christ in the first of his *Chronicles of Narnia*, titled *The Lion, the Witch and the Wardrobe.* In one of the most revealing scenes of the book, the veracity of Jesus' testimony is marvelously portrayed when Lucy, having gone through the enchanted wardrobe and discovered the magical country of Narnia, is confronted by her unbelieving siblings. Although her brother Edmund has also discovered Narnia by going through the wardrobe, he denies it to Peter and Susan, saying that he and Lucy were only "pretending" about another country in the wardrobe. While Peter and Susan have always found Lucy to be more truthful and reliable than Edmund in the past, Lucy's talk of enchanted woods and the Faun are simply too much for the older siblings to believe. So Peter, worried that Lucy is either going mad or turning into a frightful liar, decides to bring the whole matter before the Professor. After he listens attentively to their story, the Professor challenges their conclusion that either Lucy is lying about her discovery of Narnia or something is wrong with her. He wants them to use their critical faculties:

> "Logic!" said the Professor half to himself. "Why don't they teach logic at these schools? There are only three possibilities. Either your sister is telling lies, or she is mad, or she is telling the truth. You know she doesn't tell lies and it is obvious that she is not mad. For the moment then and unless any further evidence turns up, we must assume that she's telling the truth." [33]

Just as Lucy has been found to be reliable in her life and testimony in the past, and should not be discredited for what seemed like a highly improbable experience in the magical world of Narnia, so also, Lewis suggests, we cannot ignore the claims of Jesus Christ about Himself. As Lucy had been found trustworthy in the past and was certainly not mad, so also Jesus Christ confronts each person with His truth claims of deity. And as Lewis earlier stated, He has left us no other option but to make a personal decision as to whether Jesus Christ is God Incarnate or not.[34]

Why We Have Certainty for the Christian Hope

In this chapter, we have observed that, despite the deep and abiding belief in Heaven over the course of history, for the past several centuries this belief in Christian orthodoxy has largely eroded. Today, amidst postmodernist thinking, we are told that there are no absolute truths; indeed, there is a lack of certainty about virtually everything in life, not only about God but also about our very existence.

But despite this age of uncertainty in which we live, we have attempted to demonstrate that faith in Christianity, while not provable in a scientific sense, is nevertheless reasonable and credible. We have looked at some of the major signposts—or marks of the truth—that suggest that the Christian faith and its implicit promise of Heaven are not only plausible but also true.

These marks of the truth, rigorously set forth by Pascal, include the following: the biblical explanation for mankind's greatness and wretchedness; the Christian Scriptures being the definitive revelation of God to mankind; the preservation of the Jewish people as a divine sign; the messianic prophecies that found their fulfillment in Jesus Christ; the miracles performed by Christ in validation of His claims of deity; the "grand miracle," Christ's bodily resurrection; the credible testimony of the disciples; and Jesus Christ's own claims to deity.

While all of these signposts of the truth are worthy of consideration, the Resurrection stands as the centerpiece of the Christian's hope of Heaven. To take away the centrality of the Resurrection, the hope of Easter, is in effect to reduce Christianity to just another religion. As we observed earlier, if one removes the miraculous from Christianity, making it simply a naturalistic religion, one takes away that which makes Christianity distinctly "Christian," particularly its promise of bodily resurrection beyond the grave.

The centrality of Christ's bodily resurrection to the Christian faith is powerfully portrayed from a seemingly unlikely source, the American novelist John Updike. In his poem "Seven Stanzas at Easter," Updike powerfully demonstrates that apart from the real, bodily resurrection of Jesus Christ, the Christian church has no true message of hope for a life beyond this futile existence. No, Updike muses, let us not "mock God with metaphor," or make the event simply a "parable," but let us undertand the centrality of the Resurrection in the Christian hope of Heaven.

"Make no mistake," wrote Updike, for if Jesus' resurrection was not bodily, with "the molecules reknit," then Christianity has no legitimate basis — "the Church will fall." [35]

CHAPTER 13

THE CHOICE OF HEAVEN

In Heaven
The police will be British
The cooks will be French
The mechanics will be German
The social directors will be Italian
And the Swiss will run it.

In Hell
The police will be German
The cooks will be British
The mechanics will be French
The social directors will be Swiss
And the Italians will run it.

—Author unknown

If I cannot smoke cigars in Heaven, I shall not go.
—Mark Twain

The one principle of Hell is—"I am my own!"
—George MacDonald

AS GLORIOUS AS THE PROMISE OF HEAVEN IS FOR THE SAINT, THERE IS NO avoiding the perplexing subject of whether *everyone* in fact gets to Heaven. While many religions of the world may not take seriously the idea of divine judgment, the warning passages in the Scriptures about the reality of Hell are sobering. Indeed, this is the most difficult of all theological issues in Christendom.

You will recall T. S. Eliot's observation, "I had far rather walk, as I do, in daily terror of eternity, than feel that this was only a children's game in which all the contestants would get equally worthless prizes in the end." Eliot's profound statement suggests that there is a seriousness to this life and that it is possible to win as well as to lose. It may seem odd to include a chapter on judgment—or Hell—in a book about Heaven. Yet if life is more than a "children's game," we would be irresponsible not to deal with it.

The choice one makes as to whether or not God exists and whether He has revealed Himself through Jesus Christ is the greatest "wager" any mortal will ever face. From a Christian worldview, the decision one makes about Jesus Christ in this life has eternal consequences for the life to come.

A host of questions come to mind when we consider the subject of Hell: Does the Bible really teach that there is a Hell? How could a good and loving God even *allow* people to end up in Hell? Does this not impugn His goodness? Do people actually choose to go to Heaven? And if there is a Hell, what is its nature, anyway? Is the torment and pain of Hell physical or spiritual? Does the punishment of Hell last forever? Do humans get another chance to go to Heaven after death?

In this chapter we will consider four facets of the doctrine of Hell. We will first consider the great disdain for the doctrine of Hell. Second, we will consider three of the common objections to Hell. Third, we will consider what might be called the necessity of Hell, or why it is reasonable to believe in the doctrine. And fourth, we will speculate as to the nature of Hell, or what it might be like.

The Disdain for the Doctrine of Hell

While the doctrine of Hell has been a theological staple of orthodox Christianity since its inception, it has fallen on hard times. In many ways, the traditional, orthodox belief in Hell is out of step with modern culture. Richard Bauckham summarizes this flight from the orthodox belief in Hell:

> Until the nineteenth century almost all Christian theologians taught the reality of eternal torment in hell. . . . Since 1800 this situation has entirely changed, and no traditional Christian doctrine has been so widely abandoned as that of eternal punishment. . . . Among the less conservative, universal salvation either as hope or as dogma, is now so widely accepted that many theologians assume it virtually without argument.[1]

What has led to this disdain for Hell? Why has modernity lost the fear of divine judgment? A number of strong psychological reasons for the abandonment of Hell exist in popular culture. One of these is the deeply cherished belief in progress, making Hell an antiquated doctrine. The Christian frequently hears the charge, "Are you living in the twenty-first century or the Dark Ages?"

Another reason is that we as a culture have lost a sense of moral absolutes. No longer does our society believe in absolute right and wrong, which has resulted in subjectivity about everything. Further, we as a culture have epitomized love and toleration as the noblest qualities of life and have consequently neglected the needful attributes of justice and truth. While it is true that justice without love is hardness of heart, it is equally true that love without justice is softness of head.

Fundamentally, our society has lost its sense of a transcendent, supernatural worldview, jettisoning God from our collective consciousness. And when you lose God, you not only lose Heaven, but Hell also. It has been relegated to the dark recesses of the modern, supposedly sophisticated mind.

The story is told of two men who lived in the same small town many years ago; each had the same last name and lived in the same neighborhood. One of the men was a clergyman, the other a businessman. The clergyman died; his family and friends had a wonderful memorial for him; and he was laid to rest. About that same time, the businessman was on a trip from the Midwest to California. He sent a telegram to his wife to let her know that he had arrived safely. But there was a terrible mistake: the telegram went to the clergyman's wife instead. It read, "Arrived safely. Heat here is terrific!"

Have you ever wondered why so many jokes deal with the afterlife? It may very well underscore the fact that we seek to trivialize the most important issues we face. And if we are discerning observers of our culture, we will note that Hell, like Heaven, has been greatly trivialized in our day.

Indeed, the doctrine has become so trivialized that it has even lost its force as a curse. We regularly hear uttered the casual remark, "Go to Hell!" Or when we are surprised and amazed, we say, "The hell it is!" Even the exclamation "dammit!" is an utterance that we may hear when someone stubs a toe or smashes a finger, but it is certainly not intended as an eternal sentence! Better to trivialize, ridicule, and yes, even joke about Hell than to reflect seriously upon it. In many ways we've refashioned Hell to meet our contemporary attitude about the afterlife. Now it refers to nothing more than when something "bad" happens in our earthly existence. In essence, the doctrine of Hell has gotten a makeover.

Interestingly, the reality of Hell and why people go there (if they go there) is undergoing tremendous transformation in our religious culture. Throughout Catholicism as well as Protestantism, there is a growing shift away from seeing Hell as genuine damnation or eternal torment, to something a bit more palatable to contemporary sensibilities. Belief in Hell has become about as politically incorrect a concept as one can find. Aside from Christian evangelicals, who continue to stand firm, many Christian denominations (as well as other religions) have become "soft" on judgment. They believe that God is too good to allow for Hell.

And if He is considered too good to allow for Hell, a more fundamental question arises, Does He really have a *right* to judge the human race? Herman Melville, author of *Moby Dick*, was never comfortable with the God of Christianity. He sensed that humanity had transcended its need for God and particularly the idea of God's righteous judgment upon the affairs of humanity. We cannot condemn our fellow man, Melville reasoned, because God Himself is on trial. Melville reveals his beliefs through the profound statement of Captain Ahab, who declares in *Moby Dick:* "Where do murderers go, man! Who's to doom, when the judge himself is dragged to the bar?" [2] Melville's words are reminiscent of C. S. Lewis's contention that God is now on trial before the tribunal of man. He is now "in the dock," to use Lewis's phrase, and found wanting before the modern world.

Writing in *USA Today*, Gerald L. Zelizer, a rabbi of a Conservative congregation, suggests three reasons for organized religions' "refashioning" of Hell. [3] First, we are religious consumers who sense a greater need for hope, peace, and love than to be saved from Hell. Second, the American psyche makes it difficult to embrace any idea of judgment, because it is our perceived birthright to be happy, and we will go so far as to even redesign Hell with a cheerful blueprint in mind! And third, there is ambiguity or lack of consensus within Christianity regarding the meaning of New Testament passages where none other that Jesus warns evildoers of the actual danger that they will be cast "into the fiery hell" (Matthew 5:22; see also Mark 9:43-48; Luke 12:5).

Ironically, at a time when many religions and Christian denominations are watering down the idea of judgment and wrath, much of our popular culture seems almost obsessed with Hell and its accompanying torment. In the video game *Avenging Angel*, players are escorted through hellish visions of throbbing, intestine-like caves, where demons rip the flesh of the damned and cries of eternal suffering echo throughout. In the film *What Dreams May Come* starring Robin Williams, moviegoers witness a ghoulish Hell that is populated with a virtual sea of heads, displaying the damned up to their necks in mud. On the graphic covers of comic books, young people encounter such titles as *Hell Hound* and *Lord of the Pit.*

Even though popular culture seems to be fascinated with Hell and judgment, it seems that fire and brimstone are out of fashion and the netherworld no longer instills fear and trepidation. Jonathan Edwards, the eighteenth-century Puritan preacher, struck fear into the hearts of his audience when he admonished them, "The pit is prepared, the fire is made ready, the furnace is now hot, ready to receive you. The flames do now rage and glow. . . . O sinner! Consider the fearful danger you are in!" [4]

To Edwards and his spiritual heirs, the eternal stakes were frightfully obvious: There is a Hell to shun and Heaven to gain. In Edwards' day, just as Heaven held great anticipation for the saint (to be in the presence of God along with other saints for eternity), so Hell and its flaming torments were *real.* And while the threat of Hell served as a powerful incentive to his fellow New Englanders, Edwards and his ilk would hardly recognize the Hell of today. Writing about the current notion of Hell, Jeffery L. Sheler in *U. S. News & World Report* observes,

> After decades of near obscurity, the netherworld has taken on a new image: more of a deep funk than a pit of fire. While the traditional infernal imagery still attracts a following, modern visions of eternal perdition as a particularly unpleasant solitary confinement are beginning to emerge, suggesting that hell may not be so hot after all. [5]

Three Common Objections to the Doctrine of Hell

From Sheler's observation it is apparent that the modern world, with its claim for enlightenment and sophistication, finds the orthodox

Christian doctrine of Hell repugnant. Let's now look at three common objections marshaled against the Christian belief in Hell: the objection to the narrowness of Christianity; the objection to the exclusivity of Christianity; and the objection to Hell based upon the premise that it impugns the goodness of God.

Is Christianity Really Narrow?

One of the most common arguments against the doctrine of Hell is generally worded something like this: "You're telling me that 75 percent of the world is nonChristian and that they are going to Hell simply because they do not worship Jesus?" Certainly one of the greatest factors influencing our thinking on this doctrine is the religious pluralism that has become the accepted norm of our day. The smuggled-in assumption is "Are not all religions essentially the same?" Religious pluralism has radically affected our thinking about Heaven as well as Hell.

"Toleration," G. K. Chesterton once mused, "is the virtue of people who do not believe in anything." Perhaps never has a statement been so true as in our modern day, not only when we talk about Hell but when we talk about other Christian doctrines as well. In a day when absolute truths are relegated to a bygone era, toleration of *all* viewpoints is extolled as the epitome of virtue.

This expression of religious pluralism was brilliantly illustrated in a *Time* magazine essay entitled "Will It Be Coffee, Tea, or He?" Writer Charles Krauthammer wrote of an experience he had in a local hospital that gives new meaning to how we perceive religious faith:

> As I checked in for an outpatient test at a local hospital last week, the admissions lady asked for the usual name, rank, serial number, insurance and ailment. Then she inquired, "What is your religious preference?" I was tempted to say, "I think Buddhism is the coolest of all, but I happen to be Jewish." My

second impulse was to repeat what Jonah said when asked by the shipmates of his foundering skiff to identify himself: I am a Hebrew, ma'am. And I fear the Lord, the God of Heaven, who made the sea and the dry land." But that would surely have got me sent to psychiatry rather than X-ray. So I desisted. In ancient times, they asked, "Who is your God?" A generation ago, they asked your religion. Today your creed is a preference. Preference? "I take my coffee black, my wine red, my sex straight and my shirts lightly starched. Oh yes, and put me down for Islam." [6]

Whatever we may glean from Krauthammer's experience, it is apparent that this is not our Father's world! We find ourselves in a fundamentally different religious environment from what our parents—and certainly our grandparents—encountered. And while the idea of a cornucopia of human religiosity is quite old, the world we live in today is drastically different. With virtually tens of millions of foreign-born people immigrating to America, our nation is becoming the adopted home of the entire world. Islam may well replace Judaism as America's second-largest religion in the coming years, and Buddhist and Hindu temples dot the landscapes not only of New York and Chicago, but increasingly of Middle America. This American religious hodgepodge was noted in an article for the *Wall Street Journal* entitled "The Age of Divine Disunity":

> If America had always been a melting pot, these days its religious practices have become a spiritual hash. Blending or braiding the beliefs of different spiritual traditions has become so rampant in America that the Dalai Lama has called the country "the spiritual supermarket." Jews flirt with Hinduism, Catholics study Taoism, and Methodists discuss whether to make the Passover seder an official act of worship. . . . The melding of Judaism with Buddhism has

become so commonplace that marketers who sell spiritual books, videotapes and lecture series have a name for it: "JewBu."[7]

As a consequence of this religious potpourri that characterizes America, many theologians and philosophers have encouraged non-judgmental attitudes toward other religions, precluding that any one religious faith could be *superior* to another. And if no one religious faith can be superior to another, then how much less the Christian doctrine that has historically taught that all will be lost apart from Jesus Christ.

In our day, any absolute claim to truth is met with disdain and considered idolatrous and illusory. And while choice is deemed good in and of itself, the only choice that cannot be tolerated is one that holds some beliefs to be true but others false. The natural implication of this thinking is that many now insist that "right action" (ethics, orthopraxy) is the criterion of true religion, whereas "right doctrine" (belief, orthodoxy) is merely divisive. Consequently, followers of other religions are viewed as possible partners in carrying out one's ethical goodwill, rather than as lost people who need to be saved.[8]

Not surprisingly, the religious plurality that characterizes the American landscape has tremendously undermined the traditional, orthodox beliefs of Christianity, including the doctrine of Hell. Os Guinness, in his brilliant book *The Gravedigger File,* refers to this religious pluralization as "The Smorgasbord Factor." He describes this cultural phenomenon as "the process by which the number of options in the private sphere of modern society rapidly multiplies at all levels, especially at the level of world views, faiths and ideologies."[9] Mindful of H. L. Mencken's observation that "nobody ever went broke underestimating the taste of the American people," Guinness argues that just as Americans love the plethora of fast-food options in our culture, so also this pluralization in the religious sphere influences how people perceive Christianity and other religions.

Another issue surrounding pluralism is that of religious identity and geography. In other words, just as the people in India are Hindu, those of Kuwait primarily Muslim, and those in Japan Shinto, are we not Christians simply because we were born and raised in America, where the Christian faith has dominated? Furthermore, the fact that the vast majority of people who have ever lived and are living today are not Christian gives us reason to reflect soberly on the narrowness of Christianity. Does it truly make sense, then, to believe that God wants to save people *only* through Christ?[10] Put succinctly, this question arises: Are all worshipers of world religions outside of Christianity condemned by God to Hell?

In recent years, as evangelical theologians have felt the brunt of religious pluralism alongside the narrow truth claims of Christianity, an honest attempt has been made to come to grips with the eternal destiny of those outside the Christian faith. Theologian and author Clark Pinnock believes that we should embrace an optimism concerning the salvation of the unevangelized and those who stand outside the Christian faith—what he calls a "wideness in God's mercy."

> The foundation of my theology of religions is a belief in the unbounded generosity of God revealed in Jesus Christ. This topic, like many others, comes down to the question of God. Who or what is God and what does he want or intend? Is he the kind of God who would be capable of sitting by while large numbers perish, or the kind to seek them out patiently and tirelessly? Does God take pleasure and actually get glory from the damnation of sinners as some traditions maintain, or is God appalled and saddened by this prospect? My reading of the gospel of Jesus Christ . . . causes me to celebrate the wideness in God's mercy and a boundlessness in his generosity towards humanity as a whole.[11]

While Pinnock and others are to be commended for their attempts to reconcile the idea of God being holy and loving in the light of the plurality of world religions, more often than not (at least in this writer's opinion), they end up accentuating the benevolence of God to the detriment of His holiness and righteousness. While an apologetic discourse dealing with the truth claims of Christianity and its implicit exclusiveness is beyond the scope of this chapter, it is important for us to realize that the Christian position is not only narrow, but also claims to be a true representation of the way things really are.

Is Christianity Really Exclusive?

One of the greatest obstacles evangelical Christians face when dealing with others is the claim of exclusivity. Many of those on the periphery of Christianity and largely ignorant of the Bible's teaching believe that Christianity is inclusive, tolerant of other world religions. Yet a broad and tolerant interpretation of the Christian faith is at odds with the biblical testimony. More specifically, such a perspective of Christianity is contrary to the claims of Jesus Christ and His disciples. According to the Bible, the idea of exclusivity and the belief that those without Christ are lost originate with none other than Jesus Himself. Consider the following words of Christ and His apostle Peter, which make a claim for His deity. Likewise, they clearly eliminate "different" ways to God other than Himself:[12]

> "I said therefore to you, that you shall die in your sins; for unless you believe that I am He, you shall die in your sins." (John 8:24)

> Jesus said to them, "Truly, truly, I say to you, before Abraham was born, I am." (John 8:58)

> Jesus said to him, "I am the way, and the truth, and the life; no one comes to the Father, but through Me." (John 14:6)

And there is salvation in no one else; for there is no other name under heaven that has been given among men, by which we must be saved. (Acts 4:12)

While one may vehemently disagree with the words and testimony of Jesus and His disciples, the one thing we must understand is that they claimed that He is the exclusive way to God. And when once we begin to grasp the exclusive nature of Christianity, it is at this point in our toleration-crazed culture when objections arise as to its validity.[13]

Some of the questions deal with the issues of sincerity of belief as well as the relativity of truth. People raise the question, "Are you telling me that all of the *sincere* people who are seeking God in other religions and in their own way outside of Christ are wrong?" Or, "Could people who are so *sincere* and passionate about their beliefs really be wrong?" The mistaken notion in such thinking is that *sincerity* has something to do with the truth of a religion. In fact, sincerity, or the lack thereof, has nothing to do with determining truth.

Not only do people feel strongly about the sincerity of other people's religious beliefs, they also are enamored with the mindset that considers anything that is narrow or exclusive to be inherently *wrong*. As Chesterton was quoted earlier in this chapter, "Toleration is the virtue of people who do not believe in anything." But the truth of the matter is that whether a religious viewpoint is narrow or not does not determine its veracity. If anything, truth, by definition, tends to be narrow and is always intolerant of error. As someone has said, while toleration in relationships is a virtue, toleration when it comes to truth is nothing but a travesty. Consequently, we may be sincere in our beliefs but sincerely right or wrong. And we may believe a certain religious position that happens to be narrow, but the narrowness does not make it inherently wrong.

While the world may chide Christians who embrace a narrow

view of salvation, in reality the Christian faith is not the only narrow religion of the world. If one examines, for instance, the five major religions of the world (Hinduism, Buddhism, Judaism, Islam, and Christianity), one will soon discover that they all make quite *different* truth claims. How each of these major religions explains such critical issues as who God is, mankind's eternal destiny, and how one obtains salvation are so different that it is impossible to declare that they are all essentially the same.

Let's consider the issue of God. While the Muslim and Jew are strong unitarians, the Hindu waxes philosophical as a monist or pantheist (all is one, God is in all) whose god is impersonal and without any knowable attributes. And while Buddhism and Hinduism have many popular sects that are largely polytheistic and pantheistic, Christianity boldly proclaims that there is only one true God, but that in the unity of the Godhead there are three coequal and eternal Persons: the Father, the Son, and the Holy Spirit.

With regard to mankind's destiny after death, the religions of the world again have quite divergent beliefs. While Muslims believe they will experience an eternal bliss of sensual pleasures and delights with Allah, Hindus believe that their future destiny can best be described as "Atman is Brahman"; they will become one with the impersonal supreme being, losing all personal identity. Buddhists also espouse the belief that individuals lose personal consciousness at death and reach their earthly aspiration to nirvana, a state of total nothingness. And while Jews have a multitude of beliefs about the afterlife, Christians believe they will retain their own individuality—though transformed—and spend eternity in Heaven in deepening communion with God and other believers.

When it comes to how the individual person achieves this destiny—or salvation—the religions of the world again differ greatly. Generally speaking, all the major religions except Christianity believe that a person's individual efforts achieve that longed-for destiny. While the Muslim devotes his or her life to performing the duties of the Five Pillars of Faith and believes the five doctrines of Islam, the Buddhist seeks liberation from repetitive reincarnations by adhering to the Four Noble Truths and the Eightfold Path. Similarly, the Hindu believes the desired state of oneness with Brahman is through multiple reincarnations, while the Jew rests upon his or her own moral life to gain God's salvation.

In contrast to all the world religions, Christianity declares that a person enters Heaven based upon his or her acceptance of Jesus Christ's substitutionary payment on the cross for his or her own sin. The apostle Paul underscores this Christian truth in his letter to the Ephesians: "For by grace you have been saved through faith; and that not of yourselves, it is the gift of God; not as a result of works, that no one should boast" (Ephesians 2:8-9). Similarly, he declares in his letter to the Galatians: "I do not nullify the grace of God; for if righteousness comes through the Law, then Christ died needlessly" (Galatians 2:21). According to Christianity, salvation is a "free gift" and cannot be earned by good works or living a good life. As the British writer Evelyn Underhill once declared, "Christianity says not, 'Do this!' but rather 'This has been done!'"

Therefore, when people say "all religions are essentially the same," perhaps the kindest remark a Christian can make is that they simply haven't done their homework. The real question to consider is not which religion is *not* narrow (because they are all narrow), but which one is true. The challenge before the Christian is to help the nonChristian audience realize that he or she is recommending the Christian faith not because it is a nice doctrine or may make them good, but because it is *true*. In his essay "Christian Apologetics," Lewis comments,

> One of the great difficulties is to keep before the audience's mind the question of Truth. They always think you are recommending Christianity not because it is *true* but because it is *good*. And in the discussion they will at every moment try

to escape from the issue "True — or False" into stuff about a good society, or morals. . . . One must keep on pointing out that Christianity is a statement which, if false, is of *no* importance, and if true, of infinite importance. The one thing it cannot be is moderately important.[14]

While Lewis rightly suggests in *Mere Christianity* that Christians need not believe that all other religions are wrong "all through" when they do differ from Christianity, he did strongly believe that Christians need to realize that Christianity is right and other religions are wrong. In his words, "Christianity is a fighting religion."[15]

We see, then, that Christianity is not the only narrow religion of the world, but that all the religions of the world make specific truth claims that are by definition equally exclusivistic. Consequently, as Lewis suggests, our challenge is to determine not which religion is not narrow, but which one is true.[16]

Doesn't Hell Impugn the Goodness of God?

Once people begin to grasp the facts that truth by definition tends to be narrow and that Christianity makes exclusivistic claims, it is only natural that the objection to the doctrine of Hell based on the benevolence or goodness of God should arise. To many, a belief in Hell is a blemish to be covered up by the cosmetic of divine love. Yet in reality, the objection is an attempt to protect the benevolent character of God, because it would be hard to worship a God who appears to be an unjust Judge. That God's redemptive love can coexist with the doctrine of Hell is surely the greatest objection to be encountered.

Often the objection sounds something like this: "You say that you believe in a God of love? Well it certainly seems to me that if God really does love people, He could somehow, some way, keep people out of Hell!" If God is infinitely good and infinitely powerful, the argument goes on, then how could He allow His creatures to suffer in Hell?

What these objectors are really saying is that if God is truly loving then *everyone* will get to Heaven, none will be lost. Yet it is important to remember that, according to the Scriptures, God's original, unspoiled creation did *not* include evil, suffering, or the reality of Hell. The first two chapters of Genesis teach that our ancestors in the Garden, Adam and Eve, were created in perfection and enjoyed a Utopian environment centered upon worship of and service to God. This original, unfallen state was free of the misery and travail that we experience.

Furthermore, Adam and Eve were given *genuine* free choice to love or reject the God who had created them for fellowship, or relationship, with Himself. Why, we may ask, did God take such a big gamble? What was the payoff that made such a momentous decision worthwhile? It seems that in God's design, the ability to freely choose or reject is essential, for only when true choice is an option can true love and a significant relationship be experienced. Thus when God created humans with a free will, He fashioned creatures who could go either right or wrong. As Lewis wrote,

> Free will, though it makes evil possible, is also the only thing that makes possible any love or goodness or joy worth having. A world of automata—of creatures that worked like machines—would hardly be worth creating. . . . Of course God knew what would happen if they used their freedom the wrong way: apparently He thought it worth the risk.[17]

Of course, we know the rest of the story—the abuse of this free will. It is the story of the Fall, what Milton referred to as man's "foul revolt." It is the sad account of the human race spurning God, choosing to go its own way rather than to obey and follow Him. And it naturally follows that because the first human family and all humans since have chosen to go our own way (the Bible refers to this human propensity as "sin"), significant and devastating consequences have resulted.

Indeed, the entire human race is tainted with such a waywardness and alienation from God (see Psalm 14:1-3; Romans 3:9-18).

In reality, the dilemma of how a good and loving God could allow Hell is the same problem as that of evil on the earth. If God is infinitely powerful and infinitely good, how can there be evil? For if He is infinitely good, He wills only the good; and if He is infinitely powerful, He can perform all that He wills. We say, can He not and should He not override the consequences of our choice to reject Him? Fundamentally, the answer to both problems is free will.

When we come to realize that mankind has true free will, we see that it, as all other gifts, is two-edged. In a way, we might even be so bold as to say that with Hell, we see the true love of God, in that God honors mankind with dignity as a moral agent who can either choose or reject His offer of forgiveness and eternal life. As much as we would like to believe that God might intervene to remove mankind's rebellion—and all would be saved—it would in effect violate the dignity of mankind. Lewis observes in *The Problem of Pain,*

> If a game is played, it must be possible to lose it. If the happiness of a creature lies in self-surrender, no one can make that surrender but himself (though many can help him to make it) and he may refuse. I would pay any price to be able to say truthfully "All will be saved." But my reason retorts, "Without their will, or with it?" If I say "Without their will" I at once perceive a contradiction; how can the supreme voluntary act of self-surrender be involuntary? If I say "With their will," my reason replies "How if they *will not* give in?" [18]

Having looked at the general disdain for the doctrine of Hell in our contemporary culture as well as at three of the most common objections, let us now turn our attention to the necessity for belief in the doctrine.

The Necessity of Hell

Of all the doctrines in Christianity, Hell is undoubtedly the most despised by our culture, the most burdensome to believe, the most difficult to defend, and probably one of the first to be dismissed. But as much as we would prefer to ignore the doctrine, for the Christian who is more concerned with what is true than with what he or she would simply like to be true, the subject must be addressed with sensitive objectivity. Let's consider some of the key reasons for believing in the doctrine of Hell: the teaching of Christ and the church; God's honoring of free will; Hell as a necessary theological complement to Heaven; and lastly, the idea that life is more than a "children's game," but rather a sacred drama where it is truly possible to win or lose.

The Teaching of Christ and the Church

Arguably the strongest reason, particularly for the Christian, to believe in Hell is the fact that Jesus Christ and the church have taught the doctrine frequently and without ambiguity. Try as we may to attempt to water down this hard doctrine, we cannot evade its centrality in the Christian worldview. Hell is unavoidable to the Christian who accepts the authority of the Christian revelation. Lewis rightly expresses this sentiment: "There is no doctrine which I would more willingly remove from Christianity than this, if it lay in my power. But it has the full support of Scripture and, specially, of our Lord's own words; it has always been held by Christendom; and it has the support of reason." [19]

What Lewis is suggesting in this powerful statement is that however undesirable and distasteful we may find the doctrine, to disbelieve in Hell is to suggest that both the Scriptures and the church lie and that Jesus Himself was a liar, for Christ believed in Hell and was far more forthright and adamant about its reality than anyone else in the Scriptures. Even Jesus' most popular and loving saying talks indirectly about Hell: "For God so loved the world, that

He gave His only begotten Son, that whoever believes in Him should not perish, but have eternal life" (John 3:16). Furthermore, Jesus speaks of Hell five times in His beloved Sermon on the Mount. If there is no Hell, or even if only a small number of people find themselves in Hell[20] (so that there is very little danger of Hell for the ordinary person), then Jesus' words are intended to merely give us a good scare—and He is not such a wonderful teacher after all!

Hence, to question the reality of Hell is tantamount to questioning the integrity of Jesus Christ as well as the entire Christian faith. In exploring the doctrine, it is good to remember Lewis's trilemma argument that was considered earlier: either Jesus was a liar, a lunatic, or the very Lord God of the universe whose words and testimony can be trusted. And if His words about Heaven can be trusted, certainly what He has said about Hell should not be taken lightly either.

God's Honoring of Free Will

Although God desires all to be saved,[21] He honors mankind with dignity as a moral agent who can choose to accept or reject His offer of forgiveness and eternal life. But a problematic question arises: Why would anyone *choose* to go to Hell if he or she could do otherwise, if it were really "up to him or her" to decide? The idea seems absurd that anyone would seriously make such a choice to spend eternity separated from God in Hell. What are we to make of this important objection?

While this is a serious concern and the choice of Hell over God would seem to be a logical absurdity, such choices have been powerfully illustrated in classic literature, which often portrays the human struggle with good and evil. One such example is presented in Graham Greene's tragic but powerful novel *The Heart of the Matter*. Greene's novel is the moving tale of Scobie, a police officer in a flyblown West African colony, who lives his life with the utmost personal integrity in contrast to the corruption that surrounds him. But when he is passed over for a promotion to be commissioner, he is forced to borrow money from an unscrupulous Syrian trader to send his wife, Louise, on holiday. She is terribly disappointed that he did not get the promotion and has become increasingly discontented with living in West Africa.

When Louise leaves Scobie, a number of small compromises vividly lead to the eventual demise of his character. He becomes involved in a sexual affair and is guilty of complicity in the murder of his servant, of whom he had become wrongfully suspicious. When Louise later returns, his life becomes even more complicated as he attempts to please both wife and mistress. As his conscience is assaulted by his immoral behavior and his love for God, Scobie sees only one way out of the shambles he has created. He chooses to take his own life.

While much of Greene's novel is worthy of theological and philosophical reflection,[22] for our concern a scene toward the end of the book reveals much about the choices we make in life. Scobie has visited his mistress, Helen, after going to Confession and then to Mass. At Confession, he refuses to promise the priest that he will stop seeing Helen. The next day, while attending Mass without absolution, he comes to the conclusion that he is damned. When he subsequently visits Helen, he reveals his hopelessness.

"I've given up hope," he said.

"What do you mean?"

"I've given up the future. I've damned myself."

"Don't be so melodramatic," she said. "I don't know what you are talking about. Anyway, you've just told me about the future — the Commissionership."

"I mean the real future — the future that goes on."

She said, "If there's one thing I hate it's your Catholicism. I suppose it comes of having a pious wife. It's so bogus. If you really believed you wouldn't be here."

"But I do believe and I am here," he said with bewilderment. "I can't explain it, but there it is. My eyes are open. I know what I'm doing. When Father Rank came down to the rail carrying the sacrament . . ."

Helen exclaimed with scorn and impatience, "You've told me all that before. You are trying to impress me. You don't believe in Hell any more than I do."

He took her wrists and held them furiously. He said, "You can't get out of it that way. I believe, I tell you. I believe that I'm damned for all eternity—unless a miracle happens. I'm a policeman. I know what I'm saying. What I've done is far worse than murder—that's an act, a blow, a stab, a shot: it's over and done, but I'm carrying my corruption around with me. It's the coating of my stomach."[23]

What is important to our discussion is that Greene portrays Scobie choosing evil "with his eyes open." Despite the prospect of damnation in full view, he chooses to continue to visit Helen. He persists in his illicit behavior and rejects any suggestion that he does not know what he is doing or believe what he is saying.

Another work that brilliantly portrays how people make choices—even risking damnation, rather than choosing God—is Lewis's *The Great Divorce*. The idea for this highly entertaining and theologically profound fictional tale of the afterlife was based on the works of the seventeenth-century Anglican divine Jeremy Taylor. In Taylor's sermon "Christ's Advent to Judgment," Lewis came across the idea of the *Refrigerium,* or Holiday from Hell. It was the opinion of some of the church Fathers that, while punishment for the damned is eternal, it is intermittent. In *The Great Divorce* Lewis sought to imaginatively portray what an infernal day excursion to Paradise might look like.[24]

The story is told in the form of a dream, with Lewis himself as the visitor in a busload of bullying, cynical, resentful, and above all, selfish men and women. They travel from the Grey City of Hell to the glorious, shimmering, bright, and substantial world of Heaven. The Grey City is laid out in astronomical distances because its ghostly, ethereal citizens are so quarrelsome that they keep moving farther and farther from each other. The same selfishness that has led to their being in Hell has continued its work of isolation and selfishness so that some of its "old" inhabitants, like Julius Caesar, Henry the Fifth, and Genghis Khan, are light years from the center![25]

The Grey City is a place of endless twilight whose inhabitants are consumed with fear. As Lewis begins his trip, he observes that although the windows on the bus are closed, the bus is full of "cruel" light. He finds himself shrinking from the faces and forms that surround him, as these faces are fixed and "full not of possibilities but of impossibilities, some gaunt, some bloated, some glaring with idiotic ferocity, some drowned beyond recovery in dreams; but all, in one way or another, distorted and faded."[26]

Instead of flames and devils with their pitchforks, Lewis sometimes portrays Hell with wry humor. It has a very active Theological Society and other "amusements." It is a place where one can have a new home or any other material thing simply by wishing for it. The only downside is that the new house will not keep out the rain and the material objects will not be anything of real substantiality that you can eat or drink or sit on. While one can have anything he or she wants simply for the asking, everything in the Grey City is devoid of essential reality, of real substance.

When the bus finally arrives in the glorious City of Heaven, the passengers depart and are greeted by such radiant people whose solidity makes the bus passengers look so transparent that they appear almost as ghosts, as man-shaped stains on the brightness of the air. Interestingly, the grass does not bend under the feet of these radiant people, and even the dewdrops are not disturbed by their walking. And as they approach the visitors departing from the bus, "the earth shook under their tread as their strong feet sank into the wet turf. A tiny haze and a sweet smell went up where they had crushed the grass and scattered the dew."[27]

While *The Great Divorce* merits significant discussion in many areas, what is germane to our particular focus is the way Lewis presents the people from the Grey City as truly having the choice to stay in Heaven. And while the book presents various cameos of people, some quite humorous and others quite sad and pathetic, it is primarily a picture of souls from Hell who *refuse* the offer to stay in Heaven. When the Big Man addresses the Driver, asking him when they have to be back at the bus, the Driver informs him that he need never come back—"You can stay as long as you please."[28] Sadly, of all the bus passengers on the holiday from Hell, only one accepts the invitation to remain in Heaven.

Throughout *The Great Divorce,* Lewis is intimating that the innumerable choices of life inevitably condition a soul for eternity and that these choices give a true reflection of the will of the individual. Toward the middle of the book, one of the Solid People who has the double appearance of an old weather-beaten shepherd and an ageless, enthroned spirit comes to offer, like Virgil in Dante's *The Divine Comedy,* to guide Lewis. This Teacher is none other than George MacDonald, the Scottish minister and novelist who had had a profound influence on Lewis's spiritual pilgrimage.[29] In perhaps the most theologically profound dialogue of the entire book, Lewis asks him what exactly these souls choose who go back to the Grey City and how could they ever choose it over Heaven.

> "Milton was right," said my Teacher. "The choice of every lost soul can be expressed in the words 'Better to reign in Hell than serve in Heaven.' There is always something they insist

on keeping, even at the price of misery. There is always something they prefer to joy—that is, to reality.[30]

Later, Lewis asks why the Solid People do not go down into Hell to rescue the Ghosts ("Would one not expect a more militant charity?"). It would do little good, says the Teacher, because few Ghosts are interested in staying in Heaven once they get there. Indeed, he continues, most Ghosts don't even want to make the trip.

> "There are only two kinds of people in the end: those who say to God, 'Thy will be done,' and those to whom God says, in the end, '*Thy* will be done.' All that are in Hell, chose it. Without that self-choice there could be no Hell. No soul that seriously and constantly desires joy will ever miss it. Those who seek find. To those who knock it is opened."[31]

While Heaven is reality itself, damned souls are what they are because they always choose something less than reality, joy, substance, and yes, even God. They prefer a substitute rather than God, while those who really seek God shall find Him.

So, granted that God honors man's free will, even if it means being separated from Him forever, what could possibly be the reason or motivation behind an individual soul choosing self over God? Let's look at one of the most memorable characters from *The Great Divorce*, the Big Ghost, who provides some insight here. This ethereal man is shocked to discover that one of his former employees, Len, himself a murderer, has been sent to instruct him and help him so that he too can remain in Heaven. Needless to say, the Big Ghost finds this arrangement to be humiliating! He vociferously protests against the very idea of a bloody murderer being sent to "help" him and insists that, while he wasn't a religious man and had his share of faults, he has done his best all his life. He proclaims that he is a decent and moral man and only wants his "rights."

> "So that's the trick, is it?" shouted the Ghost, outwardly bitter, and yet I thought there was a kind of triumph in its voice. It had been entreated: it could only make a refusal: and this seemed to it a kind of advantage. "I thought there'd be some damned nonsense. It's all a clique, all a bloody clique. Tell them I'm not coming, see? I'd rather be damned than go along with you. I came here to get my rights, see? . . . I didn't come here to be treated like a dog. I'll go home. That's what I'll do." . . . In the end, still grumbling, but whimpering also a little as it picked its way over the sharp grasses, it made off.[32]

This episode serves as a significant clue to why people make the decisive and intelligible choice of evil and self over God and Heaven. It is apparent that the Big Ghost feels a certain triumph (from his perspective at least), a certain advantage, because he is able to maintain his feelings of superiority. Because he feels he has been treated unfairly, he savors his indignation so that it gives him a sense of power and control over the situation. As George MacDonald once said, "The by-word of Hell is, 'I am my own.'"

Even if it means eternal separation from Himself and from the accompanying promise of happiness and joy, God cannot and will not override free will. In *The Problem of Pain*, Lewis declares,

> I willingly believe that the damned are, in one sense, successful, rebels to the end; that the doors of hell are locked on the *inside*. . . . They enjoy forever the horrible freedom they have demanded. . . . In the long run the answer to all those who object to the doctrine of hell is itself a question: "What are you asking God to do?" To wipe out their past sins and, at all costs, to give them a fresh start, smoothing every difficulty

and offering every miraculous help? But He has already done so, on Calvary. To forgive them? They will not be forgiven. To leave them alone? Alas, I am afraid that is what He does.[33]

In our day, it is often incorrectly taught or implied that Hell is forced on the damned, that they are "sent to Hell" against their will. Yet this would go against the fundamental reason for Hell's existence: our free choice and God's honoring of that choice. When we come to understand that Hell is freely chosen, the problem then becomes not so much reconciling Hell with God's love, but reconciling Hell with human choice. And if we think about such a choice, we may rightly conclude that someone would have to be insane to choose Hell over Heaven! But isn't the deliberate rejection of joy and truth what sin is all about? Indeed, the doctrine of sin essentially means that the human race is spiritually insane.[34]

A Theological Complement to Heaven

If God's honoring of mankind's free will provide the basis for Hell, this next reason suggests how God has provided a "place" for those who choose to spend eternity away from Him.

Oxford University philosopher Richard Swinburne sets forth an important defense for the orthodox view of Hell when he asks the question, "Why is it that you have to have right beliefs and a good will (one that desires God, salvation, and heaven) to go to heaven? Why are people with wrong beliefs and a bad will left out?"[35] Swinburne's answer is twofold. First, Heaven is the kind of place where people with wrong beliefs and bad wills would not fit in. According to Swinburne, Heaven is a place where people will eternally enjoy a deep, abiding, and worthwhile happiness, not a shallow one based on the mere possession of pleasant sensations. Furthermore, this happiness is obtained by freely choosing to participate in activities that are in line with one's true beliefs, activities deemed to be truly worthwhile. These tasks include developing a friendship with God as well as deepening our relationships with others who share that friendship.

Heaven, therefore, is not a reward for good action, but rather the home for good people. As such, Heaven intensifies and fulfills a certain type of life that can be chosen in this present life, albeit in an undeveloped form. Only people of a certain sort are suited for Heaven, specifically those with true beliefs about what it is like and those who want to be there for the right reasons.

Those people with different beliefs about what a good life looks like or about Heaven itself will practice different activities, so that even if they are seeking the good in some sense, their character will develop differently from that of the Christian. Not only people with a bad will, but also people with a good will but with false beliefs about God, Jesus Christ, and Heaven will not be properly suited for life in Heaven.

Consequently, if Heaven is suitable for people of a certain kind (those with right beliefs and right desires, who truly want to be there), then Hell is a place for people of a different character who freely choose to be there. As we observed in the previous section, because God cannot and will not force His love upon anyone, Hell is His provision for such people. Hell is God's quarantine for those who refuse His offer of Heaven.

In a sense, Hell is God's provision not only for what people truly desire, but also for what they have in fact become. Perhaps this is what the apostle Paul was alluding to when he declared in 2 Thessalonians 1:9 that "these will pay the penalty of eternal destruction, away from the presence of the Lord." It seems that this relational isolation that they desire involves banishment from the presence and purposes of God. It is absorption into the abyss of the self, the road that is finally and irrevocably taken, the road east of Eden.

Furthermore, Hell seems to be the logical answer to all the suffering, injustice, and evil that pervades our present world. While the atheist and skeptic scoff at the idea of a benevolent and omnipotent God due to our blighted existence here on earth, God's holiness and justice seem to demand the existence of Hell, where retribution and rewards will be meted out in a judicious way. Because God is holy, one day He will put an end to all the evil, pain, and suffering of this life—"He shall wipe away every tear from their eyes; and there shall no longer be any death; there shall no longer be any mourning, or crying, or pain. . . . And there shall no longer be any curse" (Revelation 21:4; 22:3).

In reality, a genuine belief in Heaven also requires the complementary belief in Hell. Those who deny Hell must also deny either Heaven or free will.

More than a Children's Game

T. S. Eliot's sober words quoted at the beginning of this chapter suggest that there is a seriousness to life and that because it is possible to win as well as to lose, the doctrine of Hell truly puts "bite" into this drama we call life.

Just as the height of a mountain is measured by the depth of the valley, so the greatness of salvation can only be appreciated by the terribleness of damnation—what we are actually saved *from*. While in the past the difficulty in accepting Christianity focused on salvation (premodern societies knew sin was real, but many doubted salvation), today it is just the opposite: modernity believes that everybody is saved, but there is no belief that there is sin to be saved from.[36]

Hell truly makes an infinite difference. And to see the difference anything makes, we simply need to remove it and see what happens. And this, of course, is largely what our enlightened society, which believes in the inherent goodness of mankind, has done. With no Hell, all roads lead to the same place, whether that place is Heaven, reincarnation, or annihilation. Whatever we may want to call it, do away with Heaven and Hell and we flatten our reality, where everyone receives, in Eliot's words, "equally worthless prizes."

Only a belief in God—with Heaven and Hell as the potential destiny for each human being—gives dignity, meaning, and purpose to life. If there is no God, then mankind's life becomes absurd and there is no ultimate meaning in this universe of ours. One is reminded of Eliot's haunting lines at the conclusion of his poem "The Hollow Men": "This is the way the world ends / Not with a bang but a whimper." [37]

If there is no God, then "all things are permitted," as Dostoyevsky wrote in *The Brothers Karamazov*. But such a cynical and nihilistic worldview is hard to live by. We intuitively sense that life has meaning and purpose and that it is not a "tale told by an idiot, signifying nothing." And because life is a sacred drama where beliefs, attitudes, and actions not only have meaning but also consequences, we realize that our desire to do the right thing is rooted in our fundamental belief in a righteous world to come. Do away with Hell and we essentially remove the basis for ethics and morality. As the apostle Paul says, "If the dead are not raised, let us eat and drink, for tomorrow we die" (1 Corinthians 15:32).[38] In reality, our moral behavior—or lack thereof—tells much about our ultimate hope beyond this world. Lewis observed, "I have met no people who fully disbelieved in Hell and also had a living and life-giving belief in Heaven." [39]

So far in this chapter, we have considered why the doctrine of Hell is so despised in our enlightened culture, as well as three of the major objections against the doctrine. We then considered why the belief in Hell is necessary. Let's now turn to discuss what might be the nature, or character, of Hell.

The Nature of Hell

What will Hell be like? Is it a place or a state of mind? Is it a place of torture and unrelenting torment? If people go there, do they have to stay forever? Will those who suffer in Hell be tormented forever, or will they eventually cease to exist?

These are all serious questions for us to consider, and our

answers will influence not only how we live our own lives, but also how we view other people who face the potential destiny of being separated from God. Generally speaking, there are three primary views about Hell's nature and duration. The traditional literalist view of Hell interprets the scriptural images in a literal fashion and affirms that the torment is everlasting. The metaphorical view of Hell affirms that the torment is everlasting but that the images of Hell speak of a greater judgment than we can even fathom with human language. The annihilationist view affirms the reality of Hell's severe torment (like the other two positions) but maintains that the end of the wicked will be destruction, not eternal suffering.[40] But before we look at these different views on the nature of Hell, let's first look at some of the key concepts and passages that deal with the "abode," or place of Hell.

The Scriptures Dealing with Hell

Although the biblical description of Hell is far from definitive, we are able to come to some fundamental conclusions based on the Old and New Testament data. As is generally the case in all of Christian theology, the Old Testament tends to present beliefs and doctrines that are somewhat nebulous—in "seed" form—and which then "blossom" into a more definitive explanation in the New Testament. This is certainly true of the doctrine of Hell.

Various words describe or include the idea of Hell or final judgment in the Old Testament. The term *sheol*, while sometimes referring to the grave itself, more often refers to the netherworld of all the dead, including both believers and unbelievers.[41] Even King David pleads for God's rescue from his enemies, because in death he is cut off from the praise and worship of God: "There is no mention of Thee in death; in Sheol who will give Thee thanks?" (Psalm 6:5). And while it is a dark mode of existence (see Job 10:21-22; Psalm 143:3), Sheol is still a place where one could talk with others (see Isaiah 14:9-20) and be reunited with friends (see Genesis 15:15; 37:35). It perhaps had two compartments (see Genesis 37:35; Deuteronomy 32:22), a lower part and a higher part, which were later in the New Testament referred to as "Abraham's bosom" and "paradise" (see Luke 16:22; 23:43). From these passages it is apparent that Sheol cannot be identified as the place of the wicked's final punishment, but is merely the Old Testament designation for where everyone goes at death.

In the New Testament, Hades, like Sheol in the Old, represents the underworld, or the realm of the dead. But after the resurrection of Jesus Christ, the nature of Hades seems to radically alter and become identified as the temporary place of banishment for the unbeliever awaiting final judgment (see Ephesians 4:8-9; 1 Peter 3:18-22; 2 Peter 3:9; Revelation 20:13-15).

The New Testament also interchangeably uses the terms *tartarus*[42] (only in 2 Peter 2:4), *Gehenna*, and *lake of fire* to describe the final state of banishment pronounced at the judgment at the end of the world (see Matthew 23:33; Revelation 20). While its derivation is obscure, *Gehenna* probably is related to the "Valley of Hinnom," which is situated between Mount Olivet and the old city of David in Jerusalem.[43]

What Do We Make of the Images of Hell?

One of the most formidable tasks in understanding the nature of Hell is the interpretation of the various images used to describe it. Jesus describes Hell in a number of ways: He calls it "the fiery hell" (Matthew 5:22); it involves being departed from Him (see Matthew 7:23); it is referred to as an "outer darkness; in that place there shall be weeping and gnashing of teeth" (Matthew 8:12; see also 13:42; 22:13; 24:51; 25:30; Luke 13:28); it is "the furnace of fire" (Matthew 13:42); it is "the unquenchable fire . . . where their worm does not die, and the fire is not quenched" (Mark 9:43,48); it is a place of torment and agony in the flame (Luke 16:22-24); and it is a place where people "receive many lashes" (Luke 12:47). The critical question is how these and similar passages are to be interpreted. Are we to take them literally or metaphorically?

Throughout the ages, the images of Hell have fascinated the Christian church. With very few exceptions, a literal interpretation of the images of Hell dominated Christian thinking from the time of Augustine until the Reformers (the fifth through sixteenth centuries). For approximately the first four centuries after Christ, there was no uniform view on the fate of the lost, yet many Christians put forth descriptions of Hell that were gruesome beyond belief. Not satisfied with the images of fire and smoke, some of the more creative pictured Hell as a bizarre horror chamber. Often dependent on early Jewish accounts of Hell, these portraits viewed the punishment as based on the *lex talionis* of the Old Testament, the measure-for-measure principle ("eye for eye, tooth for tooth," Exodus 21:24; Leviticus 24:20). In short, whatever member of the body sinned, that member would be punished more than any other in Hell. Thus in early Christian literature we find blasphemers hanging by their tongues; adulterous women, who plaited their hair to entice men, dangling over a boiling mire by their necks or hair; and murderers cast into pits filled with venomous reptiles, worms filling their bodies. Those who chatted idly during church stand in a pool of burning sulphur and pitch.[44]

Even the great theologian Augustine, whose writings on Hell (like his other writings) left a deep and lasting impression on Western theology, believed that the torment of damnation was best understood to be primarily bodily, although it also could involve spiritual torment. In his opinion, the Scriptures were silent regarding the spiritual pain of the damned.[45] Origen of Alexandria and Gregory of Nyssa (a theologian of the fourth century) thought Hell was more a place of spiritual suffering, of remorse and separation from God. Origen even believed that the punishment of Hell was remedial and that even the worst of sinners could be rehabilitated and ultimately find their way to Paradise. His universalist view was rejected, however, by the church leaders at the Council of Constantinople in A.D. 543.

In the fourteenth century, the Italian poet Dante Alighieri fueled these earlier speculations about damnation with the publication of *The Divine Comedy*. Dante immortalized the literalist view of Hell as he imagined a place of absolute terror where the damned writhe and scream while the blessed bask in the glory of Eternal Light. Furthermore, he suggested that the saints in Heaven will derive pleasure from contemplating the torments of the damned. In Dante's Hell, people must endure thick, burning smoke that chars their nostrils, and some remain forever trapped in lead cloaks, a claustrophobic nightmare.

Faced with imaginations that had run riot, theologians during the Reformation, primarily Martin Luther and John Calvin, began to regard Hell as a real place to be understood in a figurative or metaphorical manner. Hell's worst agonies, they suggested, were the terror and utter despair of spending eternity cut off from God. While understanding that the torment of Hell is to be understood metaphorically, Calvin nonetheless believed that the pain it signifies is quite real and intense. He urges us to "lay aside the speculations, by which foolish men weary themselves to no purpose, and satisfy ourselves with believing, that these forms of speech denote, in a manner suited to our feeble capacity, a dreadful torment, which no man can comprehend, and no language can express." [46]

While a number of conservative, evangelical Christians continue to embrace a literalist view of Hell where fire and brimstone are actually part of the furnishings, it seems that a metaphorical understanding of these ghastly images of Hell is a more accurate interpretation. Perhaps the strongest reason for such a view is the conflicting language the New Testament uses to describe Hell. For instance, how could Hell be literal fire when it is also described as darkness (see Matthew 3:10,12; 5:22; 7:19; 8:12; 13:40,42,50; 22:13; 25:30; 2 Peter 2:17; Jude 13)? It would seem that fire and darkness are mutually exclusive terms. It is doubtful that the writers of the New Testament ever intended their words to be taken literally.

Consider Jude, who describes Hell as "eternal fire" in verse 7, but then further depicts it as "the blackest darkness" in verse 13.

Furthermore, we have the other images of Hell in the New Testament, which seem to defy being taken in a literal manner. As we have already seen, the wicked are said to weep and gnash their teeth (see Matthew 8:12; 13:42; 22:13; 24:51; 25:30; Luke 13:28), "their worm does not die" (Mark 9:48), and they "receive many lashes" (Luke 12:47).

In contrast to the literalist interpretation, the metaphorical view gives proper weight to the legitimacy of biblical symbolism and sees Hell as an endless, conscious torment of those consigned to damnation. In addition to the Reformation theologians Calvin and Luther, recent evangelical scholars who have embraced the metaphorical understanding of the nature of Hell include such prominent figures as J. I. Packer, Leon Morris, John Stott, and C. S. Lewis.

If the charge is made that the metaphorical understanding doesn't offer a strong enough picture of how terrible the judgment of Hell might be, the simplest reply is that these images are to be taken quite seriously. In fact, they are to be taken with utmost seriousness because they point to something more horrible than the literal images denote. Packer cautions us when he observes, "Do not try to imagine what it is like to be in hell. . . . The mistake is to take such pictures as physical descriptions, when in fact they are imagery symbolizing realities . . . far worse than the symbols themselves." [47]

Annihilation or Eternal Suffering?

While the metaphorical understanding of the nature of Hell seems to be the most appropriate way to view the terrible images of Hell, let's briefly consider the view of annihilationism. This view, while accepting the reality of Hell and that many will in fact be lost eternally, sees the end of the wicked to be destruction and not eternal suffering. While the traditional teaching of the church—that the lost will suffer unending conscious torment in Hell—has repeatedly been challenged by universalists (who believe all will be saved) since the third century, from the time of the Reformation annihilationism has emerged as a minority position.

In recent years, a number of notable evangelical scholars have embraced annihilationism, including Clark Pinnock, theology professor at McMaster Divinity College in Hamilton, Ontario; theologian John Wenham; John R. W. Stott, founder of the London Institute for Contemporary Christianity; and Philip E. Hughes, a noted Anglican clergyman and author. Proponents of annihilationism argue that the traditional belief in unending torment serves no remedial purpose and paints a portrait of God as a vindictive despot incompatible with that of the loving Father revealed in Jesus Christ.

Further, some annihilationists claim that the traditional view of Hell as being eternal, conscious punishment is based more on the Platonic notion of the innate immortality of the soul than on the Bible. In their thinking, the immortality of which the Christian is assured— "eternal life"—is not inherent within himself or his soul, but is bestowed by God. Thus this view is also sometimes referred to as "conditional immortality." With annihilationism, everyone survives death and participates in the final resurrection. And while the believer is given immortality through his or her participation in Christ's resurrection, the judgment passed upon unbelievers is extinction. Consequently, unbelievers undergo everlasting punish*ment*—destruction—but not everlasting punish*ing*—or eternal torment.

Advocates of annihilationism generally base their belief on New Testament passages that warn of "eternal destruction" (2 Thessalonians 1:9) and "the second death" (Revelation 20:14) as well as Jesus' admonition not to fear men, who can kill only the body, but rather God, "who is able to destroy both soul and body in hell" (Matthew 10:28).

Without question, the primary basis and appeal of annihilationism is an attempt to protect the benevolence of God. The ethical argument is raised, "How can Christians possibly project a God of such cruelty and vindictiveness as to inflict 'everlasting torment' upon His creatures, however sinful they may have been? Such a God would be more like Satan than the God of the Bible!"

While such an effort to defend the goodness of God is commendable, some significant difficulties are inherent in this position. First of all, it needs to be stressed that the traditional view on Hell—of unending torment—is not a picture where God is actively torturing people forever and ever. Granted, there will be everlasting, conscious torment in varying degrees according to the lives people have lived here on earth,[48] but the essence of that torment seems to be relational in nature: banishment from God, His Heaven, and all that it encompasses.

What is more, the traditional doctrine of Hell as being "eternal, everlasting, forever," has strong biblical support for connoting precisely what it suggests—it is *unending*. While annihilationists argue that the word "eternal" refers to the permanence of the judgment and not its duration, the normative meaning of the word "eternal" argues for the traditional view of Hell.[49] Furthermore, several passages make a strong case that the final states of the just and unjust are precisely analogous—both are conscious, continuous modes of existence, both with resurrection bodies—except for their respective destinations. When the biblical writers use the word "eternal," they use it to refer not only to the punishment of the lost, but also to the bliss of the righteous (see Matthew 25:46). This suggests a parallel that goes beyond the permanence of the pronounced judgment. The unending joy of the redeemed stands in bold contrast to the unending torment of the lost. The Scriptures, and Jesus in particular, are quite emphatic that resurrection is the appointed end for every human being. If Heavenly bliss is endless, so is Hellish agony:

> "And many of those who sleep in the dust of the ground will awake, these to everlasting life, but the others to disgrace and everlasting contempt." (Daniel 12:2)

"Do not marvel at this; for an hour is coming, in which all who are in the tombs shall hear His voice, and shall come forth; those who did the good deeds to a resurrection of life, those who committed the evil deeds to a resurrection of judgment." (John 5:28-29)

What Is the Essence of Hell?

While these passages clearly address the reality of Hell and the fact that it is everlasting, we need to consider what the essence of Hell might be like. We have already suggested that the idea of God as a cosmic sadist, who vindictively delights in eternally tormenting people, is not an accurate picture of how the Bible presents Hell. Generally speaking, Christian theologians have traditionally described Hell with three different aspects: punishment, pain, and privation.[50] With respect to the idea of punishment, it may be helpful to distinguish between punishment seen as positive law or natural law. The punishments of positive law are chosen by the punisher (and if applied to God, would seem to impugn His goodness, because He could have chosen differently): "If you disobey what I've told you to do, you'll be grounded for a week!" The punishments of natural law are intrinsic rather than extrinsic and therefore are necessary rather than chosen: "If you drive too fast and recklessly, you'll endanger your life."

Understanding the punishment of Hell as an aspect of natural law helps us better understand the biblical perspective of mankind's alienation from and rebellion against God. For instance, when God commanded Adam and Eve not to eat the forbidden fruit and they violated His command, divorcing their wills (and ours) from God's, then the disastrous consequence was both physical and spiritual death. Consequently, when the punishment of Hell is seen in light of natural law, virtue becomes its own reward and vice its own punishment. Therefore, when humans freely refuse the gracious offer of God, they must necessarily find death and misery as the inevitable punishment. Because God honors human beings with true free choice, He ultimately gives those in Hell precisely what they want: to be separate from Him, Heaven, and His eternal purposes to bring blessedness and joy to those in fellowship with Him. And while Hell is in fact God's retributive punishment against evildoers who cannot withstand the holiness of His gaze, it nonetheless is also rightly seen as the fulfillment of what they have become. As Lewis observed,

> The characteristic of lost souls is "their rejection of everything that is not simply themselves." Our imaginary egoist has tried to turn everything he meets into a province or appendage of the self. The taste for the other, that is, the very capacity for enjoying good, is quenched in him except in so far as his body still draws him into some rudimentary contact with an outer world. He has his wish — to live wholly in the self and to make the best of what he finds there. And what he finds there is Hell.[51]

It naturally follows that when people decisively choose against a God of ultimate joy and happiness, their refusal must necessarily include joylessness as well as pain. We earlier observed concerning the images of Hell that they most likely are to be understood metaphorically and not literally. Similarly, the pain of Hell most likely is internal rather than external.

Because we were designed for relationship, perhaps the greatest pain and anguish to be felt in Hell is that terrible burning within the heart for fellowship with God, which can never be satisfied in inanimate things. The medieval scholastics referred to this as *poena damni*, "the pain of missing Heaven," which they understood to be the pain and anguish of having no contact with the One who is the source of all peace.

However, it may be that the punishment, sorrow, and shame of

Hell involve both mental and physical anguish. If all human beings have resurrection bodies for their eternal destinies, physical pain might logically follow from the spiritual torment. Jerry L. Walls, in his book *Hell: The Logic of Damnation*, expresses this possibility:

> I do not think the fire of hell is literal, nor do I think hell is an ingeniously contrived place of the greatest possible pain and agony. I do, nevertheless, think hell includes physical distress. My reason for this involves an appeal to the traditional Christian belief that the damned as well as the blessed will be resurrected in their bodies. If the damned will have bodies in hell, it seems only natural to suppose that there will be a bodily dimension to their suffering.[52]

Not only will Hell involve the punishment that is inevitable due to mankind's freely rejecting God and the attendant pain that must naturally accompany such rejection, it also involves privation of God. Because God is not simply one among many sources of joy but is in reality its ultimate source, any attempt to find joy and happiness outside of Him is doomed to failure. Furthermore, because all joys and pleasures have their origin in Him (pleasures are, as Lewis suggested, "patches of godlight in the woods of our experience"[53]), the privation of God is the privation not just of some joy but of all joy. This aspect of Hell may in fact be the most terrible and hideous of all.

Two New Testament passages are highly suggestive of what privation of God may be like: Matthew 25:41,46, and 2 Thessalonians 1:6,8-9. In the first instance, Jesus follows an extended discourse concerning His glorious return to earth with a warning of the coming judgment that awaits those who are not in a proper relationship with Him. In the other passage, the apostle Paul tells the suffering believers of Thessalonica that though they suffer persecution, God's righteous judgment will one day prevail.

"But when the Son of Man comes in His glory, and all the angels with Him, then He will sit on His glorious throne. And all the nations will be gathered before Him; and He will separate them from one another, as the shepherd separates the sheep from the goats; and He will put the sheep on His right, and the goats on the left. Then the King will say to those on His right, 'Come, you who are blessed of My Father, inherit the kingdom prepared for you from the foundation of the world.' . . . Then He will also say to those on His left, 'Depart from Me, accursed ones, into the eternal fire which has been prepared for the devil and his angels.' . . . And these will go away into eternal punishment, but the righteous into eternal life." (Matthew 25:31-34,41,46)

For after all it is only just for God to repay with affliction those who afflict you, . . . dealing out retribution to those who do not know God and to those who do not obey the gospel of our Lord Jesus. And these will pay the penalty of eternal destruction, away from the presence of the Lord and from the glory of His power. (2 Thessalonians 1:6,8-9)

As Matthew 25 suggests, those in Hell are "separated" from Jesus Christ; as 2 Thessalonians 1:8-9 teaches, those in Hell are "away from the presence" of the Lord. Hell, therefore, seems to be banishment from God's presence, His purposes, and His followers.

Moreover, it may be that Heaven and Hell have the same objective reality, but are simply perceived differently by those in the two respective places. Unlike Heaven, which is the ultimate Reality, Hell is the abdication of that Reality and thus may be simply a "state of mind." In Lewis's *The Great Divorce*, the Teacher replies to Lewis's question:

"Then those people are right who say that Heaven and Hell are only states of mind?" "Hush," said he sternly. "Do not blaspheme. Hell is a state of mind—ye never said a truer word. And every state of mind, left to itself, every shutting up of the creature within the dungeon of its own mind—is, in the end, Hell. But Heaven is not a state of mind. Heaven is reality itself. All that is fully real is Heavenly." [54]

In such a scenario, Hell is unsubstantial and Heaven is the ultimate reality. Heaven is the fire of God's love, which is His essential being (see Hebrews 12:29), and the damned possibly find themselves in the same place as the saved—in Heaven, the only true reality. Yet they hate it because it is their Hell, while the saved delight in it because it is their Heaven. It might be compared to two people sitting side by side at a rock concert or an opera: the very thing that is Heaven to one is Hell to the other. [55] Dostoyevsky portrays this beautifully through the words of Markel in *The Brothers Karamazov*: "Don't cry. Life is paradise and we are all in paradise, only we don't want to know it, and if we wanted to we'd have heaven on earth tomorrow." [56]

Consequently, though the damned do not love God, He loves them, and this is the essence of their torment. The love of God is an objective fact and the wrath of God may very well be the human projection of the wrath of those in Hell upon Him. It is not unlike pouting children who do not get their way and who misinterpret their loving parents' affections as a threat to their autonomy. Just as a child sulks and wants to have its own way, so the damned in Hell remain steadfast in their impenitent hearts toward God, forever refusing the Divine guest of their soul. While He stands at the door and knocks (see Revelation 3:20), if the door remains locked "from the inside," it becomes the door of Hell. Hell is therefore our declaration of independence against our divine Husband and as such is not so much passive suffering as it is active rebellion.

On the human plane, this can happen to an ordinary person who seemingly is safe from the dangers of Hell. In Lewis's short story "The Shoddy Lands," Peggy's self-centeredness shuts her off not only from her boyfriend's pleading, but also from the benevolent request of Another:

> And now I became aware that two noises had been going for a long time; the only noises I ever heard in that world. . . . The one was faint, but hard. . . . But how shall I describe the other knocking? It was, in some curious way, soft . . . but unendurably heavy, as if at each blow some enormous hand fell on the outside of Shoddy Sky and covered it completely. And with that knocking came a voice at whose sound my bones turned to water: "Child, child, child, let me in before the night comes."[57]

Like Peggy, those in Hell hate God because He demands that they repent, but that hurts their pride, because such a request is the very death knell of egotism. They see God as the very enemy of what they cherish most deeply: their own autonomy.

One of the serious questions that frequently comes up concerning Hell is whether or not the damnation of even one soul in Hell might destroy the joy of Heaven. In other words, does not the pain and suffering of Hell in fact veto the joy of Heaven? Lewis addresses this difficult issue in *The Great Divorce*. At one point, Lewis and his imaginary guide, the Teacher, watch a procession of Bright Spirits followed by young boys and girls. Then follows the Lady in whose honor all this was done, whose name on earth was Sarah Smith. As the procession stops, the Lady is approached by two Ghosts—a Dwarf who is holding by a chain a tall, theatrical man, much bigger than himself. The Dwarf, named Frank, was Sarah's husband on earth. The tall Ghost—the "Tragedian"—is that part of Frank who has struck so many poses that he has become a separate self. Frank is so desperate to be needed, so ready to use blackmail for what he considers love, that it is now nearly all that is left of him. Despite Sarah's plea for him to remain, Frank insists on having his way, unmoved by his feelings of self-pity. Listen to the Teacher's response to Lewis's penetrating question dealing with those in Hell who would love to spoil the joy of those in Heaven.

> "What some people say on earth is that the final loss of one soul gives the lie to all the joy of those who are saved." "Ye see it does not." "I feel in a way that it ought to." "That sounds very merciful: but see what lurks behind it." "What?" "The demand of the loveless and the self-imprisoned that they should be allowed to blackmail the universe: that till they consent to be happy (on their own terms) no one else shall taste joy: that theirs should be the final power: that Hell should be able to *veto* Heaven.". . . "Either the day must come when joy prevails and all the makers of misery are no longer able to infect it: or else for ever and ever the makers of misery can destroy in others the happiness they reject for themselves." [58]

As sad as the story of Lewis's fictional Frank is, God cannot and will not allow the damned, who insist on getting their way, to "veto" the happiness of Heaven. While the damned may delight in getting their own way, their existence through eternity will not be so much the beginning of a new, immortal life in torment as it is the end of a life of rebellion. For while to enter Heaven is to become more human than we ever succeeded in being on earth — or could possibly imagine — to enter Hell is perhaps nothing less than being banished from humanity. What goes to Hell is perhaps not fully a person, but the remains of a person banished to the darkness, away from God, "the outer rim where being fades away into nonentity." [59]

Epilogue: No Ordinary People

One cannot deeply believe in Heaven if one does not also believe in Hell. And especially for the Christian, who believes in the truth claims of the Scriptures concerning the threat of judgment in the life to come, this is no mere theological exercise. It is a sobering account of one of the two eternal destinies that lies before every man and woman who has ever lived. To be unmoved by the gravity of this sacred, human drama, in which it is possible to win as well as to lose, is truly not to care for our fellow human beings. This interesting dream of the great German theologian Karl Barth shows his deep concern for the destiny of people.

> One day I came to Karl Barth and he was very nervous. I saw this and asked him what had happened. Then, as was typical for him, he said, "I had a very awful dream." And Barth had a very great sense for dreams. I asked him, "What have you dreamt?" He said, "I was dreaming that a voice asked me, 'Would you like to see hell?' And I said, 'Oh, I am very interested to see it once.'" Then a window was opened and he saw an immense desert. It was very cold, not hot. In this desert there was only one person sitting, very alone. Barth was depressed to see the loneliness. Then the window was closed and the voice said to him, "And that threatens you?" So Barth was very depressed by this dream. Then he said to me, "There are people who say I have forgotten this region. I have not forgotten. I know about it more than others do. But because I know of this, therefore I must speak about Christ. I cannot speak enough about the gospel of Christ." [60]

In Barth's dream, Hell was a solitary person in a cold desert—absolute loneliness. And just as this dream of Hell threatened Barth, so it threatens and grips us. Every now and then we feel the cool wind of that desert cut deeply into our own hearts, and we feel that same loneliness, like the person sitting alone in that immense desert. And sometimes, because the loneliness is so real in our own lives, because we're having a hell of a time in this life, we have no trouble believing in Hell.

Because he knew of the reality of Hell, Barth could not stop speaking enough about God's appointed way out of Hell through the finished work of His Son, Jesus Christ. This very passion for the eternal destiny of others so gripped the heart and soul of the apostle Paul that he declared, "I . . . wish that I myself were accursed, separated from Christ for the sake of my brethren" (Romans 9:3). Similarly he proclaimed that "we are ambassadors for Christ, as though God were entreating through us; we beg you on behalf of Christ, be reconciled to God. He made Him who knew no sin to be sin on our behalf, that we might become the righteousness of God in Him" (2 Corinthians 5:20-21).

For Christians, there can be few higher callings and purposes than that we would see ourselves as "ambassadors," as messengers of hope and salvation in this hopeless and dying world. There is probably a no more fitting conclusion to this chapter on the frightening reality of Hell than a passage from Lewis's sermon "The Weight of Glory." In this sermon, arguably the most powerful and memorable that Lewis ever penned or preached, he addressed the students at Oxford in the University Church of St. Mary the Virgin. He warns his hearers—and you and me—not to think too much of our own future glory, but rather paints a sobering picture of why we should be concerned for the eternal destiny of others.

> It may be possible for each to think too much of his own potential glory hereafter; it is hardly possible for him to think too often or too deeply about that of his neighbor. . . . It is a serious thing to live in a society of possible gods and goddesses, to remember that the dullest and most uninteresting person you talk to may one day be a creature which, if you saw it now, you would be strongly tempted to worship, or else a horror and a corruption such as you now meet, if at all, only in a nightmare. . . . There are no *ordinary* people. You have

never talked to a mere mortal. Nations, cultures, arts, civilizations — these are mortal, and their life is to ours as the life of
a gnat. But it is immortals whom we joke with, work with,
marry, snub, and exploit — immortal horrors or everlasting
splendors.[61]

CHAPTER 14

THE CHARACTER OF HEAVEN

"Yes," my friend said. "I don't see why there shouldn't be books in Heaven. But you will find that your library in Heaven contains only some of the books you had on earth." "Which?" I asked. "The ones you gave away or lent." "I hope the lent ones won't still have all the borrowers' dirty thumb marks," said I. "Oh yes they will," said he. "But just as the wounds of the martyrs will have turned into beauties, so you will find that the thumb-marks have turned into beautiful illuminated capitals or exquisite marginal woodcuts."

—C. S. Lewis

WHILE THE MAIN FOCUS OF OUR JOURNEY SO FAR HAS DEALT WITH OUR longings for Heaven, we now briefly address some oft-asked questions about what our lives in Heaven may be like.[1]

Most of us have found ourselves dreaming about the glorious life of Heaven. To be human is to be curious about Heaven and to have at least had passing thoughts about what it might hold. And if it is true that Heaven will be the believer's eternal destiny, then it is only proper to examine some of the Scriptures and to consider some of the insights of the great theologians and philosophers who have seriously reflected on Heaven.

What might Heaven in fact be like? Where is Heaven, anyway? Will we have bodies in Heaven? Will there be time in Heaven? What in the world will we do in Heaven? Will it be an eternally boring experience? Will we all be equal in Heaven? These and a host of other questions come to mind. We will look at three separate matters in this chapter. First, we will consider the central biblical teachings on the nature of Heaven. Second, we will look at the ineffability of Heaven (that it is in fact beyond our human comprehension). And third, we will offer some theological musings on some of the most commonly asked questions about Heaven.

Central Biblical Teachings

One of the important biblical teachings concerning Heaven is that in some mystical yet true sense, Heaven has already begun for believers who have personally appropriated Jesus' accomplished work on the cross for the forgiveness of their sins. Paul even goes so far as to tell us that believers are already citizens of Heaven (see Philippians 3:20).

Heaven exists as a real place and is not to be understood as some imaginary realm or simply as the hope of children's fairy tales or grand fantasy novels. It is not simply a state of mind or some kind of psychological reality, nor is it a place just for spirits. Just as Jesus' resurrection appearances were bodily in nature, so our heavenly nature will be bodily, because our bodies will be like His (see Philippians 3:21; 1 John 3:2). As was earlier discussed, either there is "pie in the sky" or there is not. And from what we considered already, we can have confidence that Heaven is a real and substantial place.

Yet it is important to realize that Heaven is not first of all a place, but primarily a spiritual life. The New Testament refers to Heaven as "eternal life," "divine life," "the kingdom of Heaven." This new, spiritual life was the divine intent of the Father in sending His Son to establish the kingdom of Heaven on earth, to inaugurate the coming of the eternal life into the temporal, to put the divine into the human, beginning first with Christ and then in the Christian (see John 1:12; 1 Corinthians 15:20,23).

Consequently, because of the Incarnation—Jesus Christ's "taking on human flesh"—when each individual personally appropriates His finished work of redemption, he or she becomes a recipient of the "new birth" and a "partaker of the divine nature" (John 3:3-6; 2 Peter 1:4). Jesus Himself declares, "Truly, truly, I say to you, he who hears My word, and believes Him who sent Me, has eternal life, and does not come into judgment, but has passed out of death into life" and again, "I am the resurrection and the life; he who believes in Me shall live even if he dies, and everyone who lives and believes in Me shall never die" (John 5:24; 11:25-26). It is by virtue of Jesus' resurrection that in this present world the believer has entered into Heaven and eternal life in some real sense.[2]

While the believer is assured in the pages of the New Testament that he or she has already entered into Heaven, we are also told that the believer will be glorified with a resurrection body and will be seated and exalted with Christ in Heaven (see Ephesians 2:6; Romans 8:11,17). Some texts suggest that we will be given positions of authority, service, and honor in God's eternal kingdom, including reigning with Him (see Matthew 20:1-16; 1 Corinthians 6:3; 2 Timothy 2:11-12; Revelation 5:9-10).

Furthermore, we are told that Heaven will be a place of great activity and joy, including fellowship with Jesus Himself. Jesus, after predicting His death, stated that He would not drink "the fruit of the vine" again until He did so with His disciples in the kingdom of God (Matthew 26:27-29). So not only will believers have the opportunity to see their Lord and Savior face to face (see 1 John 3:2), but also to spend eternity in His presence (see John 14:2-3; Revelation 22:4).

In addition to the promised fellowship with Jesus, there will be a collective aspect in Heaven, which will include all the saints through the ages. The Old Testament emphasizes a corporate resurrection of the entire nation—the righteous will rise together (see Isaiah 26:19; Daniel 12:1-3). In the New Testament, Paul similarly speaks of the dead and living believers being raised together, sharing in this marvelous event at the Lord's coming, known as the *parousia* (see 1 Thessalonians 4:16-17). Consequently, it seems that we will be reunited with our believing loved ones who died before us and that a true fellowship and "communion of the saints" will be shared among believers in Heaven (see Matthew 8:11; 1 Corinthians 12:13; Revelation 21:26-27).

Another important aspect of the promised life of Heaven centers on the redemption or re-creation of the entire cosmic order, thus ushering in a new, righteous world. This new life promised in Heaven is not just a pleasant, Utopian world where people are happy but continue to get sick and die. Rather, the biblical picture of Heaven envisions a world where people will never experience death again (see John 11:25-26), and where our old enemies, pain and suffering, are forever banished from our new, eternal dwelling with God (see Revelation 7:15-17; 21:1-4).

In Heaven even the fallen creation itself will be redeemed. For just as believers who await the world to come long to be clothed with their immortal, resurrection bodies, so also all of creation elicits "groanings unto glory," eagerly awaiting its ultimate redemption where righteousness dwells without evil (see Romans 8:19-23; 2 Peter

3:13; Revelation 21:25-27). This "new heaven" and "new earth" (Revelation 21:1) will be the perfect complement for His redeemed people, who will spend eternity deepening their relationship with God and their fellow saints as well as enjoying the splendor of this new and righteous home, Heaven.

Having looked at some of the more central teachings on Heaven, let's now turn to consider how the idea of Heaven is beyond our human comprehension. Heaven is, as Augustine described God, ineffable.

The Ineffability of Heaven

Throughout the Scriptures, a number of metaphors and other figures of speech are employed to describe Heaven. And while Jesus declares that the kingdom of God has been prepared from the very "foundation of the world" (Matthew 25:34) and often alludes to a number of particulars about Heaven, it is also true that much remains a mystery. It is beyond our ultimate comprehension in this life. "We see in a mirror dimly, but then face to face," Paul writes (1 Corinthians 13:12). Furthermore, he seems to intimate as much when he declares, "Things which eye has not seen and ear has not heard, and which have not entered the heart of man, all that God has prepared for those who love Him" (1 Corinthians 2:9).

While unfathomable surprises may await us, we still have a number of longings in this mortal life that Heaven will surely satisfy. One such longing is our desire for *peace and tranquility,* beautifully portrayed in such Scriptures as Psalm 23:1-3 where the Lord is seen as the Shepherd who satisfies the innermost needs of His people by leading them to green pastures and restful waters. This same motif is observed in the New Testament where Jesus provides "living water" to the Samaritan woman at the well (John 4:13-14) and where He is depicted as the Good Shepherd who calls His sheep by name and leads them out to find pasture (see John 10:1-16). Likewise, the Lamb who sits on the throne becomes the Shepherd who guides His people to springs of living water, so that they no longer experience pain and suffering, because He "shall wipe every tear from their eyes" (Revelation 7:17).

Another longing that we anticipate will be satisfied in Heaven is *rest and comfort*. The psalmist declares that God is blessed, because He "daily bears our burden" (Psalm 68:19; 81:6-7). And Jesus promises rest to those "who are weary and heavy-laden.... For My yoke is easy, and My load is light" (Matthew 11:28-30). This theme of rest—so fundamental to the very nature of God and the worship of Israel (as seen in the institution of the Sabbath; see Genesis 2:1-3; Exodus 20:8-11)—is addressed in the New Testament as well. In Hebrews 4:1-11, the writer stresses that while rest may be entered into one day, "there remains ... a Sabbath rest for the people of God" (verse 9).

In addition to peace, rest, and comfort, we also have longings in this life for *protection and security*. The psalmist pictures God as a shelter for His people when he declares, "He who dwells in the shelter of the Most High will abide in the shadow of the Almighty.... He will cover you with His pinions, and under His wings you may seek refuge; His faithfulness is a shield and bulwark" (Psalm 91:1,4). Similarly, Jesus portrays Himself as the protector of the Jewish people when He laments to them that He "often ... wanted to gather your children together, the way a hen gathers her chicks under her wings, and you were unwilling" (Matthew 23:37). And in the book of Revelation, Heaven is portrayed as the place where the need for refuge and protection is preeminently met:

> And I saw a new heaven and a new earth; for the first heaven and the first earth passed away, and there is no longer any sea. ... And I heard a loud voice from the throne, saying, "Behold, the tabernacle of God is among men, and He shall dwell among them, and they shall be His people, and God Himself shall be among them." (21:1,3)

And while we can look ahead to having the needs of peace, rest, and security met in Heaven, we are still confronted with the daunting task of trying to understand the metaphors frequently used to describe Heaven, particularly in the apocalyptic book of Revelation. For instance, in the latter chapters of that book, Heaven is described as "the holy city, new Jerusalem, coming down out of heaven from God, made ready as a bride adorned for her husband" (21:2). John further tells us that this holy city had "the glory of God. Her brilliance was like a very costly stone, as a stone of crystal-clear jasper" (21:11). This New Jerusalem "had a great and high wall, with twelve gates, and at the gates twelve angels; and names were written on them, which are those of the twelve tribes of the sons of Israel" (21:12). Most of these verses emphasize the beauty of the New Jerusalem—the dwelling of God.

When we read such glorious pictures of the life to come, if we are truthful with ourselves we must admit that these descriptions of Heaven are baffling to our human understanding. Are we to understand such passages literally or metaphorically? As we have seen earlier, while we have a clear sense about the certainty, the hope, and the promise of Heaven, there is much about the nature of Heaven that we simply do not know in detail. For just as God and His ways are incomprehensible to our finite human understanding (see Job 5:9; Romans 11:33), it should not surprise us that Heaven, His abode, is also ultimately beyond human categories of thought. As Augustine observed in the fifth century, it is easier to say what God is not than to say what He is. He is *ineffabilis*.

Our current cultural use of language is often at odds with the traditional Jewish and Christian use of language. This makes it difficult to truly grasp the intent of the traditional language used to describe Heaven. Modernity seeks to make a dichotomy between what it deems to be true and false, or as it sees it, "fact" and "fiction." It believes that statements are "literally true" if they are used to support scientific or historic "facts," but regards statements using metaphors as poetic and fanciful, but not fundamentally "true." In reality, a literal interpretation should be used to describe what the author intended to say. And the word "literal" when referring to the meaning of the Bible has generally meant not only what the writer of the text intended, but also what God intends.[3]

Because "literal" has taken on a pejorative sense in modern culture, it may be best to avoid using the term and to use the word "overt" instead. In our understanding of a biblical text we will seek to determine whether the text suggests an "overt" meaning or a "symbolic" one. When Jesus refers to His interlocutors as hypocrites (see Matthew 22:18), it is perhaps best to read this in an overt sense. Other statements are best read in the symbolic sense, such as when Jesus warns those who have a log in their own eye not to condemn those with a speck in theirs (see Matthew 7:3-5). Similarly, the statement that God's "throne is in heaven" is rarely meant in an overt sense, but usually is intended as a metaphor of God's sovereignty. In his excellent book *A History of Heaven: The Singing Silence,* Jeffrey Burton Russell suggests that there are some important reasons why the Bible's statements about Heaven focus primarily on the symbolic sense that is communicated through metaphors:

> Traditional Jewish and Christian thinkers recognized that metaphor expresses a deeper reality than can be attained through the overt sense . . . a sense of contemplation and wonder are at least as important for understanding the world as efforts to determine facts. . . . God is a poet at least as much as a scientist or a historian. God is the great poet, the maker (Greek *poietes)* of the universe, and his meaning is eternally expansive. . . . Thus heaven is best understood as metaphor. And not only is language about heaven metaphor; heaven is itself the metaphor of metaphors.[4]

The bottom line? Our experience in Heaven will be far beyond what we can imagine.

Theological Musings on Heaven

Let's now consider some of the particular questions often raised about Heaven: Where is Heaven, anyway? If we are to have resurrection bodies in Heaven, what will they be like? Will we experience time in Heaven, even though Heaven is eternal? What will we do in Heaven? Will we know everything in Heaven? Will we know each other? And lastly, will we possibly be equal in Heaven?

Where Is Heaven?

Is Heaven in space? In other words, is it a place that has physicality? As we earlier observed, there is a tendency for the materialist to use the terms "real" and "material" synonymously. In his or her mind, therefore, something is considered a real place if it is a material place. This approach makes an erroneous division of reality, creating a false separation between objective matter and subjective spirit. Pose the question "Where is Heaven?" from such a perspective and there are only two possible answers: Heaven exists as (1) an objective, material place, like a faraway planet, or (2) a subjective, psychological, nonmaterial, nonspatial place, essentially a state of mind.

Thus, while the wooden literalist "objectivizes" Heaven so as to believe that it is up in the sky, or beyond the sky (although few would suggest that we could get there by a rocket ship!), the modernist takes the equally erroneous position when he "subjectivizes" Heaven, so that it is simply "in your heart" or "in your life." The problem with the latter view is that if Heaven simply resides in our hearts, death is outrageous, because it kills Heaven. While the literalist makes Heaven relative to earth and the modernist makes Heaven relative to us, is it not more appropriate to make Heaven relative to God? Consequently, a better answer is that Heaven is where God is.

Yet it does seem reasonable to believe that Heaven is a *place*—that it has a spatial dimension—because we will have resurrection bodies in Heaven (see 1 Corinthians 15:35-53).[5] The apostle Paul goes so far as to distinguish our physical bodies, which inhabit physical space, from our future resurrection bodies, which inhabit spiritual space (see 1 Corinthians 15:44). But we should be careful not to say spiritual space is that which is mental, subjective, or psychological. Rather, in some mystical yet real sense, Heaven is an objectively real place—independent of the mind but nonetheless a spiritual place.

What Will Our Bodies Be Like in Heaven?

In an earlier chapter, I mentioned that *Harper's* magazine published a compilation of fascinating, illuminating, and shocking facts that had appeared in their popular "Harper's Index" feature over the years. Under the heading "Psychology" were some provocative statistics about how we feel about our bodies. For instance, only 4 percent of Americans said that they would change nothing about their looks, even if they could. Another interesting tidbit dealt with cosmetic surgery: surgeons remove approximately 200,000 pounds of fat from Americans each year, but they also implant about 60,000 pounds of silicone and collagen each year. Interestingly, while only 13 percent of American women considered themselves pretty, some 28 percent of American men considered themselves handsome![6] Needless to say, we Americans are obsessed with our bodies and how we look.

When we think about the transitory nature of this life, it's only natural that we wonder what our bodies will be like in Heaven. This reminds me of an advertisement for biofeedback training I saw a few years ago, which read, "If you wear out your body ... *then* where do you plan to live?"

When it comes to the matter of life beyond the grave, humanity has come up with essentially five basic answers to the question of what we become after we die.[7] First is the view of *annihilation,* typical of modern-day materialism, which essentially says that at death, *poof,* we cease to exist. *Nada.* Death ends it all, except for our reputations and memories that live on after us. A second view might be called the view of *mythology,* the view of many ancient tribes and cultures that while we survive death, it is only as ephemeral ghosts, pale shadows of the people we once were. A third perspective is the belief of *reincarnation,* which says that we come back to earth in another mortal body on our journey toward spiritual enlightenment.[8] A fourth view is *Platonism,* which believes that at death each individual's disembodied spirit becomes liberated, surviving as a pure spirit, like an angel. Accordingly, Platonism teaches the immortality of the soul and maintains that the body has imprisoned the spirit until it is released at the time of death. A fifth view is that of *cosmic consciousness,* which is the essential teaching of both Hinduism and Buddhism. In this view—unlike materialism, which believes that death is everything (because we cease to exist)—death becomes nothing, because we are already everything and death cannot change that. According to cosmic consciousness, the only thing that survives death is the only thing that was real before death, because the material body is illusion. In this view of death, the individual soul loses all dignity and personhood, because the only thing that matters is the perfect, the eternal, the One, Atman.

In contrast to these five basic answers that the human race has concocted for what happens at death, it is only in Christianity that we become *something more* than we were before death. It is the startling, surprising idea of a new, greater, resurrected body. God seems to delight in coming up with creative oddities in His creation. He is, in fact, "the Great Iconoclast."[9]

Just as we observed that it is too simplistic to see Heaven as being purely spiritual (and that it has some sort of materiality), likewise the Christian teaching that we will have glorified, resurrected bodies strikes our normal sensibilities as a bit difficult to fathom. Yet the fact of the matter is that "spiritual" to premodern cultures did not mean "immaterial." Consequently, the origin of the popular heresy that the place of Heaven, like our Heavenly existence, is purely spiritual is paradoxically modern-day materialism.[10]

But in the Great Resurrection chapter, 1 Corinthians 15, the apostle Paul speaks of Christians receiving a "spiritual body,"[11] which sounds like a contradiction in terms. Yet as Jewish tradition has always held that life in the other world is life in the body, so also the New Testament writers never referred to an individual's "immortal soul" or "immortal spirit." These early Christian writers understood that union with God was a union of the whole human—both body and soul—with Him.

In this important biblical chapter concerning the bodily resurrection, Paul first lays out the *certainty* and *necessity* of Christ's resurrection, essentially stating that if Christ has not been bodily raised, then "your faith is worthless; you are still in your sins. . . . If we have hoped in Christ in this life only, we are of all men most to be pitied" (verses 17,19). He then sets forth the *continuity* between the natural body and the resurrection body (see verses 35-38), the *superiority* of the resurrection body (see verses 42-50), and the *mystery* of the resurrection (see verses 51-57), that in fact not everyone will see death, but some will be "changed, in a moment, in the twinkling of an eye, at the last trumpet" (verses 51-52).

Therefore, when we consider what these spiritual bodies will be like in Heaven, we are instructed to look at the body of Jesus Christ, because our bodies will resemble His own resurrection body. As the apostle John declares, "It has not appeared as yet what we shall be. We know that, when He appears, we shall be like Him" (1 John 3:2).[12] In many ways, the resurrected body of Christ was viewed as His earthly one, one that eats, drinks, breathes, circulates blood, and fires neurons. After His crucifixion and resurrection, He let Thomas touch His wounds (see John 20–21). Furthermore, the resurrected Christ ate fish (see Luke 24:42-43). While His resurrection body perhaps did not necessitate it, eating may still be a central aspect of the kingdom life.

Still, while Christ's resurrection body was His own, it was qualitatively *different* from the body He was born with, as well as from His body at the Transfiguration (see Matthew 17:1-8). He could on occasions appear quite different from His known identity in this life, as when the disciples did not recognize Him on the road to Emmaus (see Luke 24:13-26).[13] Somehow, it seems our resurrected bodies, however different, are the physical bodies we now inhabit. Yet they are bodies that will one day become imperishable, incorruptible, and immune from illness, frailty, or blemish.

Somehow this new, glorified body emerges from the old, earthly body. The earthly body is replaced or exchanged for the spiritual body, or the physical body "puts on" the spiritual body, as if the earthly body were an undergarment.[14] As Lewis observed,

> The records represent Christ as passing after death (as no one has passed before) neither into a purely . . . "spiritual" mode of existence nor into a "natural" life such as we know, but into a life which has its own, new Nature. . . . That is the picture—not of unmaking but of remaking. The old field of space, time, matter, and the senses is to be weeded, dug, and sown for a new crop. We may be tired of that old field; God is not.[15]

While God provides for us in Jesus a picture of the resurrection life, a life not of unmaking but of remaking, it is not unfair to ask, "Is it really necessary for us to have a *body* in Heaven?" Again, what possibly lurks behind this question is the subtle, Gnostic tendency that many of us have, which elevates the spiritual over the material. For whatever reasons, we often shun the idea of the *materiality* of Heaven in favor of the *spirituality* of Heaven.

And while much could be said about why "glorified bodies" are necessary in Heaven,[16] perhaps one reason that God will give us glorified bodies is because bodies can do things that no mere spirit can do. Angels may in fact have much greater intelligence, will, and power than we, but they cannot feel a gentle breeze by the ocean, smell a sumptuously delectable meal, or be mesmerized by a Bach cantata. Only Christianity truly glorifies the senses.[17]

No, the God of Christianity, as seen through the promised glorified body, delights in materiality and the physical senses. And just as He took pleasure after His creation of the cosmos, declaring that it was "very good" (Genesis 1:31), so He again displays His delight for the physical when He became one of us, when deity took on humanity, which we refer to as the Incarnation (see John 1:14). God invented the senses, perhaps to reveal the unique and irreplaceable tang of the particular in our human consciousness of each and every thing in the universe.[18] Therefore, the Christian is never to make the mistake of seeing joys and pleasures as distinct from the earthly and material blessings of this world (see 1 Timothy 4:4-5). This certainly applies to the glorified, resurrection body that we anticipate, which will not diminish but will increase our sense of pleasure and delight in God and the world to come. As Lewis wrote,

> They, of all men, must not conceive spiritual joy and worth as
> things that need to be rescued or tenderly protected from
> time and place and matter and the senses. Their God is the
> God of corn and oil and wine. . . .

> These small and perishable bodies we now have were given to
> us as ponies are given to schoolboys. We must learn to man-
> age: not that we may some day be free of horses altogether
> but that some day we may ride bare-back, confident and
> rejoicing, those greater mounts, those winged, shining and

world-shaking horses which perhaps even now expect us with impatience, pawing and snorting in the King's stables.[19]

Will There Be Time in Heaven?

One of the most perplexing concepts to consider about Heaven is the matter of time. We earlier addressed the fact that time is one of the clues of transcendence given by God to suggest the reality of Heaven. And the fact that we are so uncomfortable with time and its passing is because God has set eternity in our hearts (see Ecclesiastes 3:11).

The concept of time is a mystery. Augustine observed in his *Confessions*,

> What is time? Who can explain this easily and briefly? Who can comprehend this even in thought so as to articulate the answer in words? Yet what do we speak of, in our familiar everyday conversation, more than of time? We surely know what we mean when we speak of it. We also know what is meant when we hear someone else talking about it. What then is time? Provided that no one asks me, I know.[20]

Like Augustine, we may often talk about time but rarely do we give much thought to actually trying to determine what time really is. We are told in the Scriptures that God stands outside of time; when He created the cosmos, He created both space and time. Consequently, there was no time before the creation. God did not, as it were, sit around in time, waiting until he felt like creating the cosmos. God is eternal and as such He subsists *outside* of time and space, although He created them both.

This picture of God's residing outside the sphere of time is expressed in the words of Moses, when he pictures the whole creation as but a brief period in God's eyes: "For a thousand years in your sight are like a day that has just gone by, or like a watch in the night" (Psalm 90:4, NIV). Similarly, the apostle Peter observes that "with the Lord one day is as a thousand years, and a thousand years as one day" (2 Peter 3:8). In the Old Testament, God reveals Himself to Moses as "I AM WHO I AM," as The Self-Existent One (Exodus 3:14). It seems that in some incomprehensible way, God sees each moment as an eternity, and eternity as a moment. Because of this multidimensional perspective, He sees the beginning as well as the end. God sees, understands, and knows all points in space-time as in one moment—*totum simul*, "all at once."

While God exists outside the realm of time, the question remains, Will there be time in Heaven, in eternity? Based on what we have observed about our resurrection bodies in Heaven, to make life in Heaven strictly timeless would seem to be virtually impossible. If the blessed dwell in Heaven eternally with God, hence timelessly, time would not seem to exist. But without time, there can be no sequence and therefore no beginning or ending of our singing a psalm to God. Despite this tension between eternity and linear time, it seems that even glorified bodies need some form of time to function, whether that means singing a hymn or just thinking a thought.[21]

Though some sense of time seems reasonable based upon the fact that we will live in glorified bodies in Heaven, yet another matter that needs to be addressed is the meaning of "eternity."[22] Popular misconceptions about eternity include seeing it as some vague, unimaginably long time or as "unending time," both of which would naturally lead to the commonly voiced sentiment about Heaven, "Isn't Heaven going to be boring—being finally made perfect and with nothing to do?!"

Perhaps a better way of understanding eternity is to see it as "timeless moments." If we think about how we presently live life, we would have to admit that oftentimes we experience these timeless moments, which may very well serve as hints of what time will be like in Heaven. Timeless moments during our lives tend to be those occasions when we are surrounded by our loved ones and friends, such as when we gather for a birthday or wedding celebration, or simply get together with good friends. As such, eternity would be a different *dimension* of time, having more dimensions than time as we presently know it, and would be more like a point as the pure present, rather than being spread out into the future like a line.[23] This image, as difficult as it is to grasp, does communicate the important truth that eternity is not "spread out" over linear time, but time in Heaven is the "simultaneous present," as God is *totum simul*. It is Now. Kreeft creates a picture of this idea of eternity: "Time is like a floor, and our lives in time are like buckets of water spilled out along that floor. Eternity is like all the water gathered together in a bucket. One of the reasons we need eternity is so that our lives can finally have that wholeness, that oneness, that all-together-ness."[24]

In fact, it may even be helpful to differentiate between temporal dimensions, just as we do with the spatial dimensions of height, width, and depth. Accordingly, we might refer to the experience of our earthly time as *chronos* time, that time that is quantitatively measured by calendars and clocks (hence, a chronometer). Similarly, our human time, which is characterized by our memories and experiences of "lived life" with our friends and loved ones, might be referred to as *kairos* time. The former is quantitative, the measurement of time, and the latter is qualitative, the living out of that time.

Consequently, while mere *chronos* time gets us nowhere because it is without character, being the mere "skin" of time (it is Ecclesiastes' futile tyranny of the passing of time), it is *kairos* time that is effulgent with color, promise, and the dimension of lived lives and shared memories. When we ask people if they had a good *time* on their vacation, we're not asking them about their watching time go by on their holiday. Rather, we're asking them, What did you *do;* what experiences did you have with your family and friends? And while *chronos* time never touches eternity, *kairos* time does.

In *chronos* there is only past and future with no present, but *kairos* time is the all-present. As such, eternity would include all pasts and futures in the "living present."

A remarkable consequence follows: in a strange and mysterious way, eternity can even change the past. For us in this temporal existence the past is dead and unchangeable, but for those whose lives touch eternity, not only is the future open to change but the past is open to change as well. For those "in eternity," time is not static and linear but dynamic and alive. The past remains open and can even be redeemed. Even our sins, mistakes, missed opportunities, and all the dead-end streets we've experienced—even death itself—can be made to "work backwards" from eternity.

In Lewis's beloved children's book *The Lion, the Witch and the Wardrobe,* we see this idea of time "working backwards" powerfully portrayed when Susan and Lucy encounter the risen Aslan after his slaying at the Stone Table. As the two girls fling themselves upon Aslan, covering him with kisses, they want to know "what it all means"—how are they to make sense of his being alive?

> "It means," said Aslan, "that though the Witch knew the Deep Magic, there is a magic deeper still which she did not know. Her knowledge goes back only to the dawn of time. But if she could have looked a little further back, into the stillness and the darkness before Time dawned . . . she would have known that when a willing victim who had committed no treachery was killed in a traitor's stead, the Table would crack and Death itself would start working backwards." [25]

A corollary of the principle that eternity can change both present and past life is found in the commonly spoken words, "Prayer changes things." We can pray for anything we do not know the outcome of—both past and present—because the One to whom we pray is not bound by time. "God," said Pascal, "instituted prayer to give to His creatures the dignity of causality." [26]

Though we await the final consummation of God's kingdom, Heaven is nevertheless a present biblical reality. In some sense, the Christian has now been "transferred ... to the kingdom of His beloved Son" (Colossians 1:13), and as such, our lives touch eternity. T. S. Eliot observes in his *Four Quartets* that to attempt to fathom the intersection of time with the timeless "is an occupation for the saint." [27]

As Eliot observes, it is generally the saint who attempts to see the interplay between time and eternity, because God has "set eternity in their heart" (Ecclesiastes 3:11). In Thornton Wilder's play *Our Town,* we are reminded of the fleeting nature of time in our lives. The play depicts a young woman, Emily, who after dying in childbirth joins the dead in a hillside cemetery. In the third act, the Stage Manager allows her to go back and observe a single day of her brief life, but the dead advise her to "choose the least important day in your life. It will be important enough." Emily selects her twelfth birthday and is soon overwhelmed by the fleeting nature of time:

"I can't. I can't go on. It goes so fast. We don't have time to look at one another. . . . I didn't realize. So all that was going on and we never noticed. Take me back—up the hill—to my grave. But first: Wait! One more look."

"Goodbye, Goodbye, world. Goodbye, Grover's Corners . . . Mama and Papa. Goodbye to clocks ticking . . . and Mama's sunflowers. And food and coffee. And new-ironed dresses and hot baths . . . and sleeping and waking up. Oh, earth, you're too wonderful for anybody to realize you."

"Do any human beings ever realize life while they live it?— Every, every minute?

The Stage Manager answers, "No. . . . The saints and poets, maybe—they do some." [28]

What Will We Do in Heaven? Won't It Be Boring?

The business of Heaven—what we will do there—is surely one of the most frequent questions. And behind the question, important as it may be, is the modern, utilitarian perspective on life: what we *do* (is this not the first question we ask when we meet someone?) is more important than who we *are*. Yet being *precedes* doing.[29] But because what we do flows out of our identity and to some extent reveals who we are, it is still important to address the question.

More often than not, our pictures of Heaven are boring. Somehow the conventional idea of walking streets of gold, playing harps, and polishing our halos doesn't exactly excite us and may in fact be not an overvaluing but a *devaluing* of what Heaven is really like. Earlier I talked about an interview media mogul Ted Turner gave a few years ago. In this interview, Turner openly ridiculed the idea of walking streets of gold and playing our harps as being a bit too boring for him. Lewis's response to such an attitude is appropriate:

> There is no need to be worried by facetious people who try to make the Christian hope of "Heaven" ridiculous by saying they do not want "to spend eternity playing harps." The answer to such people is that if they cannot understand books written for grown-ups, they should not talk about them. All the scriptural imagery (harps, crowns, gold, etc.) is, of course, a merely symbolical attempt to express the inexpressible. . . .
>
> People who take these symbols literally might as well think that when Christ told us to be like doves, He meant that we were to lay eggs.[30]

But even if we do not share Turner's sentiments, we may still have serious reservations about Heaven because we cannot conceptualize what a life of perfection will be like. Fundamentally, we fear boredom, and earth seems tremendously more interesting than Heaven. Seen in such a light, death is truly a great terror, because our only options are agony or boredom. Can happiness truly exist without work to be done? But what in the world can we do to improve on perfection? Will there not be a need for my PalmPilot or Day-Timer in Heaven? I've met a number of people who have finally retired from a life of work—and guess what? Many are bored out of their heads! They miss the work, the excitement, and the challenge that are part of the workplace experience. Could Heaven possibly be the Giant Retirement Party, the Ultimate Letdown? Let's hope not!

One of the most thoughtful perspectives on this subject deals with our relationships in Heaven and how they will be deepened and will continue to grow throughout eternity. In his book *Thinking about Religion*, Richard Purtill offers some interesting insights about three human tasks we may have in Heaven, in this order: (1) understanding our earthly life "by Godlight," (2) sharing all other human lives, and (3) exploring God.[31] Purtill suggests that we will first review our past life with divine understanding and appreciation of every single experience, both good and evil; we will milk all our meaning dry. Perhaps in some mysterious way, this divine illumination that we then possess may help to shed light on the hurts, pains, and disappointments of this earthly life. We possibly will see for the first time that in some way unknown to us in *chronos* time, they actually have contributed to our common good, our "growth."[32]

The second aspect of our development in Heaven might involve what could be referred to as the "communion of the saints." Just as we saw in the previous chapter that Hell is primarily known for its *absence* of relationships, so Heaven may well be most characterized by the deepening of relationships, both with one another and with God. That is, just as we have milked our own meaning dry, we may do the same with others' lives, getting to know them more intimately and completely than we could ever have known them on earth. In contrast to

Eastern religion's quest for personal and private ecstasy, the biblical portrait of Heaven tends to describe the glorious experience of Heaven as being not a private but a communal affair.[33] It seems that through the worshiping community here upon earth (the church), God is preparing us for our eternal destiny (see Acts 2:42-47; 1 Peter 2:4-12).

When these two preliminary lessons are complete—when we know, love, understand, and appreciate completely everything we and everyone else have experienced, then we are perhaps spiritually mature enough to begin the endless and fascinating task of learning, exploring, and loving the inexhaustible Person of God. This contemplation of God, commonly referred to as the Beatific Vision, cannot be boring because it is entered into with other souls who have been matured by the first two tasks. This contemplation of God will not be a static, boring experience of simply staring at God but rather a dynamic, unending exploration of God and His attributes.

Therefore, this threefold aspect that is envisioned for Heaven involves three essential relationships: knowing ourselves, knowing others, and knowing God. While it would be presumptuous to suggest a hard-and-fast sequential order for these relational components, it is true that only in our relationship with others and with God can we truly begin to love ourselves correctly, love others compassionately, and love God completely.[34] Russell rightly observes,

> Heaven is not dull; it is not static; it is not monochrome. It is an endless dynamic of joy in which one is ever more oneself as one was meant to be, in which one increasingly realizes one's potential in understanding as well as love and is filled more and more with wisdom. . . . Humans are at their most real in heaven. . . . The glow of glory lights heaven and unites creator and creatures in a circuit of love.[35]

Another exciting aspect of Heaven may involve our exploration of the cosmos. While this may seem a bit far-fetched, it may very well be that in Heaven time is malleable, expandable, compressible, and even reversible. To God, time is "silly-putty time," and He plays it like an accordion player.[36] Consequently, because we live in Him, we too may eventually share the same relationship to time. We are given hints of this possible relationship to time in Jesus' post-resurrection appearances, when He seems to come and go at will (see John 20:19–21:14). Imagine if we could travel by an earthly time machine back to sixteenth-century England! While in such a scenario we would still be only outside observers, heavenly time travel could possibly involve an experience that might be quite close to the reality itself, not unlike the "virtual reality" that is being created by sophisticated computer graphics in our age. Lewis observes in *Letters to Malcolm: Chiefly on Prayer,*

> Don't run away with the idea that when I speak of the resurrection of the body I mean merely that the blessed dead will have excellent memories of their sensuous experiences on earth. I mean it the other way round; that memory as we know it is a dim foretaste, a mirage even, of a power which the soul, or rather Christ in the soul . . . will exercise hereafter. It need no longer . . . be private to the soul in which it occurs. I can now communicate to you the fields of my boyhood—they are building-estates today—only imperfectly, by words. Perhaps the day is coming when I can take you for a walk through them.[37]

Will We Know Everything in Heaven?

The question of how much we will know in Heaven is also frequently discussed. We sometimes hear someone say, "I can't wait to get to Heaven; then I'll know and understand *everything!*" While the comment is well intentioned, I'm not sure that we will in fact know everything there is to know. It is sometimes argued that Paul's statement in 1 Corinthians 13:12 supports such a conclusion: "For we now see in a mirror dimly, but then face to face; now I know in part, but then I shall know fully just as I also have been fully known." While this passage obviously means that we will have a clearer, truer picture of life and heavenly matters, it doesn't teach that we will be omniscient. First Corinthians 12–14 deals with the proper exercise of spiritual gifts in the body of Christ. And while in chapter 12 Paul addresses the general use of these gifts and their mutual interdependence, in chapter 13 his focus is on the vast superiority of love above all other gifts. His point is that while all the gifts given by God are at best transient, love will abide; it never fails (see verses 8-13). Thus, while the gifts of prophecy, tongues, and knowledge will cease (see verse 8), when the perfect comes, the imperfect will be done away with.[38] Thus Paul is essentially saying that when the whole truth is directly seen, the reflected glimpses of truth will be abandoned.

Furthermore, the idea of our acquiring omniscience in Heaven has some other serious problems, one of which is confusion between Heaven and divinity. Just as Christ from eternity past entered into time, taking on humanity permanently, so we, who share in the divine life and have become partakers of the divine nature (see John 5:24; 2 Peter 1:4), will still maintain our humanity throughout eternity. So it is only reasonable to conclude that, because we will remain human and therefore finite in Heaven, our knowledge likewise will remain finite.

Another reason omniscience will not be a part of our life in Heaven is the "downside" of what it would be like to know everything. Have you ever thought about how much more responsibility would be entailed with more knowledge? Is it not in fact true that only omnipotence could bear the tremendous burden of omniscience and that only God's shoulders are strong enough to carry the burden of infinite knowledge without losing the joy?[39]

If we really think about it, being omniscient might be more like Hell than Heaven! That is, because we will retain our distinctive, individual humanness in Heaven, we need to continue to learn, to make progress, and to hope for tomorrow's new challenges. Part of what makes us distinctive as human beings is our curiosity about life. To think that we would simply know everything would flatten out our experience in Heaven. Even in Heaven, as great and as glorious as that will be, we will still maintain our humble creatureliness or childlikeness. As Kreeft observes,

> Our first and last wisdom in Heaven is Socratic, just as it is on earth: to know how little we know. If there is no end of the need for humility in the moral order (the saint is the one humble enough not to think he is a saint), the same is true of the intellectual order (the wise man is the one humble enough to know he has no wisdom) ... by Heavenly standards all of us, even in Heaven, are children. And by the standard of the *infinite*, inexhaustible perfection of God, we remain children forever. Happy children, fulfilled children, but children.[40]

Will We Know Each Other in Heaven?

Although this question was addressed earlier in our discussion concerning the communion of the saints, let's consider it in a bit more detail. While the Scriptures promise an abiding fellowship among the saints (see Matthew 8:11; John 14:3), Jesus' post-resurrection appearances to His disciples and the fact that they knew Him and recognized Him seem to imply that we too will recognize one another. Communion of persons in some way necessitates some kind of personal recognition. In George MacDonald's words, "Shall we be greater fools in Paradise than we are here?" [41]

But it is only natural, because of our inherent curiosity, to raise a number of questions when it comes to our physical appearance in Heaven. What will be the relationship between husband and wife in

Heaven? Is there sex in heaven? What are we to make of those who have imperfections or disfigured bodies in this life? Will their resurrection bodies resemble their earthly bodies? And what age will we appear to be after receiving our resurrection bodies? As we delve into such questions, we can only offer speculations or guesses as to what lies in store for us in Heaven.

What will be the relationship of husband and wife in Heaven? It seems reasonable to assume that just as we will recognize other believers that we have known in our earthly lives, we most assuredly will recognize and continue to grow in our relationships with all of our family loved ones. Unfortunately, many thoughtful Christians have heard sermons or been taught in Bible studies that marriage no longer exists in Heaven. The passage that is commonly used to support this position is Matthew 22:30, where Jesus declares, "For in the resurrection they neither marry, nor are given in marriage, but are like angels in heaven." While an exhaustive exegetical study of this passage is beyond the scope of this work, it is helpful to understand the context of this passage for us to properly interpret the verse under consideration. In the previous verses, it is apparent that the Pharisees are attempting to ensnare Jesus (Matthew 22:15,18). Some of the Sadducees approach Him with a philosophical and theological conundrum (see verses 23 and following). In contrast to the Pharisees, who believed in the supernatural, the Sadducees were the wealthy power brokers of the day, who not only accepted the Pentateuch (the first five books of the Old Testament) as their Scriptures, but more important to our passage, also did not believe in the bodily resurrection from the dead. In the hypothetical situation they pose to Jesus, where a woman is married to seven successive brothers, they ask Him, "In the resurrection [which we don't believe in, anyway!] therefore whose wife of the seven shall she be? For they all had her" (verse 28).[42] Jesus' response to them is direct, penetrating, and invariably misunderstood!

"You are mistaken, not understanding the Scriptures, or the power of God. For in the resurrection they neither marry, nor are given in marriage, but are like angels in heaven. But regarding the resurrection of the dead, have you not read that which was spoken to you by God, saying, 'I am the God of Abraham, and the God of Isaac, and the God of Jacob'? He is not the God of the dead but of the living." (Matthew 22:29-32)

Jesus here turns the tables on His adversaries, rebuking these "religious naturalists" because of their unbelief in the power of God to raise His people from the dead. Ironically, He quotes from the book of Exodus, supposedly one of the five books they accepted as Scripture, but chides them for not understanding that "He is not the God of the dead but of the living." The point of Jesus' words is that in the resurrection, in the world to come, there will no longer be any need for the institution of marriage to bring children into the world, to fulfill the levirate law, because in Heaven there is no death. His comparison of angels to people in Heaven is simply that they are both alive and cannot die.[43]

Therefore, while this passage does suggest that marriage as we now know it will not exist in Heaven for procreational purposes, the passage does not teach that earthly marital relationships will cease to exist. In fact, to say that marital relationships will cease to exist would be to ignore some of the most important purposes of marriage given in the Bible. Some of these purposes behind God's design for marriage include the fact that (1) in the covenant of marriage we see a spiritual manifestation of the image and personality of God (see Genesis 1:27), and consequently, our sexuality and gender are an intrinsic part of our human nature; (2) marriage is intended to help meet the personal, relational needs of man and woman, because we were not intended to live solitary lives but rather with companionship (see Genesis 2:18); (3) marriage makes possible the procreation mandate of God to "be fruitful and multiply" (see Genesis 1:28

and following), which is normative for the human race; (4) in the covenant of marriage we are provided an important means for our spiritual sanctification and maturity (see Ephesians 5:22-33; Luther declared that "God has ordained two primary means for our edification—the Church and marriage"); (5) the covenant of marriage provides us with an earthly picture of the spiritual relationship between Jesus Christ and His Bride, the church (see Ephesians 5:29-32); and (6) the marriage relationship has been given by God as a means for husband and wife to experience the joys of sexual pleasure (see Song of Solomon; 1 Corinthians 7:1-4; 1 Timothy 4:1-5).

Will there be sex in Heaven? Some might think that such a question has no warrant in such an important and high-minded discussion, yet what else dominates our television programs, literature, film, and so much of our thought life? In reality, we probably do not think too much about sex, but too little of what sex is all about. Truly, there is no subject in the world about which there is more heat and less light.[44]

Interestingly, the Bible suggests that a significant correlation exists between sexuality and spirituality. In fact, the euphemistic expression used in the Old Testament to connote sexual relations— for a man to "know" a woman (Hebrew *yadah*)—is also used in the spiritual sense of someone "knowing" the Lord. The apostle Paul goes so far as to say that the reason sexual immorality is wrong is because "the body is not for immorality, but for the Lord; and the Lord is for the body.... The one who joins himself to the Lord is one spirit with Him" (1 Corinthians 6:13,17). On the subject of the sexuality of Heaven, Kreeft makes this provocative statement:

> The God of the Bible is not a monistic pudding in which differences are reduced to lumps, or a light that out-dazzles all finite lights and colors. God is a sexual being, the most sexual of all beings. This sounds shocking to people only if they see sex only as physical and not spiritual, or if they are Unitarians

rather than Trinitarians. . . . There is therefore sex in Heaven because in Heaven we are close to the source of all sex. As we climb Jacob's ladder the angels look less like neutered, greeting-card cherubs and more like Mars and Venus.[45]

Whatever we may believe about sexuality in Heaven, it seems clear that the sexual intimacy enjoyed here on earth is at least a "mere foretaste" of pleasures to come in Heaven. If sexual relations should for some reason not be a part of the glorified life, it is only because there is something much *better* to do. As Lewis wrote,

> I think our present outlook might be like that of a small boy who, on being told that the sexual act was the highest bodily pleasure should immediately ask whether you ate chocolates at the same time. On receiving the answer "No," he might regard absence of chocolates as the chief characteristic of sexuality. In vain would you tell him that the reason why lovers in their carnal raptures don't bother about chocolates is that they have something better to think of. The boy knows chocolate; he does not know the positive thing that excludes it. We are in the same position. We know the sexual life; we do not know, except in glimpses, the other thing which, in Heaven, will leave no room for it.[46]

What about those who have imperfections or disfigured bodies in this life? Will their resurrection bodies resemble their earthly bodies? As we consider the glorified bodies that believers are promised (because we will "be like Him," 1 John 3:2), one of the most provocative features of Christ's post-resurrection appearances is the fact that His new, glorified body still had its crucifixion wounds, its stigmata. He went so far as to show these wounds to Thomas to authenticate His identity (see John 20:24-29). Even in some modern instances, there are reports from credible individuals who are visited by their deceased loved ones, who still bear the marks of their sufferings.[47] It may be that while many of the cosmetic features of the body that are judged "imperfections" by human standards are in fact badges of beauty when freely accepted and offered to God.[48] And while the beauty prized and coveted by the world is often empty and superficial, there is a deeper, resilient beauty—a heavenly beauty—that marvelously portrays the beauty of character or soul. Perhaps the glorified, resurrection body will be made beautiful by the character of the individual—his or her soul—and not simply by its physical appearance.

What age will we appear to be after receiving our resurrection bodies? We know that these glorified bodies will not die or grow old. Yet we again need to remind ourselves that in Heaven, time is not measured by physical time (*chronos*), but only by soul time (*kairos*). Consequently, because time is differently related to the soul and the soul is differently related to the body, it is difficult to determine how age might be revealed in Heaven. What is interesting is that we sometimes do see hints of Heaven's agelessness here on earth. Lewis's description in *The Great Divorce* of the Solid People he encountered in "the High Country" provides us with a glimmer of the "agelessness" of Heaven: "Some were bearded but no one in that company struck me as being of any particular age. One gets glimpses, even in our country, of that which is ageless—heavy thought in the face of an infant, and frolic childhood in that of a very old man."[49]

Will We All Be Equal in Heaven?

One of the greatest characteristics of our modern culture is our egalitarian mindset, the desire for everybody to be equal. If this were the case in heaven, it likely would be terribly dull. Can you imagine what it would be like to have no heroes, no role models for your children, and only yourself to look up to? The modern fixation on equality is perhaps one of the greatest blind spots of modernity and is the opposite form of the pride embraced by the ancients, who understood hierarchy as an essential part of reality. While the old, aristocratic form of pride was the desire to be better *than others,* the modern, democratic form of pride is the desire not to have anyone *better than yourself.*[50]

Yet if one looks at life in general—mathematics, architecture, music, literature, and all of life under the sun—there is a natural justice, a distinctiveness that informs life. In an article a number of years ago, a writer lamented the loss of moral absolutes in our society, so he asked his Volvo mechanic how he saw the problem. The mechanic replied simply, but precisely, "We've lost hierarchy." And so it is in our modern world, where democracy and equality reign supreme as inviolable virtues. And yet the structure of reality in a theistic universe presumes distinctives in our world, such as Heaven and Hell, right and wrong, good and evil.

It seems to be the divine style to see justice, but not equality, in everything in life. Not the flat, dull repetition that would characterize equality, but the uniqueness that characterizes life, and in particular, human relationships. In his book *Letters to Malcolm: Chiefly on Prayer,* Lewis makes a sobering observation about any desire that we may have to have a little "chit-chat" with any of the Great Ones:

> My grandfather, I'm told, used to say that he "looked forward to having some very interesting conversations with St. Paul when he got to heaven." Two clerical gentlemen talking at ease in a club! It never seemed to cross his mind that an encounter with St. Paul might be rather an overwhelming experience even for an Evangelical clergyman of good family. But when Dante saw the great apostles in heaven they affected him like *mountains.* There's lots to be said against devotions to saints; but at least they keep on reminding us that we are very small people compared with them. How much smaller before their Master?[51]

So then, will we all be equal in Heaven? I love Kreeft's response, "By God's grace, no! How awful that would be!" [52] And not only will we not all be equal in Heaven, the corollary of this is that some will be elevated above others. That is to say, there will be heavenly rewards given to believers for their faithful service during their time upon earth. Certainly, a central teaching of the New Testament is that the good works performed by a Christian are in no way the basis of salvation, because salvation is the free gift of God's mercy personally appropriated by faith. Nevertheless, it is the saving grace of God performing its work in the individual believer that issues forth into good works. [53]

The New Testament is replete with examples of how earthly sacrifice now will result in being rewarded in Heaven. In the Sermon on the Mount, Jesus boldly proclaims to those who suffer persecution, "Rejoice, and be glad, for your reward in heaven is great, for so they persecuted the prophets who were before you" (Matthew 5:12). He also advises His followers, "Do not to lay up for yourselves treasures upon earth, where moth and rust destroy, and where thieves break in and steal. But lay up for yourselves treasures in heaven, where neither moth nor rust destroys, and where thieves do not break in or steal" (Matthew 6:19-20). The apostle Paul speaks of the importance of living the Christian life with self-control and bodily discipline, "lest possibly, after I have preached to others, I myself should be disqualified" (1 Corinthians 9:27). In his epistle to the Colossians, he encourages them with these words: "Whatever you do, do your work heartily, as for the Lord rather than for men; knowing that from the Lord you will receive the reward of the inheritance. It is the Lord Christ whom you serve" (Colossians 3:23-24). [54]

Today many Christians seem embarrassed to speak of rewards, as though the idea of receiving rewards is somehow "unspiritual." In his magnificent sermon "The Weight of Glory," Lewis suggests that such a view stems from unselfishness being more highly valued than love. In other words, a negative has replaced a positive so that unselfishness carries with it the suggestion not primarily of our securing good things for others, but rather of going without them ourselves, so that our abstinence and not their happiness is the important point. Lewis comments,

> The New Testament has lots to say about self-denial, but not about self-denial as an end in itself . . . and nearly every description of what we shall ultimately find if we do so contains an appeal to desire. . . . Indeed, if we consider the unblushing promises of reward and the staggering nature of the rewards promised in the Gospels, it would seem that Our Lord finds our desires, not too strong, but too weak. We are half-hearted creatures, fooling around with drink and sex and ambition when infinite joy is offered us, like an ignorant child who wants to go on making mud pies in a slum because he cannot imagine what is meant by the offer of a holiday at the sea. We are far too easily pleased.[55]

As Lewis suggests, our self-denial—securing good things for others, demonstrating our love for them—is strongly commended by our Lord, and we will be rewarded for such. The assessment of our good works is referred to in the New Testament as the judgment seat of Christ. The apostle Paul declares that "we must all appear before the judgment seat of Christ, that each one may be recompensed for his deeds in the body" (2 Corinthians 5:10).[56]

While it is difficult to know precisely the basis for this judgment for rewards, a few principles seem to govern it. First, rewards seem to be based upon a believer's life after his or her conversion and essentially deal with his or her living a life well pleasing to God (see Ephesians 2:9-10; 2 Corinthians 5:9). Second, rewards for the believer are not based merely on what might be termed "religious" work, but on *all* work. Because all of life is sacred, we will be rewarded accordingly (see Colossians 3:23-24). Third, God's evaluation of the believer's life will be based upon all that has been given to him or her in the way of time, treasures, talents, and truth. Fundamentally, we are stewards of everything that we possess and all that we are (see 1 Corinthians 4:1-8). It seems that in some sense (only God knows), everything that has been granted to us in this life is given to us as a spiritual opportunity to build God's kingdom.[57] Fourth, our motivation for living the Christian life seems to be important in God's reckoning of rewards. Paul declares that we should serve from a pure heart, "not grudgingly or under compulsion; for God loves a cheerful giver" (2 Corinthians 9:7). With this in mind, it's hard to believe that the elder brother of the prodigal son, who "never neglected a commandment" of his father's (Luke 15:29), was going to be rewarded for his "obedience." And a fifth principle that seems to govern rewards is that God's justice is not ours and His assessment may not be according to our human standards of justice. This is beautifully illustrated in the parable of the vineyard workers recorded in Matthew 20:1-16. Christ tells of how a landowner gave the *same* compensation to workers who went into the fields at 5 P.M. as to those who went out at 9 A.M. Americans tend to get quite upset with this parable: "The landowner is unfair, and it's outrageous that he would give the same amount to those who work one hour as those who have worked all day!" Yet Jesus declares that He has a right to do what He wishes with what is His own, thus "the last shall be first, and the first last" (Matthew 20:16).[58]

Another important issue concerns what might be the *nature* of Heaven's rewards. The promise of Scripture may be roughly reduced to five particular areas. We are promised, first, that we shall be with Christ; second, that we shall be like Him; third—and with a great amount of imagery—that we shall have "glory"; fourth, that we shall, in some sense, be fed or feasted or entertained; and finally, that we shall have some sort of official position in the universe—ruling cities, judging angels, even being pillars of God's temple.[59]

While it is impossible to know for sure, it seems safe to say that whatever the rewards may be, they certainly won't be physical ornaments that we parade around Heaven for our own glory! While some view the rewards as being synonymous with the believer's eternal life with God (see 2 Timothy 4:8; James 1:12; 1 Peter 5:4), it is more likely that rewards may relate to our further ability or capacity for spiritual growth, development, and service to the Lord (see Matthew 25:21-23).

Whatever we may conclude about the nature of the rewards, there seems to be a tendency among Christian teachers to either over-spiritualize or overmaterialize the rewards, with the result that we are either "ruling cities," conducting business as usual, or "casting our crowns" at the feet of the Lord. Like Heaven itself, our rewards may be both spiritual and physical. Luther surely spoke very good sense when he compared humanity to a drunkard who, after falling off his horse on the right, falls off it the next time on the left. We need to strive for balance.

As we close this chapter, having considered a number of questions about our eternal destiny—Heaven—for which we were created, we would do well to reflect on the doctrine of Christ's Second Coming, when this present world will be brought to an abrupt end. In the words of John Donne, "What if this present was the world's last night?" And Lewis wrote,

> A man of seventy need not be always feeling (much less talking) about his approaching death: but a wise man of seventy should always take it into account. . . . Women sometimes have the problem of trying to judge by artificial light how a dress will look by daylight. That is very much like the problem of all of us: to dress our souls not for the electric lights of the present world but for the daylight of the next. The good dress is the one that will face that light. For that light will last longer.[60]

CONCLUSION

If I find in myself a desire which no experience in this world can satisfy, the most probable explanation is that I was made for another world. If none of my earthly pleasures satisfy it, that does not prove that the universe is a fraud. Probably earthly pleasures were never meant to satisfy it, but only to arouse it, to suggest the real thing. . . . I must keep alive in myself the desire for my true country, which I shall not find till after death. . . . I must make it the main object of life to press on to that other country and to help others do the same.

—C. S. Lewis

In Alister McGrath's excellent book *The Unknown God: Searching for Spiritual Fulfillment*, he begins with the observation made by a noted philosopher that when people had plenty to eat, they turned their minds to thinking great thoughts.[1] The point he was making is simple: Before one can do any serious thinking, one has to make sure that physical needs are met. But having satisfied our physical hunger, people become aware of a more profound kind of hunger — a longing for something that will truly satisfy.

Lewis's words quoted above from *Mere Christianity* speak eloquently to our unsatisfied desires in this life and provide a fitting conclusion to our consideration of Heaven. As we have seen, the spirit of our age, the Zeitgeist, is strongly adverse to orthodox Christian belief in a true Heaven and Hell. To borrow again from Walker Percy, those of us who believe in Christianity are like those who have found a treasure hidden in the attic, but most of the people we encounter are those who have "moved to the suburbs," who are "bloody sick of the old house of orthodoxy."

So what are we to do? If we are Christians, it is easy to be overwhelmed by the animosity and charges of being narrow-minded that often greet our convictions. But despite such opposition, I believe that God, through the world He has made and the way He has made us, has left us numerous signposts of His presence in our world. And despite the world's dismissal of the reality of Heaven and Hell, if we will simply appeal to people to listen to their hearts, they will soon discover for themselves that our world intimates another life to come. "The heart has its reasons, of which reason knows nothing," Blaise Pascal observed. Through our pains and sorrows, our lack of contentment, our pleasures and joys, and even in the daily humdrum of our mundane lives (yes, even in our work and play), we sense that a drama is being played out and that we are the actors on the stage.

Composer John Cage's response to the question, Why are we here? — "No *why*, just here" — does not satisfy. Our hearts tell us that our lives have meaning and purpose, and this is in part because God has put eternity into our hearts (see Ecclesiastes 3:11). We are creatures being prepared for eternity. Consequently, there is a divine discontent built into the very fabric of our lives; this world cannot make us happy. We were made for another world—Heaven.

We also considered a number of reasons why the Christian can have an abiding confidence in the Christian faith, that it is first and foremost true and therefore a reliable guide about Heaven. As we saw, the testimony and reliability of the Christian Scriptures substantiate the Person and work of Jesus Christ and make a strong argument for the truth claims of Christianity. And as difficult as the doctrine of Hell is, we saw that in a true sense, Hell authenticates that God takes evil seriously and that His true love for man is shown as He honors free choice.

Heaven and Hell put bite into this drama we call life. T. S. Eliot's observation is worth repeating: "I had far rather walk, as I do, in daily terror of eternity, than feel that this was only a children's game in which all the contestants would get equally worthless prizes in the end." If it is possible to win in this game called life, then it is also possible to lose. Pascal, whose writings we considered in chapter 12, "The Certainty of Heaven," was perhaps best known for his idea known as "The Wager." In a nutshell, Pascal argues that we can be wrong in two ways: by wagering on the God of Christianity when there is no God, or by wagering on there being no God when there is a God. The second wager loses *everything;* the first loses *nothing.* The second wager is therefore the most stupid wager in the world, and the first is the wisest.[2]

Christianity, like atheism or agnosticism, is a "faith" position. It cannot be empirically proven any more than the others. The writer to the Hebrews declares that faith is "the assurance of things hoped for, the conviction of things not seen" (Hebrews 11:1). Biblical faith, therefore, is a personal response to the credible evidence at hand.

In light of the credibility of the Christian faith, we who are Christians should boldly and unapologetically, yet humbly, stand up for our Christian beliefs. Further, we should see ourselves like the Danish philosopher Søren Kierkegaard (and Pascal) saw himself— with a mission "to smuggle orthodox Christianity back into Christendom." You see, the world has jettisoned not so much orthodox Christianity, but a *caricature* of the Christian faith. And while the world may look at the Christian hope of Heaven simply as wishful thinking, the truth of the matter is that either there is "pie in the sky" or not. If not, then Christianity is nothing more than an interesting but antiquated relic, fit only for a museum.

As Christians, we have a tremendous opportunity to reach out to people who, despite their successes and achievements, still have no hope and are "without God in the world" (see Ephesians 2:12). The apostle Peter goes so far as to say that Christians, because they have received the mercy of God and are now God's very possession, are to be trophies of His grace as they "proclaim the excellencies of Him who has called you out of darkness into His marvelous light" (1 Peter 2:9).

We are to be about helping others find that "other country," that Lewis alludes to. I like the way Anne Lamott describes her pilgrimage to Christianity in her best-selling *Traveling Mercies: Some Thoughts on Faith*. With an exuberant mix of passion, insight, and humor, she takes us on a journey through her painful past to illuminate her devout—albeit unusual—walk of faith. On the first page of the book she confesses,

> My coming to faith did not start with a leap but rather a series of staggers from what seemed like one safe place to another. Like lily pads, round and green, these places summoned and then held me up while I grew. Each prepared me for the next leaf on which I would land, and in this way I moved across the swamp of doubt and fear. When I look back at some of these early resting places . . . I can see how flimsy and indirect a path they made. Yet each step brought me closer to the verdant pad of faith on which I somehow stay afloat today.[3]

Notes

Introduction

1. John Updike, "Pigeon Feathers," in *Pigeon Feathers and Other Stories* (New York: Fawcett Columbine, 1987), pp. 135-138.
2. Walker Percy, "Novel-Writing in an Apocalyptic Time," in *Signposts in a Strange Land,* Patrick Samway, ed. (New York: Farrar, Straus & Giroux, 1991), p. 159.

Chapter 1: The Trivialization of Heaven

1. Karen S. Peterson, "Don't Tell 'Immortals' Nothing Lasts Forever," *USA Today,* July 29, 1992, D1. Charles Paul Brown, founder of the movement and a former retail fashion buyer and nightclub singer before discovering in 1960 that he was immortal, said "it was like a new intelligence flooding my body."
2. For just a few examples of the Christian hope of Heaven, see Matthew 5:12,20; John 6:38; 14:1-3; 1 Corinthians 2:9; Philippians 3:20; Hebrews 11:8-16; and 1 Peter 1:4.
3. Walker Percy, *Lost in the Cosmos: The Last Self-Help Book* (New York: Washington Square Press, 1983), p. 7.
4. See Peter Kreeft, *Heaven: The Heart's Deepest Longing* (San Francisco: Ignatius Press, 1989), pp. 11-12.
5. James Sire, *The Universe Next Door* (Downers Grove, IL: InterVarsity, 1976), pp. 23-24.
6. Sire, p. 85. Sire further describes the progression in worldviews following nihilism: because man cannot live with such a despairing view of life, existentialism (both atheistic and theistic and represented by such writers as Albert Camus) came into vogue in the mid-1900s in an effort to transcend such a dark perspective of life. Concerning the

West's interest in Eastern religion in the 1960s, Sire notes that the movement represents "a retreat from Western thought. The West ends in a maze of contradictions, acts of intellectual suicide and a specter of nihilism that haunts the dark edges of all our thought. Is there not another way? Indeed, there is—a very different way. With its antirationalism, its syncretism, its quietism, its lack of technology, its uncomplicated life-style and its radically different religious framework, the East is extremely attractive. Moreover, the East has an even longer tradition than the West. Sitting, as it were, next door to us for centuries have been modes of conceiving and viewing the world that are poles apart from ours. Maybe the East, that quiet land of meditating gurus and simple life, has the answer to our longing for meaning and significance" (pp. 138-139).

7. These observations of T. S. Eliot are taken from the dated but excellent article by D. Bruce Lockerbie, "Laughter Without Joy: The Burlesque of Our Secular Age," *Christianity Today,* October 7, 1977, pp. 14-16.

8. Quoted by D. Bruce Lockerbie, "Laughter Without Joy: The Burlesque of Our Secular Age," *Christianity Today,* October 7, 1977, pp. 14-16.

9. See Lockerbie, p. 14.

10. Blaise Pascal, *Pensées,* 149, A. J. Krailsheimer, trans. (New York: Penguin Books, 1966), pp. 77-78.

11. Malcolm Muggeridge, *The End of Christendom* (Grand Rapids, MI: Eerdmans, 1980), p. 20. Leslie Fiedler quote cited by Muggeridge from *Trousered Apes* by Duncan Williams. On Fiedler's quote, Muggeridge perceptively observes, "You might think that was a somewhat pessimistic way of looking at things, but it isn't really. I conclude that civilizations, like every other human creation, wax and wane. By the nature of the case there can never be a lasting civilization any more than there can be a lasting spring or lasting happiness in an individual life, or lasting stability in a society. It's in the nature of man and of all that he constructs to perish, and it must ever be so" (p. 21).

12. Kreeft, pp. 12-13.

13. The following are from Tom Willett, "Contemporary American Attitudes about God," *The Door,* September-October 1993, p. 11.

14. Gary Larsen, *The Far Side Calendar,* September 16, 1996 (Kansas City, MO: Andrews and McNeel, 1995).

15. C. S. Lewis, "Answers to Questions on Christianity," in *God in the Dock: Essays on Theology and Ethics* (Grand Rapids, MI: Eerdmans, 1970), p. 58. Lewis makes a similar point when he declares, "I quite

agree that the Christian religion is, in the long run, a thing of unspeakable comfort. But it does not begin in comfort; it begins in the dismay I have been describing, and it is no use at all trying to go on to that comfort without first going through that dismay. In religion, as in war and everything else, comfort is the one thing you cannot get by looking for it. If you look for truth, you may find comfort in the end: if you look for comfort you will not get either comfort or truth—only soft-soap and wishful thinking to begin with and, in the end, despair. Most of us have got over the pre-war wishful thinking about international politics. It is time we did the same about religion." *Mere Christianity* (New York: Macmillan, 1943), p. 25.

16. C. S. Lewis, *Surprised by Joy: The Shape of My Early Life* (New York: Harcourt Brace Jovanovich, 1955), p. 211.

17. Lewis, "Man or Rabbit?" in *God in the Dock,* pp. 108-109.

18. See further C. S. Lewis, *The Problem of Pain* (New York: Macmillan, 1962), pp. 144-145.

19. Thomas Howard, *Chance or the Dance?* (San Francisco: Ignatius Press, 1989).

20. See Peter Kreeft, *Everything You Ever Wanted to Know About Heaven . . . but Never Dreamed of Asking* (San Francisco: Ignatius Press, 1990), p. 17.

21. Flannery O'Connor, *A Good Man Is Hard to Find and Other Stories* (New York: Harcourt Brace Jovanovich, 1955), p. 28.

22. Jill Peláez Baumgaertner, *Flannery O'Connor: A Proper Scaring* (Chicago: Cornerstone, 1988), p. 127.

23. Paul Johnson, *The Quest for God: A Personal Pilgrimage* (New York: HarperCollins, 1996), p.1.

24. Ingmar Bergman, *The Seventh Seal,* in *Four Screenplays of Ingmar Bergman,* L. Malmstrom and D. Kushner, trans. (New York: Simon & Schuster, 1960), p. 150.

25. Frederick Buechner, "The Annunciation," in *The Magnificent Defeat* (San Francisco: HarperCollins, 1966), p. 65.

26. C. S. Lewis, "The Weight of Glory," in *The Weight of Glory and Other Addresses* (Grand Rapids, MI: Eerdmans, 1965), pp. 4-5.

Chapter 2: The Secularization of Heaven

1. Pronounced Ko-helleth or Ko-hellet. The word is connected with the Hebrew for "assembling," and its form suggests some kind of office-bearer. There are many attempts at translating this title, including "Ecclesiastes," "The Preacher," "The Speaker," "The Spokesman,"

"The Philosopher." We could appropriately add the title, "The Professor"! Some argue that the writer's title, his style of Hebrew, and his attitude toward rulers (suggesting that of a subject rather than a monarch; for example, see Ecclesiastes 4:1-2; 5:8-9; 8:2-4; 10:20) may point to a person other than King Solomon. Yet other passages strongly suggest that King Solomon is the author (1:1,12,16; 2:4-9; 7:26-29; 12:9; compare 1 Kings 2:9; 3:12; 4:29-34; 5:12; 10:1-8).

2. Derek Kidner, *The Message of Ecclesiastes* (Downers Grove, IL: Inter-Varsity, 1976), Author's Preface, p. 13.

3. Quoted in Donald W. McCullough, *Waking from the American Dream* (Downers Grove, IL: InterVarsity, 1988), pp. 174-175.

4. Peter Kreeft, *Three Philosophies of Life* (San Francisco: Ignatius Press, 1989), p. 20. I am indebted to Kreeft for many of these insights from his excellent book on Ecclesiastes as an apologetic to post-Christian culture.

5. See Kidner, p. 34.

6. See Kreeft, p. 20.

7. Quoted in Lisa Grunwald, "Is It Time to Get Out?" *Esquire*, April 1990, p. 141.

8. Kidner, p. 19.

9. See Kreeft, p. 23. J. I. Packer has suggested the following structure for the book: chapters 1–2: Problem Number One — Life's Failure to Satisfy; chapters 3–5: Problem Number Two — God's Inscrutability; chapters 6–8: The Worth of Wisdom, Despite Everything; and chapters 9–12: The Way of Wisdom, Despite Everything. This outline is taken from Packer's addresses at the Ozark Bible Conference, 1981. Another perspective he offered at the conference was chapters 1–2, "What Is Felt in God's World" (non-satisfaction); chapter 3, "What Is Fixed in God's World" (God's lordship); chapters 4–5, "What Is Seen in God's World" (misery); chapters 6–8, "What Is Valuable in God's World" (wisdom); and chapters 9–12, "What Is to Be Cultivated in God's World" (how to cope with life).

10. Ecclesiastes 1:3, TEV. This specific word for "gain" (Hebrew *yatar*) comes from the world of commerce and business and is found only in the book of Ecclesiastes. It is not unlike Jesus' remark, "What does it *profit* a man to gain the whole world, and forfeit his soul?" (Mark 8:36, my italics). Kidner remarks, "This is not the only place where Christ and Qoheleth speak the same language" (pp. 24-25).

11. G. S. Hendry makes these excellent observations about Qoheleth's intentions: "Qoheleth writes from concealed premises, and his book is in reality a major work of apologetic. . . . Its apparent worldliness is

dictated by its aim: Qoheleth is addressing the general public whose view is bounded by the horizons of the world; he meets them on their own ground, and proceeds to convince them of its inherent vanity. This is further borne out by his characteristic expression 'under the sun,' by which he describes what the NT calls 'the world.'. . . His book is in fact a critique of secularism and of secularized religion." See further the introduction to the article "Ecclesiastes" in *The New Bible Commentary Revised* (Downers Grove, IL: InterVarsity, 1970), p. 570.

12. See Kreeft, p. 35.

13. T. S. Eliot, "Choruses from 'The Rock,'" Chorus I, *T. S. Eliot Selected Poems* (New York: Harcourt Brace Jovanovich, 1964), p. 107.

14. Quoted in D. Bruce Lockerbie, *The Cosmic Center: The Supremacy of Christ in a Secular Wasteland* (Portland, OR: Multnomah, 1977), p. 28.

15. Kidner makes this insightful observation about Qoheleth's preoccupation with pleasure: "(He) is looking for something beyond it and through it, for this is more than simple indulgence. It is a deliberate flight from rationality, to get at some secret of life to which reason may be blocking the way. . . . Here we are brought very near to our own times with their cult of the irrational in its various forms, from romanticism down to the addict's craving for strange states of consciousness; and down still further into the nihilism which cultivates the ugly, the obscene and the absurd, not as a frolic but as an attack on reasonable values" (p. 31).

16. Quoted in *Current Books* (Bethesda, MD: Capital Communications Group, LLC), Fall/Winter 1993, p. 88. From John-Roger and Peter McWilliams, *Wealth 101: Wealth Is Much More Than Money* (Los Angeles: Prelude Press).

17. Cited in McCullough, p. 73.

18. Quoted in Tom Morris, *If Aristotle Ran General Motors* (New York: Henry Holt, 1997), p. 12.

19. Tom Barry, "Ted Turner's Mission," *Georgia Trend*, March 1996, pp. 18-22.

20. Kreeft, pp. 44-45.

21. Franz Lidz, "An Invasion of Privacy," *Sports Illustrated*, September 9, 1996, p. 72.

22. Quoted in Thomas Cahill, *How the Irish Saved Civilization* (New York: Doubleday, 1995), p. 97.

23. Kreeft, pp. 22-23.

24. Saint Augustine, *Confessions*, bk. I, i (1), Henry Chadwick, trans. (Oxford: Oxford University Press, 1991), p. 3.

25. George Herbert, "The Pulley," in *George Herbert: The Complete English Works, Everyman's Library,* Ann Pasternak Slater, ed. (New York: Knopf, 1908), p. 156.

Chapter 3: The Heart Has Its Reasons

1. Quoted in Woody Allen, "My Speech to the Graduates," *The New York Times,* August 10, 1979, A25.
2. Woody Allen, "The Scrolls," in *Without Feathers* (New York: Random House, 1972), p. 23. The title to this book is obscure until one notices the epigram at the beginning, which accurately reveals his cynical and nihilistic worldview. A line of one of Emily Dickinson's poems says, "Hope is the thing with feathers," but to Allen, this world is ultimately despairing, without hope.
3. C. S. Lewis, "Transposition," in *The Weight of Glory and Other Essays* (New York: Macmillan, 1949), pp. 28-29. Lewis elsewhere argues persuasively against any kind of reductionistic thinking that attacks the religious worldview as being something merely psychological. His apologetic is powerfully portrayed in his work *Miracles,* in which he shows the naïveté of a materialistic naturalism: "The whole process of human thought, what we call Reason, is equally valueless if it is the result of irrational causes. . . . The Naturalist cannot condemn other people's thoughts because they have irrational causes and continue to believe his own which have (if Naturalism is true) equally irrational causes. The shortest and simplest form of this argument is that given by Professor J. B. S. Haldane in *Possible Worlds* (p. 209). He writes: 'If my mental processes are determined wholly by the motions of atoms in my brain, I have no reason to suppose that my beliefs are true . . . and hence I have no reason for supposing my brain to be composed of atoms.'" *Miracles* (New York: Macmillan, 1946), pp. 219-220.
4. Quoted in Malcolm Muggeridge, *Christ and the Media* (Grand Rapids, MI: Eerdmans, 1977), p. 62.
5. C. S. Lewis, "Meditation in a Toolshed," in *God in the Dock: Essays on Theology and Ethics* (Grand Rapids, MI: Eerdmans, 1970), p. 212. On the relevance of this to the material and spiritual world, Lewis continues: "The people who look at things have had it all their own way; the people who look along things have simply been browbeaten. It has even come to be taken for granted that the external account of a thing somehow refutes or 'debunks' the account given from inside. . . . It is perfectly easy to go on all your life giving

explanations of religion, love, morality, honour, and the like, without having been inside any of them. And if you do that, you are simply playing with counters. You go on explaining a thing without knowing what it is" (pp. 213-214).

6. Blaise Pascal, *Pensées*, 423, 424, A. J. Krailsheimer, trans. (New York: Penguin Books, 1966), p. 154.

7. Pascal, 188, p. 85.

8. Harriet Beecher Stowe, *Uncle Tom's Cabin (or, Life among the Lowly)*, *The Minister's Wooing, Oldtown Folks* (New York: Literary Classics of the United States, 1982), pp. 352-354.

9. Hans Walter Wolff, *Anthropology of the Old Testament* (Philadelphia: Fortress Press, 1974), pp. 46-47. Wolff further states, "The most important word in the vocabulary of Old Testament anthropology is generally translated 'heart.' In its commonest form, *leb*, it occurs 598 times in the Hebrew Old Testament; and in the form *lebab* 252 times. In addition the Aramaic *leb* occurs once, in the book of Daniel, and *lebab* seven times. Altogether, therefore, it can be found 858 times, which makes it the commonest of all anthropological terms. Moreover, in contrast to the other main concepts, it is almost exclusively applied to man. . . . But it is to be feared that the usual translation 'heart' for *leb(ab)* leads our present-day understanding astray" (p. 40). Another Old Testament scholar, Aubrey R. Johnson, makes these significant observations about the heart: "For all that the heart is thus brought so often into relation with man's psychical life at the emotional level, it is as the seat or instrument of his intellectual and volitional activity that it figures most prominently in Israelite thinking. Thus the term for 'heart,' besides being used with a force which approximates to what we should call 'mind' or 'intellect.'" Aubrey R. Johnson, *The Vitality of the Individual in the Thought of Ancient Israel* (Cardiff: University of Wales Press, 1964), p. 77.

10. Peter Kreeft, *Heaven: The Heart's Deepest Longing* (San Francisco: Ignatius Press, 1980), p. 36.

11. Walker Percy, *The Moviegoer* (New York: Ballantine Books, 1960), pp. 9-10.

12. "Uncle Jules is the only man I know whose victory in the world is total and unqualified. He has made a great deal of money, he has a great many friends, he was Rex of Mardi Gras, he gives freely of himself and his money. He is an exemplary Catholic, but it is hard to know why he takes the trouble. For the world he lives in, the City of Man, is so pleasant that the City of God must hold little in store for him." Percy, *The Moviegoer*, p. 25.

13. Frederick Buechner, "Message in the Stars," in *The Magnificent Defeat* (San Francisco: HarperCollins, 1966), p. 47.

Chapter 4: Our Universal Unhappiness

1. Taken from *I've Got Tears in My Ears from Lyin' on My Back in My Bed While I Cry Over You: Country Music's Best (and Funniest) Lines*, compiled by Paula Schwed (Kansas City, MO: Andrews and McMeel, 1992).
2. Daniel Boorstin, *The Image: A Guide to Pseudo-Events in America* (New York: Atheneum, 1987), p. 4. Boorstin makes a telling observation about our culture when he relates how the idea of "greatness" has changed in the last half of the twentieth century, moving from hero to celebrity: "One of the oldest of man's visions was the flash of divinity in the great man. . . . Two centuries ago when a great man appeared, people looked for God's purpose in him; today we look for his press agent" (p. 45).
3. Boorstin, p. 5.
4. Charles Colson, "Madison Avenue's Spiritual Chic," *Christianity Today*, January 12, 1998, p. 80.
5. Quoted in Colson, p. 80.
6. Cynthia Crossen, "Americans Have It All (But All Isn't Enough)," *The Wall Street Journal*, September 20, 1996, R1.
7. See further Richard A. Swenson, M.D., *Margin: Restoring Emotional, Physical, Financial, and Time Reserves to Overloaded Lives* (Colorado Springs: NavPress, 1992), p. 22.
8. Cited in D. Bruce Lockerbie, *The Cosmic Center: The Supremacy of Christ in a Secular Wasteland* (Portland, OR: Multnomah, 1986), p. 69.
9. Albert Camus, "The Adulterous Woman," in *Exile and the Kingdom*, Justin O'Brien, trans. (New York: Knopf, 1957), p. 33.
10. Peter Kreeft, *Heaven: The Heart's Deepest Longing* (San Francisco: Ignatius Press, 1989), p. 58.
11. Walker Percy, *The Moviegoer* (New York: Ballantine Books, 1960), p. 73.
12. Malcolm Muggeridge, "Happiness," in *Jesus Rediscovered* (New York: Doubleday, 1979), p. 179. Muggeridge remarks, "The sister-in-law of a friend of Samuel Johnson was imprudent enough once to claim in his presence that she was happy. He pounced on her hard, remarking in a loud, emphatic voice that if she was indeed the contented being she professed herself to be then her life gave the lie to every research of humanity" (p. 179).

13. Quoted in Peggy Noonan, "Why We Feel So Bad," *Forbes Magazine*, September 14, 1992, p. 65. Addressing the cultural shift that has transformed the American culture, Noonan continues, "Somewhere in the Seventies, or the Sixties, we started expecting to be happy, and changed our lives (left town, left families, switched jobs) if we were not. And society strained and cracked in the storm. . . . I think we have lost the old knowledge that happiness is overrated—that, in a way, life is overrated. We have lost, somehow, a sense of mystery— about us, our purpose, our meaning, our role. Our ancestors believed in two worlds, and understood this to be the solitary, poor, nasty, brutish and short one. We are the first generations of man that actually expected to find happiness here on earth, and our search for it has caused such—unhappiness. The reason: If you do not believe in another, higher world, if you believe only in the flat material world around you, if you believe that this is your only chance at happiness—if that is what you believe, then you are not disappointed when the world does not give you a good measure of its riches, you are despairing" (p. 65).

14. Peter Kreeft, *Christianity for Modern Pagans* (San Francisco: Ignatius Press, 1993), p. 169.

15. Blaise Pascal, *Pensées*, 70, 136, A. J. Krailsheimer, trans. (New York: Penguin Books, 1966), pp. 48, 67.

16. See Kreeft, *Christianity for Modern Pagans*, p. 169.

17. Quoted in Kreeft, *Heaven*, p. 53.

18. Walker Percy, "Novel-Writing in an Apocalyptic Time," in *Signposts in a Strange Land*, Patrick Samway, ed. (New York: Farrar, Straus and Giroux, 1991), pp. 162-163.

19. C. S. Lewis, *Till We Have Faces* (New York: Harcourt Brace Jovanovich, 1956), p. 74.

20. Jon Katz, *Running to the Mountain: A Journey of Faith and Change* (New York: Villard, 1999), pp. 6-7.

21. C. S. Lewis, *The Problem of Pain* (New York: Macmillan, 1962), p. 115.

Chapter 5: Our Sense of Alienation

1. Malcolm Muggeridge, *Chronicles of Wasted Time, Chronicle I: The Green Stick* (New York: Quill, 1982), p. 18.

2. Malcolm Muggeridge, *Jesus Rediscovered* (New York: Doubleday, 1979), pp. 47-48.

3. Quoted in Donald W. McCullough, *Waking from the American Dream* (Downers Grove, IL: InterVarsity, 1988), pp. 199-200.

4. Thomas Kellner, "Resurrection Insurance," *Forbes,* August 24, 1998, p. 45.

5. Thomas Lynch, "The Day the Gravedigger Died," *Esquire,* May 1999, pp. 88-89.

6. Thomas Lynch, *The Undertaking: Life Studies from the Dismal Trade* (New York: Norton, 1997), p. 33.

7. Malcolm Muggeridge, *Confessions of a Twentieth-Century Pilgrim* (San Francisco: Harper & Row, 1988), p. 144. Muggeridge continues his reflections as he recalls a month spent in sunny Florida in his latter years: "This basic fact of death is today highly unpalatable, to the point that extraordinary efforts are made ... to keep death out of sight and mind. ... A month spent in Florida in the company of fellow geriatrics gave me some idea of the lengths to which the old are induced to go in order to distract their thoughts from their impending demise. In, let us call it, Sunshine Haven, everything was done to make us feel that we were not really aged, but still full of youthful zest and expectations; if not teenagers, then keen-agers, perfectly capable of disporting ourselves on the dance floor, the beach, or even in bed. Withered bodies arrayed in dazzling summer wear, hollow eyes glaring out of garish caps, skulls plastered with cosmetics, lean shanks tanned a rich brown, bony buttocks encased in scarlet trousers ... the cadavers are scented and anointed and dressed for their obsequies in their exotic best, down to underclothes; in Sunset Haven, pre-cadavers likewise array themselves for social occasions like young debutantes and their squires out on a spree, and behave accordingly, though sometimes with creaking joints and inward groans" (pp. 142-143).

8. Joshua Levine, "Dr. Pangloss, Meet Ingmar Bergman," *Forbes,* March 30, 1992, p. 96.

9. Levine, p. 96.

10. See Peter Kreeft, *Heaven: The Heart's Deepest Longing* (San Francisco: Ignatius Press, 1989), p. 13.

11. Paul Johnson, *The Quest for God* (New York: HarperCollins, 1996), pp. 131-133.

12. Peter Kreeft, *Christianity for Modern Pagans* (San Francisco: Ignatius Press, 1993), p. 141.

13. Johnson, pp. 134-135.

14. C. S. Lewis, *Miracles: A Preliminary Study* (New York: Touchstone Books, 1996), p. 169.

15. John Updike, *Rabbit at Rest* (New York: Ballantine Books, 1990), p. 16.

16. Tim Hansel, *When I Relax I Feel Guilty* (Elgin, IL: David C. Cook,

1979), pp. 67-68. The article is taken from Leslie B. Flynn, *It's About Time* (Newtown, PA: Timothy Books, 1974), p. 39.

17. Alan Lightman, *Einstein's Dreams* (New York: Warner, 1993), pp. 28-30. In another fable, dated 28 June 1905, a family is having a picnic on the bank of the Aare, ten kilometers south of Bern. A young man, his wife, and his grandmother sit on a blanket, eating smoked ham, cheese, sourdough bread with mustard, grapes, and chocolate cake. As they eat and drink, and the couple's daughters frolic in the grass, a gentle breeze comes over the river and they breathe in the summer air. Then something arrests their attention. Suddenly, a flock of birds flies overhead. The young man leaps from the blanket to chase after them. He is soon joined by others, who have spotted the birds from the city. One bird alights in a tree, and a woman climbs the trunk, attempting to catch the bird, but it jumps to a higher branch. As the woman hangs helplessly in the tree, another bird is seen eating seeds on the ground. Two men sneak up behind it, carrying a giant bell jar. But the bird takes to the air, joining the rest of the flock. Now the birds fly through the town. Lightman poetically describes the significance of the birds: "Because this flock of nightingales is time. Time flutters and fidgets and hops with these birds. Trap one of these nightingales beneath a bell jar and time stops. . . . The children, who alone have the speed to catch the birds, have no desire to stop time. For the children, time moves too slowly already. . . . The elderly desperately wish to halt time, but are much too slow and fatigued to entrap any bird" (pp. 172-175).

18. Kreeft, *Heaven*, pp. 70-73.

19. Sheldon Vanauken, *A Severe Mercy* (San Francisco: Harper & Row, 1977), p. 93. In a similar vein, Lewis comments on our surprise at the passing of time when he observes, "We are so little reconciled to time that we are even astonished at it. 'How he's grown!' We exclaim, 'How time flies!' as though the universal form of our experience were again and again a novelty. It is as strange as if a fish were repeatedly surprised at the wetness of water. And that would be strange indeed; unless of course the fish were destined to become, one day, a land animal." *Reflections on the Psalms* (New York: Harcourt Brace Jovanovich, 1958), p. 138.

20. See Thomas Howard, *Christ the Tiger* (San Francisco: Ignatius Press, 1990), p. 120.

21. Lewis, *Miracles*, p. 169.

22. Malcolm Muggeridge, *The End of Christendom* (Grand Rapids, MI: Eerdmans, 1980), p. 16.

23. Quoted in Muggeridge, *The End of Christendom,* pp. 27-28.

24. See Genesis 11.

Chapter 6: Transcendence in Literature and Film

1. See Peter Kreeft, *Heaven: The Heart's Deepest Longing* (San Francisco: Ignatius Press, 1989), pp. 110-111.

2. Thomas Howard, *Chance or the Dance? A Critique of Modern Secularism* (San Francisco: Ignatius Press, 1969), pp. 11-12.

3. G. K. Chesterton, *Orthodoxy* (San Francisco: Ignatius Press, 1995), pp. 14-15.

4. Chesterton, pp. 29-33. He continues, "The ordinary man has always been sane because the ordinary man has always been a mystic. He has permitted the twilight. He has always had one foot in earth and the other in fairyland. . . . His spiritual sight is stereoscopic, like his physical sight: he sees two different pictures at once and yet sees all the better for that. . . . The whole secret of mysticism is this: that man can understand everything by the help of what he does not understand" (pp. 32-33).

5. The New Testament frequently addresses this issue of symbol and reality. The writer to the Hebrews contrasts the "earthly" and "heavenly" high priest, that is, the earthly priest appointed to offer sacrifices for the nation versus the heavenly high priest par excellence, Jesus Christ. He states that, in contrast to the earthly high priest, "we have such a high priest, who has taken His seat at the right hand of the throne of the Majesty in the heavens, a minister in the sanctuary, and in the true tabernacle, which the Lord pitched, not man" (Hebrews 8:1-2). Further, the offerings of the earthly high priests "serve at a sanctuary that is a copy and shadow of what is in heaven" (8:5, NIV). See further Hebrews 9:23 and 10:1, where the items of the holy tabernacle as well as the Law are to be seen as only "copies" or "shadow[s] of the good things to come and not the very form of things" (10:1). The issue of symbol and reality is further seen in the covenant of marriage, which is a deep and abiding symbol of Christ's union with His Bride, the church: "This mystery is great; but I am speaking with reference to Christ and the church" (Ephesians 5:32). Furthermore, in the two ordinances given by our Lord to the church—water baptism and the Lord's Table—a wealth of meaning is contained in the symbolic "earthly" elements of water, representing spiritual cleansing, and the bread and blood, representing His body and blood. To participate in the Lord's Table is thus a participation in the life offered

through the new covenant that Jesus Christ inaugurated (see further Romans 6 and 1 Corinthians 11).

6. See Kreeft, pp. 118-119.

7. Alfred Kazin, *God and the American Writer* (New York: Vintage Books, 1997), p. 3.

8. Kazin, p. 16. In his afterword, Kazin observes, "Mark Twain, the first of the best-selling prima donnas of the modern American novel, was in old age still trying to dispose of the Presbyterian God who like a bad fairy at his birth was to poison every success with guilt" (pp. 256-257).

9. D. Bruce Lockerbie, *Dismissing God* (Grand Rapids, MI: Baker, 1998), p. 15.

10. C. S. Lewis, "Learning in War-Time," in *The Weight of Glory and Other Addresses* (Grand Rapids, MI: Eerdmans, 1949), pp. 50-51.

11. Jack Kroll, "Map of Greeneland," *Newsweek,* April 15, 1991, p. 75.

12. Reynolds Price, "At the Heart," in *A Common Room: Essays 1954-1987* (New York: Atheneum, 1989), p. 405.

13. C. S. Lewis, "On Three Ways of Writing for Children," in *Of Other Worlds: Essays and Stories* (New York: Harcourt Brace, 1966), pp. 24-25.

14. C. S. Lewis, *The Voyage of the Dawn Treader* (New York: Macmillan, 1952), pp. 1-2.

15. To the charge that fairy tales give children a false impression of the world, Lewis writes in his essay "On Three Ways of Writing for Children," "I think no literature children could read gives them less of a false impression. . . . It would be much truer to say that fairy land arouses a longing for he knows not what. It stirs . . . him (to his life-long enrichment) with the dim sense of something beyond his reach and, far from dulling the actual world . . . gives it a new dimension of depth. He does not despise real woods because he has read of enchanted woods: the reading makes all real woods a little enchanted" (pp. 29-30).

16. J. R. R. Tolkien, "On Fairy Stories," in *A Tolkien Reader* (New York: Ballantine Books, 1966), p. 37.

17. C. S. Lewis, *The Silver Chair* (New York: Macmillan, 1953), pp. 158-159.

18. This phrase in Lewis's *The Lion, the Witch and the Wardrobe,* as well as Lucy's going "further up and further in" to the wardrobe, is Lewis's way of intimating that Christianity cannot be reduced to mere facts and data. The Christian faith displays a mysticism that is greater than this physical world, and Narnia is his portrayal of this other world.

19. For two provocative critiques of the impact of the visual medium on culture, see Neil Postman's *Amusing Ourselves to Death: Public Discourse in*

the *Age of Show Business* (New York: Penguin Books, 1985); and Malcolm Muggeridge's *Christ and the Media* (Grand Rapids, MI: Eerdmans, 1977), which curiously has a foreword by evangelist Billy Graham.

20. Terry Teachout, "How We Get That Story," *The Wall Street Journal,* August 6, 1999, W11. Observes Teachout, the music critic for *Commentary,* "We are not accustomed to thinking of art forms as technologies, but that is what they are—which means they can be rendered moribund by new technological developments, in the way that silent films gave way to talkies and radio to TV. Well into the 18th century, for example, most of the West's great storytellers wrote plays, not novels. But the development of modern printing techniques made it feasible for books to be sold at lower prices, allowing storytellers to reach large numbers of readers individually; they then turned to writing novels, and by the 20th century the theatrical play had begun to be widely regarded as a cultural backwater. To be sure, important plays continue to be written and produced, but few watch them, unless they are made into movies."

21. Cited in Teachout, W11.

22. Quoted in Bob Minzesheimer, "Mixing Movies and Mysticism," *USA Today,* January 12, 1998, D1.

23. Minzesheimer, D1.

24. Woody Allen, "The Condemned," in *Side Effects* (New York: Random House, 1975), p. 15.

25. Woody Allen, "Conversations with Helmholtz," in *Getting Even* (New York: Random House, 1966), p. 121.

26. James Nuechterlein, "Godless and Guiltless, a Disorderly Cosmos," *The New York Times,* October 15, 1989, H15 and following.

27. Quoted in Marcia Pally, "Crime Story," *Film Comment,* November-December 1989, pp. 11-15.

28. Allan Bloom, *The Closing of the American Mind* (New York: Simon & Schuster, 1987), pp. 144-146.

29. Woody Allen, "My Speech to the Graduates," *The New York Times,* August 10, 1979, A25.

30. Thomas Merton, *Disputed Questions* (New York: Farrar, Straus & Giroux, 1960), p. 166.

31. Alexander Theroux, "The Real Menace: It's All Those Pretentious Musings on the 'Stars Wars' Series," *The Wall Street Journal,* May 14, 1999, p. W15. Theroux finds Lucas and his Star Wars films to be quite troubling: "As it happens, Mr. Lucas's 'intergalactic fantasy' is cobbled together from Japanese samurai swords and mempo masks,

fascist uniforms, naval jumpsuits, World War I German blaster guns and monsters from Greek mythology, all draped around various oversimplified medieval 'evil empire' fables. It's all very kitschy and reductive—shallow." Theroux rightly chides Bill Moyers' interview with Lucas in *Time* magazine: "He interviewed Mr. Lucas as if he were Hans Kung or the Dalai Lama. 'Ultimately, isn't Star Wars about transformation?' asks Mr. Moyers. (The answer, not surprisingly, is yes.) The interview concludes with theologian Lucas, head in hand, deep in thought, pondering the verities, leaving us with one more bet-hedging mouse masquerading as a mountain: 'I think there is a God. No question. What that God is or what we know about that God, I'm not sure.' Now that is what I call going out on a limb."

32. Cited in Paul F. M. Zahl, "Stephen King's Redemption," *Christianity Today,* March 6, 2000, p. 82.

33. Zahl, p. 82.

34. Geoffrey Hill, *Illuminating Shadows: The Mythic Power of Film* (Boston: Shambhala Publications, 1992), p. 3.

35. Michael J. Cusick, "A Conversation with Philip Yancey," *Mars Hill Review,* Premier Issue, 1994, pp. 93-94.

Chapter 7: Our Experience of Pain and Suffering

1. C. S. Lewis, *The Problem of Pain* (New York: Simon & Schuster, Touchstone, 1996), p. 23.

2. Annie Dillard, *Holy the Firm* (New York: Harper & Row, 1977), pp. 35-36, 46-47.

3. C. S. Lewis, *A Grief Observed* (New York: The Seabury Press, 1961), p. 9. Lewis's faith was greatly tested by the death of his wife. The BBC production of Lewis's life, *Shadowlands,* left the viewer with the mistaken notion that Lewis had jettisoned the Christian faith.

4. In the preface to his book *The Problem of Pain,* Lewis makes the stark confession to his readership that when Mr. Ashley Sampson suggested writing the book, he asked to be allowed to write it anonymously, because "if I were to say what I really thought about pain, I should be forced to make statements of such apparent fortitude that they would become ridiculous if anyone knew who made them . . . but Mr. Sampson pointed out that I could write a preface explaining that I did not live up to my own principles! This exhilarating programme I am now carrying out . . . ." (p. 9).

5. Cited in Peter Kreeft, *Making Sense Out of Suffering* (Ann Arbor, MI: Servant Books, 1986), p. 15.

6. Kreeft, pp. 43-44.

7. Fyodor Dostoyevsky, *The Brothers Karamazov* (London: Penguin Books, 1958), pp. 285-287.

8. C. S. Lewis, *Mere Christianity* (New York: Macmillan, 1942), p. 31. Lewis makes the similar admission in *The Problem of Pain* when he observes, "If the universe is so bad, or even half so bad, how on earth did human beings ever come to attribute it to the activity of a wise and good Creator? Men are fools, perhaps; but hardly so foolish as that" (p. 13).

9. Frederick Buechner, "Atheist," in *Wishful Thinking: A Theological ABC* (New York: Harper & Row, 1973), pp. 2-4.

10. See Kreeft, p. 32.

11. Peter Kreeft, *Three Philosophies of Life* (San Francisco: Ignatius Press, 1989), p. 61.

12. Paul Tournier, *Creative Suffering*, Edwin Hudson, trans. (San Francisco: Harper & Row, 1982), p. 98.

13. Lewis, *The Problem of Pain*, pp. 35-36.

14. Lewis, *The Problem of Pain*, pp. 36, 38.

15. Dorothy L. Sayers, *Creed or Chaos?* (New York: Harcourt Brace, 1949), p. 4.

16. See Philip Yancey, "The Day I'll Get My Friends Back," *Christianity Today*, April 3, 1995, p. 120.

17. C. S. Lewis, *The Last Battle* (New York: Macmillan, 1956), pp. 183-184.

Chapter 8: Our Experience of Pleasures and Joys

1. *The Harper's Index Book,* vol. 3, Charis Conn and Lewis H. Lapham, eds. (New York: Franklin Square Press, 2000), pp. 103, 105, 135, 179, 190.

2. The word "hedonism" derives from the Greek words for pleasure and sweetness. One of the earliest proponents of hedonism was Epicurus (341-270 B.C.), the founder of Epicureanism. To Epicurus, pleasure was considered the first and natural good, the canon by which all choices were to be made.

3. Cited in D. Bruce Lockerbie, *The Cosmic Center: The Supremacy of Christ in a Secular Wasteland* (Portland, OR: Multnomah, 1973), p. 68.

4. Neil Postman, *Amusing Ourselves to Death: Public Discourse in the Age of Show Business* (New York: Penguin Books, 1985), pp. vii-viii.

5. G. K. Chesterton, *Orthodoxy* (John Lane Company, 1908; reprint, San Francisco: Ignatius Press, 1995), p. 70.

6. C. S. Lewis, *Mere Christianity* (New York: Macmillan, 1943), p. 75. Lewis concludes from this that anyone who grew up in a different

world would similarly think that there was something equally odd about the state of our sexual instinct. Lewis adds that one critic said that if he found a country in which such strip-tease acts dealing with food were popular, he would conclude that the people of that country were starving. He meant, of course, to imply that such things as the strip-tease act resulted not from sexual corruption but from sexual starvation: "Everyone knows that the sexual appetite, like our other appetites, grows by indulgence. Starving men may think much about food, but so do gluttons; the gorged, as well as the famished, like titillations" (p. 76).

7. Garrison Keillor, "It's Good Old Monogamy That's Really Sexy," *Time,* October 17, 1994, p. 71.

8. Robert Farrar Capon, *The Supper of the Lamb—A Culinary Reflection* (New York: Farrar, Straus & Giroux, 1989), p. xiii.

9. Isak Dinesen, *Babette's Feast and Other Anecdotes of Destiny* (New York: Vintage Books, 1988), p. 27.

10. Cited in Tim Hansel, *When I Relax I Feel Guilty* (Elgin, IL: David C. Cook, 1979), pp. 44-45.

11. Chesterton, pp. 69-70.

12. C. S. Lewis, *Letters to Malcolm: Chiefly on Prayer* (New York: Harcourt Brace Jovanovich, 1963), pp. 89-91.

Chapter 9: Celebrating the Daily Humdrum

1. *Webster's New Collegiate Dictionary* (Springfield, MA: Merriam-Webster, 1977), p. 1017.

2. C. S. Lewis, *Mere Christianity* (New York: Macmillan, 1943), pp. 6-7.

3. *Webster's,* p. 261.

4. Jill Lawrence, "Excuse Me, But . . . Whatever Happened to Manners?" *USA Today,* December 16, 1996, p. 1.

5. See Mark Caldwell, *A Short History of Rudeness: Manners, Morals, and Misbehavior in Modern America* (New York: Picador USA, 1999).

6. Donald McCullough, *Say Please, Say Thank You: The Respect We Owe One Another* (New York: Perigee Books, 1999).

7. McCullough has some intriguing chapter titles, such as "Don't Show Up at the Wedding in a Baseball Cap"(Showing Respect with What You Wear); "*Repondez, S'il Vous Plait*" (Being Considerate of Others' Plans); "Hold Your Wind" (Trying Not to Offend with Bodily Grossness); "Be First to Reach for the Tab" (Developing a Generous Spirit); "Go Home Before Your Host Falls Asleep" (Not Abusing the Gift of Hospitality); "Don't Let Your Dog Romance My Leg" (Remembering Not Everyone Shares Your Interests).

8. Ned Crabb, "Dress to Regress," *The Wall Street Journal,* June 25, 1999, W13.

9. Alvaro de Silva, ed., *Brave New Family: G. K. Chesterton on Men and Women, Children, Sex, Divorce, Marriage & the Family* (San Francisco: Ignatius Press, 1990), pp. 12-13.

10. G. K. Chesterton, "The Policeman as a Mother," in *The New Witness,* November 14, 1919, cited in de Silva, p. 141.

11. Quoted in de Silva, p. 223.

12. Charles Williams, *The Forgiveness of Sins* (Grand Rapids, MI: Eerdmans, 1984), p. 117.

13. G. K. Chesterton, "The Home of the Unities," in *The New Witness,* January 17, 1919, cited in de Silva, p. 24.

14. Why do we do this? Because as humans, created in the image of God, we are carrying out our dominion and rule in the world. Because God is a God who makes distinctions (Genesis 1:4), we also, created in His image, make distinctions in life. This also serves as a basis for moral absolutes.

15. Thomas Howard, *Hallowed Be This House* (San Francisco: Ignatius Press, 1976). Many of the observations made in this chapter on the various functions of rooms in a house are derived from Howard's excellent book.

16. Garrison Keillor, *The Book of Guys* (New York: Viking Penguin, 1993), p. 13.

17. Howard, p. 47.

18. Thomas Howard, *Chance or the Dance? A Critique of Modern Secularism* (San Francisco: Ignatius Press, 1969), pp. 40-41.

19. Howard, *Hallowed Be This House,* pp. 87-88.

20. Roger Shattuck, *Forbidden Knowledge* (New York: Harcourt Brace, 1996), pp. 1, 4-5.

21. Derek Kidner, *Genesis: An Introduction and Commentary* (Downers Grove, IL: InterVarsity, 1967), p. 69.

22. Howard, *Hallowed Be This House,* pp. 102-103.

23. Lewis, *Mere Christianity,* pp. 77-78.

24. Howard, *Chance or the Dance?,* pp. 124-126.

25. Howard, *Hallowed Be This House,* p. 106.

26. Howard, *Hallowed Be This House,* p. 21.

Chapter 10: Transcendence in Our Work

1. Garrison Keillor, *The Book of Guys* (New York: Viking Penguin, 1993), pp. 11, 14.

2. Michael S. Kimmel, "What Do Men Want?" *Harvard Business Review*, November-December 1993, p. 50.

3. Kimmel, p. 50.

4. Michael S. Kimmel, *Manhood in America: A Cultural History* (New York: The Free Press, 1996), p. 9.

5. Douglas LaBier, *Modern Madness* (Reading, MA: Addison-Wesley, 1986), p. 25.

6. Cited in Kimmel, "What Do Men Want?" p. 52.

7. T. S. Eliot, "Choruses from 'The Rock,'" in *Selected Poems* (New York: Harcourt Brace Jovanovich, 1936), pp. 107-108.

8. Leonard Woolf, as quoted in Tom L. Eisenman, *Temptations Men Face* (Downers Grove, IL: InterVarsity, 1990), p. 41.

9. See Thomas Howard, *Hallowed Be This House* (San Francisco: Ignatius Press, 1976), pp. 10-11.

10. Quoted by Donald. W. McCullough, *Waking from the American Dream* (Downers Grove, IL: InterVarsity, 1988), p. 55.

11. Quoted by Doug Sherman and William Hendricks, *Your Work Matters to God* (Colorado Springs, CO: NavPress, 1987), p. 201.

12. Quoted by Os Guinness, *The Call: Finding and Fulfilling the Central Purpose of Your Life* (Nashville: Word, 1998), p. 2.

13. Guinness, p. 29. Guinness's book is a stimulating Christian apologetic for work as needing the transcendent dimension to provide significance and purpose in life.

14. Old Testament scholar Allen P. Ross comments on Genesis 2:15: "The LORD God took the man and put him into the garden of Eden to *cultivate* it and *keep* it" (emphasis added), and observes, "the two infinitives (translated 'to serve it' and 'to keep it') are also significantly chosen. These two verbs are used throughout the Pentateuch for spiritual service. 'Keep' (*samar*) is used for keeping the commandments and taking heed to obey God's Word; 'serve' (*abad*) describes the worship and service of the Lord, the highest privilege a person can have. Whatever activity the man was to engage in in the garden (and there is no reason to doubt that physical activity was involved), it was described in terms of spiritual service to the Lord." Allen P. Ross, *Creation and Blessing: A Guide to the Study and Exposition of the Book of Genesis* (Grand Rapids, MI: Baker, 1988), p. 124.

15. Cited in Guinness, p. 34. Guinness also quotes William Perkins, whom he refers to as the great "door-opener" of the truth of calling to the English-speaking world: "The action of a shepherd in keeping sheep . . . is as good a work before God as is the action of a judge in

giving sentence, or of a magistrate in ruling, or a minister in preaching" (p. 35).

16. William Griffin of Macmillan Publishing Company gives an illuminating description of Sayers in the foreword to the collection of her essays entitled *The Whimsical Christian:* "There was a touch of whimsy about the way she looked and the way she sounded. She was slender as a young girl, stout as an adult, and tall enough to fill G. K. Chesterton's robes as president of the Detection Club—and he was six feet from crown to ground and four feet around the middle. She could sing, and her voice in conversation could be like a high wind, according to C. S. Lewis; no small wind himself, he ascribed the tone to her keen mind and extraordinary zest. She liked parties, and when the women withdrew from the room to discuss their ailments, she continued to converse with the men on the great theological and philosophical issues. She smoke and drank in the manner of the best-known Christian apologists of the century." *The Whimsical Christian* (New York: Macmillan, 1987), p. x.

17. Dorothy L. Sayers, "Why Work?" in *Creed or Chaos?* (New York: Harcourt Brace, 1949), p. 56. In the essay "Creed or Chaos," from the collection *The Whimsical Christian,* Sayers' words sound hauntingly prophetic of our current day when she states: "a Christian doctrine of work is very closely related to the doctrines of the creative energy of God and the divine image in man. The modern tendency seems to be to identify work with gainful employment. . . . The fallacy is that work is not the expression of man's creative energy in the service of society, but only something he does in order to obtain money and leisure. A very able surgeon put it to me like this: 'What is happening is that nobody works for the sake of getting the thing done. The result of the work is a by-product; the aim of the work is to make money to do something else. Doctors practice medicine not primarily to relieve suffering, but to make a living. . . . Lawyers accept briefs not because they have a passion for justice, but because the law is the profession that enables them to live." See further Dorothy L. Sayers, *The Whimsical Christian* (New York: Macmillan, 1987), pp. 49-50.

18. See Guinness, pp. 198-199.

19. C. S. Lewis, "Good Work and Good Works," in *The World's Last Night and Other Essays* (New York: Harcourt Brace Jovanovich, 1959), pp. 71, 80.

20. Tom Morris, *If Aristotle Ran General Motors* (New York: Henry Holt, 1997), pp. xiii-xiv.

21. Morris suggests that these four verities represent the four basic dimensions to all human experience and are as important now as they ever have been: the intellectual dimension (which aims at truth); the aesthetic dimension (which aims at beauty); the moral dimension (which aims at goodness); and the spiritual dimension (which aims at unity). He believes that the most successful companies will cultivate a corporate culture characterized by these four basic dimensions.

22. I believe these three perspectives on happiness mirror the three major philosophies of life: happiness through pleasure (Western materialism); happiness through personal peace (Eastern mysticism); and happiness through participation in something significant and fulfilling (Christian theism). Quotes supporting these various views on happiness are taken from Morris's excellent book.

23. Cited in Morris, p. 12. Morris also quotes Publius Cornelius Tacitus, who rightly observed that pleasure, as good as it may be, is not synonymous with happiness: "Many who seem to be struggling with adversity are happy; many, amid great affluence, are utterly miserable" (p. 12). Have truer words ever been spoken?

24. Frederick Buechner, "Vocation," in *Wishful Thinking: A Theological ABC* (New York: Harper & Row, 1973), p. 95.

25. Cited in Morris, p. 17.

26. See Morris, p. 17.

27. George Herbert, "The Elixir," in *The Complete English Works,* Everyman's Library, Ann Pasternak Slater, ed. (New York: Knopf, 1908), p. 180.

Chapter 11: Transcendence in Our Play

1. These statistics are from Mortimer B. Zuckerman, "Whistling While We Work," *U. S. News & World Report,* January 24, 2000, p. 72.

2. Gordon Dahl, *Work, Play, and Worship in a Leisure-Oriented Society* (Minneapolis: Augsburg, 1972), p. 12.

3. Josef Pieper, "Leisure and Its Threefold Opposition," in *Josef Pieper: An Anthology* (San Francisco: Ignatius Press, 1989), p. 140.

4. Pieper, "What Is a Feast?" in *Josef Pieper: An Anthology,* pp. 151-152. Derek Kidner makes this interesting comment on God's rest from creation in Genesis 2:3: "God's finished task is sealed in the words 'he rested' (2,3; literally 'ceased'; from *sabat,* the root of 'sabbath'). It is the rest of achievement, not inactivity, for He nurtures what He creates." *Genesis: An Introduction and Commentary* (Downers Grove, IL: InterVarsity, 1967), p. 53. Rest (*sabbath*) would become a central

aspect of Israel's worship in the Old Testament (Exodus 20:8-11; 23:10-12); and Jesus Christ teaches the abiding principle of rest for humanity when He declares, "The Sabbath was made for man, and not man for the Sabbath" (Mark 2:27).

5. Norman Maclean, *A River Runs Through It and Other Stories* (Chicago: The University of Chicago Press, 1976), p. 1.

6. Maclean, pp. 3-4.

7. Maclean, p. 2.

8. John Feinstein, *A Good Walk Spoiled: Days and Nights on the PGA Tour* (Boston: Little, Brown, 1995).

9. M. Scott Peck, *Golf and the Spirit: Lessons for the Journey* (New York: Harmony Books, 1999), p. 3.

10. Feinstein, pp. xvi-xvii.

11. Cited in Feinstein, p. xvii.

12. Jay Tolson, *Pilgrim in the Ruins: A Life of Walker Percy* (New York: Simon & Schuster, 1992), p. 27. To better understand the writings of Walker Percy, see the excellent treatment by Linda Whitney Hobson, *Understanding Walker Percy* (Columbia, SC: The University of South Carolina Press, 1988).

13. John Updike, "Moral Exercise," in *Golf Dreams: Writings on Golf* (New York: Knopf, 1996), pp. 44-45.

14. Michael Murphy, *Golf in the Kingdom* (New York: Penguin Arkana, 1972), pp. 164-166. "Hamartiology" derives from the Greek word *hamartia* and is properly understood as the Christian doctrine that describes man's ethical failure, his "missing the mark" before a righteous and holy God. A central New Testament passage that describes the plight of humanity is in the epistle to the Romans, where the apostle Paul declares, "All have sinned [*hamarton*] and fall short of the glory of God" (Romans 3:23).

15. Cited in Feinstein, p. xix.

16. Peck, pp. 4-5.

17. Updike, pp. 46-48.

18. Cited in Robert D. Linder, "Why Baseball Is Better Than Football, Especially for Republicans," *Mars Hill Review*, Number 14, Summer 1999, p. 62.

19. Annie Dillard, *Diamonds Are a Girl's Best Friend: Women Writers on Baseball*, Elinor Nauen, ed. (Boston: Faber and Faber, 1993), p. 55.

20. George F. Will, *Men at Work: The Craft of Baseball* (New York: Harper Perennial, 1991), p. 2. Will also observes, "Success in life has been described as the maintained ecstasy of burning with a hard, gemlike

flame. John Updike, in his famous essay on Ted Williams, spoke of his radiating 'the hard blue glow of high purpose.' Updike said 'For me, Williams is the classic ballplayer of the game on a hot August weekday before a small crowd, when the only thing at stake is the tissue-thin difference between a thing done well and a thing done ill'" (p. 5).

21. James V. Schall, S. J., "The Seriousness of Sports," in *Another Sort of Learning* (San Francisco: Ignatius Press, 1988), p. 223.

22. Thomas Boswell, *Why Time Begins on Opening Day* (New York: Penguin Books, 1984), p. 288.

23. A. Bartlett Giamatti, "Baseball and the American Character," in *A Great and Glorious Game: Baseball Writings of A. Bartlett Giamatti*, Kenneth S. Robson, ed. (Chapel Hill, NC: Algonquin Books of Chapel Hill, 1998), pp. 64-65.

24. C. S. Lewis, *Letters to Malcolm: Chiefly on Prayer* (New York: Harcourt Brace Jovanovich, 1963), pp. 92-93.

Chapter 12: The Certainty of Heaven

1. Peter Kreeft, *Everything You Ever Wanted to Know About Heaven . . . but Never Dreamed of Asking* (San Francisco: Ignatius Press, 1990), pp. 17-19.

2. Gene Edward Veith Jr., *Postmodern Times: A Christian Guide to Contemporary Thought and Culture* (Wheaton, IL: Crossway Books, 1994), pp. 43-44.

3. C. S. Lewis, *Surprised by Joy: The Shape of My Early Life* (New York: Harcourt Brace Jovanovich, 1955), p. 211.

4. C. S. Lewis, *Mere Christianity* (New York: Macmillan, 1943), pp. 17-18.

5. Kenneth Boa and Larry Moody, *I'm Glad You Asked* (Wheaton, IL: Victor, 1982), pp. 18-19.

6. Agnosticism derives from the Greek word *ginowsko*, with the alpha *privative* denoting negation prefaced to the word, meaning "not knowable." There are actually two forms of agnosticism: the "hard" kind says that we can't know if God exists, which is self-defeating (how can anyone say that they know for sure that they can't know anything for sure!); the other is a "soft" agnosticism. Soft agnostics claim that they simply do not know if there is a God. Such people are generally open to consider the reasonable evidence for theism.

7. Cited in Thomas V. Morris, *Making Sense of It All: Pascal and the Meaning of Life* (Grand Rapids, MI: Eerdmans, 1992), p. 47.

8. Blaise Pascal, *Pensées*, 12, A. J. Krailsheimer, trans. (New York: Penguin Books, 1966), p. 34.

9. Many of these observations about Pascal's contributions concerning the reasonableness of the Christian faith are taken from Morris's excellent book, *Making Sense of It All: Pascal and the Meaning of Life* (Grand Rapids, MI: Eerdmans, 1992).

10. Pascal, 114, 130, pp. 59, 62.

11. Pascal, 24, 36, 73, pp. 36, 38, 49.

12. Pascal, 747, p. 257.

13. Lewis, *Mere Christianity*, p. 29.

14. Pascal, 454, pp. 176-177.

15. Walker Percy, *The Thanatos Syndrome* (New York: Ivy Books, 1987), p. 134.

16. Pascal, 487–488 deal especially with a number of prophecies that applied to Jesus Christ: His precursor (Malachi 3); He will be born a child (Isaiah 9); He will be born in the town of Bethlehem (Micah 5); He is to be the victim for the sins of the world (Isaiah 34,53, etcetera); He is to be the cornerstone (Isaiah 28:16); pp. 194-195.

17. Pascal, 332, p. 129.

18. Interestingly, it has been observed that one-fourth of the Bible was "prophetic" at the time of its writing. And of the over three hundred messianic prophecies that are contained in Scripture, the odds of any ten of these being fulfilled by any one person, as they were by Jesus Christ, is the slim probability of one in ten to the seventeenth power!

19. C. S. Lewis, "Religion and Science," in *God in the Dock: Essays on Theology and Ethics* (Grand Rapids, MI: Eerdmans, 1970), pp. 72-75.

20. Robert Jastrow, *God and the Astronomers*, 2d ed. (New York: Norton & Company, 1992), p. 107.

21. Pascal, 734, p. 255.

22. Various inadequate explanations have been put forth over the years to explain away the biblical assertion that Jesus was in fact raised from the dead. Among these, some have suggested that His friends stole the body (compare Matthew 28:11-15); His enemies stole the body (yet why would the Romans or Jews steal the body when this is precisely what they sought to avoid?); and the Swoon Theory, which suggests that Jesus did not really die, but was resuscitated. In terms of His post-resurrection appearances, suggestions have been made that the witnesses lied or hallucinated or that the entire story of Jesus' resurrection is a fabricated legend that was circulated by the early church. It takes more faith to believe these spurious explanations than to simply take the biblical accounts at face value for what they

purport to have happened. On these and other related issues, see the excellent discussion by Kenneth Boa and Larry Moody, *I'm Glad You Asked* (Wheaton, IL: Victor, 1982).

23. Marcus J. Borg and N. T. Wright, *The Meaning of Jesus: Two Visions* (San Francisco: HarperSanFrancisco, 1998), pp. 129-131.

24. Borg and Wright, pp. 121-122.

25. Listen to Wright's concluding remarks about the challenge the data presents to our worldview and about where he believes the evidence leads us: "At this point the theologian or philosopher can and must step in and ask: do we in fact have good grounds for ruling the straightforward solution out of a court a priori? The answer to that will depend, of course, on your worldview: on what you believe about God, the world, yourself, and a host of other things. . . . It is no good falling back on 'science' as having disproved the possibility of the resurrection. Any real scientist will tell you that science observes what normally happens; the Christian case is precisely that what happened to Jesus is not what normally happens. For my part, as a historian I prefer the elegant, essentially simple solution rather than the one that fails to include all the data: to say that the early Christians believed that Jesus had been bodily raised from the dead, and to account for this belief by saying that they were telling the truth" (Borg and Wright, pp. 124-125). Wright provides even greater substantiation for the bodily resurrection of Jesus in a way that only a historian could capture. He recounts that while first-century Jewish burial did include the body being initially laid on a slab in a cave and wrapped in cloth with spices, there was a second stage to the burial process. A year or later after the flesh had decomposed, relatives or friends would return to collect the bones and place them in an ossuary, a box roughly two feet by one foot by one foot, which would then be stored away either in the recesses within the cave or elsewhere. In other words, the burial of Jesus as recorded in the Gospels was only the first stage of an intended two-stage burial. Wright observes, "So, did anyone ever think of going back to the tomb to collect Jesus' bones and put them in an ossuary? No, they didn't! The whole early church knew that Jesus' body wasn't in the tomb. They believed that God had raised Jesus to life again, transforming his body in the process. . . . If the disciples had believed that what they called the 'resurrection' was just a 'spiritual' event, leaving the body in the tomb, someone sooner or later would have had to go back to collect Jesus' bones and store them properly. . . . Even those

contemporary scholars who deny that Jesus was raised bodily from the dead are clear that all the early Christians thought he had been, and that they made it the basis of their whole lives. . . . So the question of the ossuaries, when we explore it thoroughly, provides paradoxically a sort of negative evidence in favor of Jesus' resurrection" See further N. T. Wright, "Grave Matters: Take Away the Resurrection and the Center of Christianity Collapses," in *Christianity Today*, April 6, 1998, pp. 51-53.

26. H. L. Mencken, *Life*, February 20, 1956.

27. Lewis, *Surprised by Joy*, pp. 223-224.

28. On the reliability of the New Testament documents, especially as it relates to the manuscript evidence and their favorable comparison with other documents of antiquity, see F. F. Bruce, *The New Testament Documents: Are They Reliable?* (Downers Grove, IL: InterVarsity, 1960); on the historicity of the New Testament, see also John Warwick Montgomery, *History & Christianity* (Downers Grove, IL: InterVarsity, 1964); a classic on the Resurrection is the book by Frank Morrison, an English journalist who set out to disprove Christianity: *Who Moved the Stone?* (Downers Grove, IL: InterVarsity, 1958). Also see William Lane Craig, *Reasonable Faith: Christian Truth and Apologetics* (Wheaton, IL: Crossway Books, 1984); and the already mentioned book by Boa and Moody, *I'm Glad You Asked*.

29. See Pascal, 322, p. 127.

30. Pascal, 822, p. 276.

31. Jesus' words immediately raised the ire of the Jewish leaders; John records in the next verse that the Jews "picked up stones to throw at Him" (John 8:59). They recognized that Jesus was making a claim to be one with the Father, who had revealed His personal, covenant name Yahweh ("I AM") to Moses in Exodus 3:14. In Jesus' statement in John 8:58 that "before Abraham was born, I am," He was making a claim of eternality, like God the Father, the Self-Existent One. The personal, covenantal name for God, Yahweh, comes from the Hebrew verb *hayah*.

32. Lewis, *Mere Christianity*, pp. 40-41.

33. C. S. Lewis, *The Lion, the Witch and the Wardrobe* (New York: Collier Books, 1950), pp. 43-45.

34. Lewis's disdain for muddled contemporary thinking is seen in the Professor's words, "Why don't they teach logic at these schools?" As Lewis had had his own imagination "baptized" by the writings of George MacDonald (particularly *Phantastes* and *Lilith*), so he

unapologetically desired that when young readers encountered the *Chronicles of Narnia* their minds be "baptized," awakened to the legitimacy of the Christian faith.

35. John Updike, "Seven Stanzas at Easter," in *Collected Poems: 1953-1993* (New York: Knopf, 1999), pp. 20-21.

Chapter 13: The Choice of Heaven

1. Richard J. Bauckman, "Universalism: A Historical Survey," *Themelios* 4 (1979), p. 48.
2. Herman Melville, *Moby Dick* (New York: Norton, 1967), p. 445.
3. Gerald L. Zelizer, "Churches Give Hell a Makeover," *USA Today,* February 21, 2000, p. 15A.
4. Quoted by Jeffery L. Sheler, "Hell Hath No Fury," *U.S. News & World Report,* January 31, 2000, p. 45.
5. Jeffery L. Sheler, "Hell Hath No Fury," *U. S. News & World Report,* January 31, 2000, pp. 45-50. In Sheler's article, a survey suggests that 64 percent of people believe there is a hell, 25 percent do not, and 9 percent are unsure.
6. Charles Krauthammer, "Will It Be Coffee, Tea, or He?" *Time,* June 15, 1998, p. 92.
7. Lisa Miller, "The Age of Divine Disunity," *The Wall Street Journal,* February 10,1999, B1.
8. For some of these observations I am indebted to Daniel B. Clendenin's excellent article "The Only Way," in *Christianity Today,* January 12, 1998, pp. 35-40.
9. Os Guinness, *The Gravedigger File: Papers on the Subversion of the Modern Church* (Downers Grove, IL: InterVarsity, 1983), p. 93.
10. Clendenin mentions some disturbing figures in his article: "In A.D. 100, about a half percent of the world population was Christian, in A.D. 1000 about 19 percent, and today—after 2,000 years of missionary effort—only about 30 percent of the world identifies itself as Christian. What can we say about the eternal destiny of this vast horde who never named the name of Christ?" (p. 36).
11. Clark Pinnock, *A Wideness in God's Mercy: The Finality of Jesus Christ in a World of Religions* (Grand Rapids, MI: Zondervan, 1992), p. 18.
12. The issue of the reliability of the Bible—and more specifically the New Testament documents—as well as the personal claims of Jesus Christ concerning His deity were covered in chapter 12, "The Certainty of Heaven." On the important "I am" phrase in these passages, especially in John 8:58, there is an unmistakable allusion to God's

revealing Himself to Moses as the Self-Existent One (Yahweh, from the Hebrew verb *hayah*) in Exodus 3:14. Jesus was clearly making a claim to be one and the same with God. If there is any doubt, notice the response of the Jews in John 8:59 to His declaration in the preceding verse: "Therefore they picked up stones to throw at Him; but Jesus hid Himself, and went out of the temple."

13. For an excellent treatment dealing with the exclusivity of Christianity, as well as other commonly asked questions, see Kenneth Boa and Larry Moody, *I'm Glad You Asked* (Wheaton, IL: Victor, 1982), pp. 126-144.

14. C. S. Lewis, "Christian Apologetics," in *God in the Dock: Essays on Theology and Ethics* (Grand Rapids, MI: Eerdmans, 1970), p. 101. The matter of determining which religion is right because all have competing truth claims, is helped by the law common to logic known as the law of noncontradiction. It essentially states that if two statements about one particular issue contradict each other, then (a) only one of them is true, or (b) they are both false. They cannot both be true. More specific to our discussion, if Christ claims to be the only way to God and Islam claims that there is another way, then either Christ is right and Islam is wrong, or Christ is wrong and Islam is right, or they are both wrong. They cannot both be right.

15. C. S. Lewis, *Mere Christianity* (New York: Macmillan, 1943), p. 31.

16. The issue of the exclusivity of Christianity should be dealt not only with objectivity but with humility as well. The Scriptures clearly teach that mankind has knowledge about God as well as his own sin, which therefore demands a response (see Romans 1:20 and following; 2:1 and following; Psalm 19; Acts 14:15 and following). Therefore, man is not ignorant about spiritual matters, but God holds him accountable for his response to the provided revelation. The question is not as to whether mankind is in total darkness about God and matters of salvation, but whether he is seeking after God. The Scriptures seem to suggest that God honors and gives further revelation to those who truly seek him wholeheartedly (see Jeremiah 29:13; Hebrews 11:6; Acts 8:26-40; Matthew 7:7-8). Most Christians grant that there are a number of mysteries about salvation that are not clearly addressed by the Scriptures. Most Christians also will choose to make at least some exceptions to the exclusivity of Christianity, specifically as to whether people must explicitly call upon Christ to be saved. This would probably include Old Testament saints, the mentally handicapped, and infants and children who die young. Nevertheless, the overall message

of salvation remains narrow. Here are some fundamental truths that are important to keep in mind when dealing with this difficult subject: First, God is perfect and just in all of His dealings. We can be confident that God will treat every person with perfect justice and love: "Far be it from God to do wickedness, and from the Almighty to do wrong" (Job 34:10). David, facing the discipline of the Lord for numbering his men, chose God's discipline over man's: "Let us now fall into the hand of the LORD for His mercies are great, but do not let me fall into the hand of man" (2 Samuel 24:14). Second, while God is infinite and beyond comprehension, we humans are finite and sinful, too often speaking authoritatively on things we don't fully comprehend. Job says, "Who is this that hides counsel without knowledge? Therefore I have declared that which I did not understand, things too wonderful for me, which I did not know" (Job 42:3). We need to cultivate a theological humility that recognizes the limits of human understanding in these difficult areas. We must confess with Paul, "How unsearchable are His judgments and unfathomable His ways!" (Romans 11:33). While it is only natural and appropriate that we should look for definitive answers to these critical questions about life and faith, the fact of the matter is that many of our questions defy complete comprehension in this life. The thoughtful Christian comes to trust and recognize not only the goodness and justice of God but also the mystery of God in matters pertaining to salvation: "For as the heavens are higher than the earth, so are My ways higher than your ways, and My thoughts than your thoughts" (Isaiah 55:9).

17. Lewis, *Mere Christianity*, pp. 37-38.
18. C. S. Lewis, *The Problem of Pain* (New York: Macmillan, 1962), pp. 118-119.
19. Lewis, *The Problem of Pain*, p. 118.
20. Jesus' words in the Sermon on the Mount actually suggest the opposite: "Enter by the narrow gate; for the gate is wide, and the way is broad that leads to destruction, and many are those who enter by it" (Matthew 7:13).
21. See 2 Peter 3:9 and 1 Timothy 2:4.
22. Graham Greene was arguably one of the greatest English writers of the twentieth century, and his works display a preoccupation with many theological issues. As a Catholic, he frequently sought to explore what faith means and how one can deal with his or her guilt before a holy God. He wrote some thirty novels but is probably best known for *The Heart of the Matter, The Power and the Glory*, and *The*

End of the Affair, which has been made into an award-winning motion picture.

23. Graham Greene, *The Heart of the Matter* (New York: Penguin Books, 1962), pp. 232-233.

24. For a remarkable amount of background information and summary of *The Great Divorce* as well as all of the writings of C. S. Lewis, see Walter Hooper's excellent work *C. S. Lewis: A Companion & Guide* (San Francisco: HarperCollins, 1996). Lewis employed the title *The Great Divorce* to describe what he believed about the reality and disparity between Heaven and Hell. He states in the preface that while William Blake's *Marriage of Heaven and Hell* attempted to make us believe that such a "marriage" is possible, "reality never presents us with an absolutely unavoidable 'either-or.' . . . This belief I take to be a disastrous error. . . . We are not living in a world where all the roads are radii of a circle and where all, if followed long enough, will therefore draw gradually nearer and finally meet at the centre: rather in a world where every road, after a few miles, forks into two, and each of those into two again, and at each fork you must make a decision. . . . I do not think that all who choose wrong roads perish; but their rescue consists in being put back on the right road." See further C. S. Lewis, *The Great Divorce* (New York: Touchstone Books, 1996), pp. 9-10.

25. Lewis's imaginative picture of Hell's inhabitants as being separated and isolated from others because of their inability to get along is the opposite of the Hell envisioned by the French existentialist Jean-Paul Sartre in his play *No Exit*. There, Hell is confined to a single room.

26. Lewis, *The Great Divorce*, p. 26.

27. Lewis, *The Great Divorce*, pp. 27, 30.

28. Lewis, *The Great Divorce*, p. 29.

29. George MacDonald did serve as a spiritual mentor to Lewis in his pilgrimage to Christianity.

30. Lewis, *The Great Divorce*, p. 69.

31. Lewis, *The Great Divorce*, p. 72.

32. Lewis, *The Great Divorce*, pp. 36-37.

33. Lewis, *The Problem of Pain*, pp. 127-128.

34. I like the way Peter Kreeft and Ronald Tacelli address this issue in their *Handbook of Christian Apologetics:* "If hell is chosen freely, the problem then becomes not one of reconciling hell with God's love, but reconciling hell with human insanity. Who would freely prefer hell to heaven unless they were insane? The answer is that all of us do at one time or another. Every sin reflects that preference. The skeptic

objects that if we freely choose hell over heaven, we must be insane; the Christian replies that that is precisely what sin is: insanity, the deliberate refusal of joy and truth. . . . Perhaps the most shocking teaching in all of Christianity is this: not so much the doctrine of hell as the doctrine of sin. It means the human race is spiritually insane." (Downers Grove, IL: InterVarsity, 1994), p. 290.

35. On the development of this justification for Hell, see Richard Swinburne, *Faith and Reason* (Oxford: Clarendon Press, 1981), pp. 143-172.

36. See Peter Kreeft, *Christianity for Modern Pagans* (San Francisco: Ignatius Press, 1993), p. 26. Kreeft goes on to rightly observe concerning modernity's rejection of Christianity, "Thus what originally came into the world as '*good* news' strikes the modern mind as *bad* news, as guilt-ridden, moralistic and 'judgmental'" (p. 26).

37. T. S. Eliot, "The Hollow Men," in *Selected Poems* (New York: Harcourt Brace Jovanovich, 1934), p. 80.

38. The apostle Paul is not here prohibiting the daily regimen of "eating and drinking" any more than the enjoyment of God's gifts of food, blessings, and abundant pleasures in life. The key is our attitude toward them, as he suggests when he declares that "everything created by God is good, and nothing is to be rejected, if it is received with gratitude; for it is sanctified by means of the word of God and prayer" (1 Timothy 4:4-5). What he is addressing in 1 Corinthians 15—the Great Resurrection Chapter—is that if there is no resurrection and if Jesus Christ was not bodily raised from the dead, then the Christian might as well lead a hedonistic lifestyle, because the basis of the Christian faith has been undermined. If there is no Resurrection, then "we are of all men most to be pitied" (1 Corinthians 15:19).

39. C. S. Lewis, *Letters to Malcolm: Chiefly on Prayer* (New York: Harcourt Brace Jovanovich, 1963), p. 76.

40. Perhaps to the consternation of some Catholic readers, I have chosen not to deal with the Roman Catholic purgatorial view on the nature of Hell. The reader is directed to the provocative presentation of this view by Zachary J. Hayes in *Four Views on Hell*, edited by William V. Crockett (Grand Rapids, MI: Zondervan, 1992), pp. 91-118. In the response of the other writers, all of whom are Protestants, it becomes clear that Protestants have always found the traditional doctrine of purgatory—an intermediate "place" between Heaven and Hell—as inadequate because of its lack of biblical support. Hayes prefers to distance himself from the traditional Roman Catholic doctrine and speaks of purgatory as a "process" that begins at death and continues

for those who need it. Clark Pinnock's comments in his response to Hayes' article are thought-provoking: "I cannot deny that most believers end their earthly lives imperfectly sanctified and far from complete. I cannot deny the wisdom in possibly giving them an opportunity to close the gap and grow in maturity after death. . . . It is obvious that Christian character is not perfectly transformed at death. Therefore, it is reasonable to hope that there might be a perfecting process after death" (see *Four Views on Hell,* pp. 129-130). Other respected writers and theologians have also seen the need for some type of "cleansing" before the believer enters Heaven. C. S. Lewis remarks, "Our souls *demand* Purgatory, don't they? Would it not break the heart if God said to us, 'It is true, my son, that your breath smells and your rags drip with mud and slime, but we are charitable here and no one will upbraid you with these things, nor draw away from you. Enter into the joy'? Should we not reply, 'With submission, sir, and if there is no objection, I'd rather be cleaned first.' 'It may hurt you know'—'Even so, sir.' " Lewis, *Letters to Malcolm,* pp. 108-109.

41. The origin of Old Testament word "Sheol" (Hebrew *sheol*) is unclear. It generally refers to the Old Testament netherworld where everyone descends at death. Its derivation may come from the Hebrew *sha'al,* "hollow hand," and therefore suggesting a "hollow place." See further "sheol," in Brown, Driver, and Briggs, *A Hebrew and English Lexicon of the Old Testament* (Oxford: Clarendon Press, 1907), p. 982.

42. As noted, *tartarus* (the Greek verb *tartaroo*) is the classical word for the place of eternal punishment and appears only once in the New Testament. It is translated in the *New American Standard Bible* as "cast them into Hell" and is here applied to the intermediate sphere of punishment for fallen angels.

43. Jesus' warning in the Sermon on the Mount about our being "guilty enough to go into the fiery hell" (Matthew 5:22) employs this word, and His audience certainly grasped His meaning. In the Old Testament, the Hinnom Valley was an abomination in Israel because it was used to burn children in sacrifice to the Ammonite god Molech (see 2 Kings 23:10; Jeremiah 7:31; 32:35). Jeremiah denounced such practices by saying that the Hinnom Valley would become the valley of God's judgment, a place of slaughter (see Jeremiah 7:32; 19:5-7). Consequently, in Jesus' day the valley was used as a refuse dump where people would burn their garbage and offal using sulphur, the flammable substance we now use in matches and gunpowder. Thus, when Jesus spoke of punishment

in the next life, what better image could He have used than the smoldering valley they called *Gehenna?*

44. For a good historical treatment on the nature of Hell, see William V. Crockett, ed., "The Metaphorical View," in *Four Views on Hell* (Grand Rapids, MI: Zondervan, 1992), pp. 43-76.

45. For an excellent discussion of the various views on the nature of Hell, see Jerry L. Walls, "Hell and Human Misery," in *Hell: The Logic of Damnation* (Notre Dame, IN: University of Notre Dame Press, 1992), pp. 139-155.

46. John Calvin, *Commentary on a Harmony of the Evangelists,* vol. I, William Pringle, trans. (Grand Rapids, MI: Eerdmans, 1949), p. 201.

47. J. I. Packer, "The Problem of Eternal Punishment," *Crux* 26 (September, 1990), p. 25. George MacDonald makes a similar point in one of his readings when dealing with the images of moth and rust: "What is with the treasure must fare as the treasure. . . . The heart which haunts the treasure house where the moth and rust corrupt, will be exposed to the same ravages as the treasure. . . . Many a man, many a woman, fair and flourishing to see, is going about with a rusty moth-eaten heart within that form of strength or beauty. 'But this is only a figure.' 'True. But is the reality intended, less or more than the figure?'" C. S. Lewis, ed., *George MacDonald: 365 Readings,* no. 22 (New York: Macmillan, 1974), p. 10

48. That there may be gradations of punishment in Hell seems to be implied in the judgment spoken of in Revelation 20:11-15, generally known as the "Great White Throne Judgment," which is the judgment of all unbelievers. This poses yet another problem for the annihilationist view. While many annihilationists believe in different degrees of torment before extinction, they still essentially anticipate only one ultimate destiny for all the wicked, an undifferentiated nonexistence. The New Testament, and Jesus in particular, declares that those who have received greater opportunities for belief will suffer more severe condemnation (see Matthew 10:15; 11:20-24; Luke 12:47-48). Would it not be hard to believe that the righteous Judge of the earth (see Genesis 18:25) would pronounce the same sentence of judgment upon the most despicable villain of human history, as upon the seemingly moral pagan?

49. While it is true that the Hebrew word *olam* and the Greek word *aionios* can on occasion refer to an age or long period of time, more often than not the terms generally mean an unending period of time.

50. For an excellent discussion of Hell, including misconceptions, objections, and what Hell is, see chapter 12, "Hell," in Peter Kreeft and Ronald K. Tacelli, *Handbook of Christian Apologetics* (Downers Grove, IL: InterVarsity, 1994), pp. 282-314.

51. Lewis, *The Problem of Pain*, pp. 122-123.

52. Walls, p. 151.

53. Lewis, *Letters to Malcolm*, p. 91.

54. Lewis, *The Great Divorce*, p. 68.

55. For a good discussion on the possible essence of Hell, see Peter Kreeft, *Everything You Ever Wanted to Know About Heaven . . . but Never Dreamed of Asking* (San Francisco: Ignatius Press, 1990), pp. 229 and following.

56. Fyodor Dostoyevsky, *The Brothers Karamazov*, pt. II, bk. VI, chap. 2, David Magarshack, trans. (New York: Penguin Books, 1958), p. 338.

57. C. S. Lewis, "The Shoddy Lands," in *Of Other Worlds: Essays and Stories*, Walter Hooper, ed. (New York: Harcourt Brace, 1966), p. 105. Lewis suggests toward the end of the story that Peggy had lost her "taste for the other," namely, seeing nature as an entrée to God: "I was, for a second or so, let into Peggy's mind; at least to the extent of seeing her world, the world as it exists for her. At the centre of that world is a swollen image of herself, remodelled to be as like the girls in the advertisements as possible. . . . The daffodils and roses are especially instructive. Flowers only exist for her if they are the sort that can be cut and put in vases or sent as bouquets; flowers in themselves, flowers as you see them in the woods, are negligible" (p. 106).

58. Lewis, *The Great Divorce*, pp. 114-118.

59. Lewis, *The Problem of Pain*, p. 127.

60. Eberhard Busch, "My Memories of Karl Barth," *Reformed Journal*, May 1986, p. 14. Cited in Donald W. McCullough, *Waking from the American Dream: Growing Through Your Disappointments* (Downers Grove, IL: InterVarsity, 1986), pp. 133-134.

61. C. S. Lewis, "The Weight of Glory," in *The Weight of Glory and Other Addresses* (Grand Rapids, MI: Eerdmans, 1949), pp. 14-15.

Chapter 14: The Character of Heaven

1. For excellent, in-depth discussions of various questions about Heaven, see especially Peter Kreeft, *Everything You Ever Wanted to Know About Heaven . . . but Never Dreamed of Asking* (San Francisco: Ignatius Press, 1990); Gary R. Habermas and J. P. Moreland, *Immortality: The Other Side of Death* (Nashville: Nelson, 1992); and Jeffrey

Burton Russell, *A History of Heaven: The Singing Silence* (Princeton, NJ: Princeton University Press, 1997).

2. It seems that Jesus and the New Testament understand Heaven to be virtually synonymous with "eternal life," a life experienced presently with God (which will be addressed later in this chapter). See, for example, John 3:16,36; 5:24; 6:51,58; Romans 6:1-11; Philippians 3:20-21; 1 Peter 1:3-5; 1 John 5:13.

3. See Jeffrey Burton Russell's excellent and lucid discussion on this issue of interpretation in his book *A History of Heaven: The Singing Silence,* (Princeton University Press, 1997), pp. 6-16.

4. Russell, pp. 8-9.

5. The fact that Jesus ascended to Heaven in a real, resurrection body, as reported by Luke in Acts 1:9-11, strongly argues that Heaven is a place. Interestingly, the angels tell the astonished disciples who are witnesses to this event that He "will come in just the same way as you have watched Him go into heaven" (verse 11). Evidently, His bodily ascension into Heaven is closely aligned to His personal, bodily Second Coming at the end of the ages.

6. Charis Conn and Ilena Silverman, eds., *What Counts: The Complete Harper's Index* (New York: Holt, 1991), pp. 160, 162. Another curious observation was that pectoral implants for men are finding a niche— for a mere 6,500 dollars in Beverly Hills, California—and that 20 percent of American men and a whopping 45 percent of American women admit to wearing uncomfortable shoes "because they look good" (p. 161).

7. See Kreeft, pp. 84-116. It seems that even these five answers as to what happens to us at the time of death can be further distilled down to three fundamental worldviews of the afterlife, each of which is mutually exclusive of the others: annihilation, reincarnation, or resurrection.

8. For a good discussion concerning the problems of reincarnation, see Habermas and Moreland, *Immortality: The Other Side of Death,* (Nelson) chapter 8, "Reincarnation—Is It True?" pp. 121-133.

9. C. S. Lewis, *A Grief Observed* (New York: Bantam Books, 1976), p. 76.

10. See Kreeft's excellent discussion of Cartesian dualism, where matter and spirit become separate ideas, in chapter 6 of his book *Everything You Ever Wanted to Know About Heaven . . . but Never Dreamed of Asking,* pp. 84 and following.

11. Literally, a *soma pneumatikon* (1 Corinthians 15:44).

12. See further Philippians 3:20-21. While the believer will have a resurrection body like Jesus', *when* the believer receives this glorified body

is not clearly known. The term "interim state" was introduced by Tertullian early in the life of the church (A.D. 160–225), though the concept had been implied by the New Testament. The tenor of the New Testament suggests that the soul is temporarily disembodied until it is clothed with immortality. While "longing to be clothed with our dwelling from heaven" (2 Corinthians 5:2), the apostle Paul still believed it was highly desirable to be in the presence of the Lord (see Philippians 1:23), which could hardly suggest a state of unconsciousness, boredom, and inactivity. See further Habermas and Moreland, *Immortality: The Other Side of Death,* chapter 7, "Life in Between."

Lewis offers this observation in *Letters to Malcolm: Chiefly on Prayer,* the last book before his death: "I don't say the resurrection of this body will happen at once. It may well be that this part of us sleeps in death, and the intellectual soul is sent to Lenten lands where she fasts in naked spirituality—a ghost-like and imperfectly human condition. I don't imply that an angel is a ghost. But naked spirituality is in accordance with his nature; not, I think, with ours. (A two-legged horse is maimed, but not a two-legged man.) Yet from that fast my hope is that we shall return and re-assume the wealth we have laid down. . . . And once again . . . the birds will sing and the waters flow, and lights and shadows move across the hills, and the faces of our friends laugh upon us with amazed recognition. Guesses, of course, only guesses. If they are not true, something better will be. For 'we know that we shall be made like Him, for we shall see Him as He is'" *Letters to Malcolm: Chiefly on Prayer* (New York: Harcourt Brace Jovanovich, 1963), pp. 123-124.

13. Most likely this was an unusual occasion where Jesus desired to withhold His identity from those around Him in His post-resurrection appearances. Luke writes that "their eyes were prevented from recognizing Him" (Luke 24:16); a similar event occurred with Mary Magdalene on her visit to the empty tomb on Easter morning. As Jesus stood beside her, she "did not know that it was Jesus . . . supposing Him to be the gardener" (John 20:14-15). Yet she did recognize Him when He spoke to her (see John 20:16). Curiously, while the disciples did not at first recognize Him by the Sea of Galilee as they were fishing, the apostle John then recognized Him, which led Peter to desert his fellow fishermen and swim to the shore to meet the Lord (see John 21:7-8)! Whatever we may conclude about His resurrection body, it is clear that while there was some sense of continuity with His earthly, physical body, it now possessed a different constitution.

Even in the Transfiguration, perhaps a "sneak preview" of the Second Coming, we are told that He was "transfigured (*metamorphe*) before them" (see Matthew 17:2). And Mark, in alluding briefly to the two disciples meeting Jesus on the road to Emmaus (Luke 24), remarks that He "appeared in a different form" (*hetera morphe*) (Mark 16:12), which suggests, by the use of the Greek word *morphe* (as opposed to *schema),* that not just His outward appearance was different, but also His inward, *essential* nature. See further G. Abbott-Smith, "*morphe,*" *A Manual Greek Lexicon of the New Testament,* (Edinburgh: T&T Clark, 1937), pp. 296-297.

14. See Russell, p. 47.
15. C. S. Lewis, *Miracles* (New York: Simon & Schuster, 1975), pp. 196-197.
16. See Kreeft, *Everything You Ever Wanted to Know About Heaven . . . but Never Dreamed of Asking,* pp. 90-97.
17. Lewis observes that while humans experience the "tingling taste of oranges," the angels have no sensory "nerves." C. S. Lewis, "On Being Human," in *Poems* (New York: Harcourt Brace Jovanovich, 1964), pp. 34-35.
18. See Kreeft, p. 91.
19. Lewis, *Miracles,* p. 214.
20. Saint Augustine, *Confessions,* XI, 14 (17), Henry Chadwick, trans. (Oxford: Oxford University Press, 1991), p. 230.
21. See Russell, p. 11.
22. The words used in the Scriptures for "eternal" are generally the Hebrew word *olam,* and the Greek word *aionios,* both of which, depending on their context, can refer to "ages, long duration, continuous existence."
23. See Kreeft, p. 153. Kreeft provides probably the most thorough treatment of time in Heaven of any recent writer in chapters 10 and 11 of his book *Everything You Always Wanted to Know About Heaven . . . .*
24. Kreeft, p. 154.
25. C. S. Lewis, *The Lion, the Witch and the Wardrobe* (New York: Macmillan, 1950), pp. 159-160.
26. Blaise Pascal, *Pensées,* 930, A. J. Krailsheimer, trans. (New York: Penguin Books, 1966), p. 320.
27. T. S. Eliot, "The Dry Salvages," in *Four Quartets,* V, 199-202, (New York: Harcourt Brace Jovanovich, 1943), p. 44.
28. Thomas Siebold, ed., "Readings on *Our Town,*" *The Greenhaven Press Literary Companion to American Literature* (San Diego, CA: Greenhaven Press, 2000), pp. 107-108.

29. On being versus doing, Lewis says, "What God cares about is not exactly our actions. What He cares about is that we should be creatures of a certain kind or quality—the kind of creatures He intended us to be—creatures related to Himself in a certain way." *Mere Christianity* (New York: Macmillan, 1943), p. 113.

30. Lewis, *Mere Christianity*, p. 106.

31. Richard Purtill, *Thinking about Religion* (Englewood Cliffs, NJ: Prentice Hall, 1978), pp. 136-152, cited in Kreeft, *Everything You Ever Wanted to Know About Heaven . . . but Never Dreamed of Asking*, pp. 52-53.

32. See further 1 Corinthians 2:8-9; 13:12; 2 Corinthians 4:16-18; and especially Joseph's profound words to his brothers, "And as for you, you meant evil against me, but God meant it for good in order to bring about this present result, to preserve many people alive" (Genesis 50:20).

33. See, for example, Exodus 24, when Moses meets God on Sinai with Aaron, Nadab, Abihu, and the seventy elders of Israel; also see the communal worship scenes in the book of Revelation, particularly chapters 14 and 19.

34. The author is indebted to his colleague Kenneth Boa, who has used this helpful, threefold division to describe how the Christian should exercise a proper love for self, others, and God. It is supported by such Scriptures as Matthew 22:34-40, Romans 12:3, and Ephesians 5:28-29. Contrary to our narcissistic culture, in the Bible we are *never* told that we need to learn to love *ourselves.* The Bible assumes that we will always put self-interests first; hence Paul's admonition to husbands to "love their own wives as their own bodies . . . for no one ever hated his own flesh, but nourishes and cherishes it" (Ephesians 5:28-29; see also Leviticus 19:18).

35. Russell, pp. 3-4.

36. See Kreeft, p. 169.

37. Lewis, *Letters to Malcolm: Chiefly on Prayer*, pp. 121-122.

38. In their commentary on 1 Corinthians, Archibald Robertson and Alfred Plummer suggest, "The argument is *a fortiori.* If adults have long since abandoned their playthings and primers, how much more will the reflected glimpses of truth be abandoned, when the whole truth is directly seen. . . . Ancient mirrors were of polished metal, and Corinthian mirrors were famous; but the best of them would give an imperfect and somewhat distorted reflection. . . . This world reflects God so imperfectly as to perplex us; all that we see is *en anigmati.*" *A Critical and Exegetical Commentary on the First Epistle of St. Paul to the Corinthians,* The International Critical Commentary Series

(Edinburgh: T. & T. Clark, 1911), p. 298. It may be that the supernatural charismatic gifts, such as tongues and prophecy, are a mere foreshadowing of Heaven's ultimate restoration after God's curse upon the *hubris* of mankind as pictured at Babel (Genesis 11). The Shinarites desire was to "build for ourselves a city . . . and . . . make for ourselves a name" (verse 4). Yet with great irony, no matter how high their tower went into the heavens, the Lord still had to come down to see their work of pride (verse 5). Just as language has been fragmented on earth since the story of Babel—resulting in diverse languages throughout the world—perhaps at Pentecost, with the disciples speaking "with other tongues" (Acts 2:4), we begin to see a shadowing of God's undoing of this curse. It is pure conjecture, but it may be that the true communion of the saints will require a better instrument of communication than any known human language, so we could return to a better, single language as was perhaps employed before the Fall and of which others are but a dim reflection.

39. See Kreeft, p. 27.

40. Kreeft, p. 28.

41. C. S. Lewis, ed., *George MacDonald: An Anthology* (London: Geoffrey Bles, 1946), p. 98.

42. The Sadducees, in their testing of Jesus, were alluding to the levirate law of the Old Testament (Deuteronomy 25:5-6). In this legislation of Israel, the next of kin—presumably a brother—would agree to marry his deceased brother's wife for the sole purpose of raising up progeny. This would safeguard the continuance of his brother's family line.

43. The parallel passage in Luke portrays the same thought: "Neither can they die anymore, for they are like angels, and are sons of God, being sons of the resurrection" (Luke 20:36).

44. See Kreeft, p. 117. Kreeft provides an entire chapter on this subject in *Everything You Ever Wanted to Know About Heaven . . . but Never Dreamed of Asking.* Most helpful are the four principles he considers fundamental to a biblical perspective on sexuality: (1) Sex is something you are, not something you do; (2) the alternative to chauvinism is not egalitarianism; (3) sex is spiritual; and (4) sex is cosmic.

45. Kreeft, pp. 126-127.

46. Lewis, *Miracles,* p. 210.

47. One interesting example is Sheldon Vanauken, an American pupil of Lewis at Oxford University. Vanauken's wife, Davy, had dark shadows under her eyes when she appeared to her husband some two years after her death, acquired through her suffering. Vanauken

recounts her appearance to him: "She looked just as she had always done, even to the slight dark circles under her eyes. I felt an immense gratitude to her, and to God for letting her come. . . . Then I couldn't resist asking her how she, in heaven, could have dark shadows under her eyes. She grinned, knowing me, and then said seriously, 'I can't tell you that. I can't tell you very much at all.'" Sheldon Vanauken, *A Severe Mercy* (San Francisco: Harper & Row, 1977), p. 222.

48. See Kreeft, p. 104.

49. C. S. Lewis, *The Great Divorce* (New York: Macmillan, 1946), p. 30.

50. This is brilliantly satirized in Lewis's essay, "Screwtape Proposes a Toast," in *The Screwtape Letters* (New York: Macmillan, 1961).

51. Lewis, *Letters to Malcolm*, p. 13.

52. Kreeft, p. 29.

53. See further Ephesians 2:8-10; 1 Thessalonians 2:13; James 2:14-26.

54. See further Philippians 4:17; 1 Thessalonians 2:19; 1 Timothy 6:18-19; 2 Timothy 4:8; James 1:12; 1 Peter 5:4; Revelation 2:10; 3:11.

55. C. S. Lewis, "The Weight of Glory," in *The Weight of Glory and Other Addresses* (Grand Rapids, MI: Eerdmans, 1949), pp. 1-2.

56. The "judgment seat of Christ" spoken of in 2 Corinthians 5:10, which is for believers only, is to be distinguished from the Great White Throne Judgment of Revelation 20:11-15, which apparently is for unbelievers, those whose "name was not found written in the book of life" (verse 15). While the New Testament presents the believer's destiny in Heaven as secure (see John 5:24; Romans 8:26-39; Ephesians 1:13-14), the testing of each believer's works may or may not result in rewards, although "he himself shall be saved" (1 Corinthians 3:10-15).

57. Two intriguing passages that have sometimes puzzled interpreters are the parable of the talents (Matthew 25:14-30) and the parable of the minas (Luke 19:11-27). In both of these parables, it is only those stewards who increase their money who receive the accolade: "to everyone who has shall more be given, but from the one who does not have, even what he does have shall be taken away" (Luke 19:26).

58. This parable follows immediately after the rich young ruler decides not to follow Jesus "for he was one who owned much property" (Matthew 19:22), and Peter's subsequent remark, "We have left everything and followed You; what then will there be for us?" (verse 27). Thus Jesus assures them, "You who have followed Me, in the regeneration when the Son of Man will sit on His glorious throne, you also shall sit upon twelve thrones. . . . But many who are first will be last; and the last, first" (verses 28,30). Jesus' words may very well be directed at Peter and any of

the other disciples who believe that they have a right of entitlement to Jesus' bounty. Jesus' words are encouraging, but cautionary. He will do what He wishes with His rewards, so any follower should be careful against any kind of presumption or self-importance.

59. See Lewis, "The Weight of Glory," p. 7.
60. C. S. Lewis, "The World's Last Night," in *The World's Last Night and Other Essays* (New York: Harcourt Brace Jovanovich, 1952), pp. 110, 113.

Conclusion

1. Alister McGrath, *The Unknown God: Searching for Spiritual Fulfillment* (Grand Rapids, MI: Eerdmans, 1999), p. 7.
2. See further Peter Kreeft's excellent book on Pascal's *Pensées* and his wager argument in *Christianity for Modern Pagans* (San Francisco: Ignatius Press, 1993), pp. 291 and following.
3. Anne Lamott, *Traveling Mercies: Some Thoughts on Faith* (New York: Pantheon Books, 1999), p. 3.

ABOUT THE AUTHOR

Barry L. Morrow is a graduate of the University of North Carolina at Chapel Hill, where he received a bachelor's degree in biology. He later attended Dallas Theological Seminary, where he graduated with High Honors, earning a Th.M. degree in Old Testament studies. He served in the pastorate for a number of years in Atlanta and is presently on staff with Reflections Ministries there. Reflections Ministries is a marketplace ministry that is committed to providing people a safe environment to consider the claims of Christianity as well as to grow in their spiritual lives.

He resides in Roswell, Georgia, with his wife, Caroleeta, and their two children, Anna and Jonathan.